My Chinese Dream

Dialogues and Encounters with Christianity

CHIARETTO YAN

甄健湘

ORBIS BOOKS
Maryknoll, New York 10545

Founded in 1970, Orbis Books endeavors to publish works that enlighten the mind, nourish the spirit, and challenge the conscience. The publishing arm of the Maryknoll Fathers and Brothers, Orbis seeks to explore the global dimensions of the Christian faith and mission, to invite dialogue with diverse cultures and religious traditions, and to serve the cause of reconciliation and peace. The books published reflect the views of their authors and do not represent the official position of the Maryknoll Society. To learn more about Maryknoll and Orbis Books, please visit our website at www.orbisbooks.com.

Copyright © 2026 by Chiaretto Yan

Published by Orbis Books, Box 302, Maryknoll, NY 10545-0302.

All rights reserved.

No part of this publication may be reproduced or transmitted in any form or by any means, electronic or mechanical, including photocopying, recording, or any information storage or retrieval system, without prior permission in writing from the publisher.

Queries regarding rights and permissions should be addressed to: Orbis Books, P.O. Box 302, Maryknoll, NY 10545-0302.

Manufactured in the United States of America

Library of Congress Cataloging-in-Publication Data

Names: Yan, Kin Sheung Chiaretto author
Title: My Chinese dream : new encounters and dialogues with Christianity / Chiaretto Yan.
Description: Maryknoll, NY : Orbis Books, [2026] | Includes bibliographical references and index. | Summary: "An effort to find areas for fruitful encounter and dialogue between Catholicism and Chinese religion and culture"— Provided by publisher.
Identifiers: LCCN 2025024193 (print) | LCCN 2025024194 (ebook) | ISBN 9781626986435 trade paperback | ISBN 9798888660850 epub
Subjects: LCSH: Christianity and other religions—Chinese | Christianity and culture—China | Catholic Church—China
Classification: LCC BR128.C4 Y36 2026 (print) | LCC BR128.C4 (ebook)
LC record available at https://lccn.loc.gov/2025024193
LC ebook record available at https://lccn.loc.gov/2025024194

*I dedicate this book to Pope Francis, for his
love for China and the Chinese people.*

*Holy Father, you once wrote me in a letter, "I encourage you
to promote dialogue on the paths of reconciliation and peace.
I bless you and all your loved ones from my heart."*

*Your words are a guiding light for my path forward.
You had inspired me through to completion of this book,
then you passed away, sending us blessings from Heaven.*

*You had always wanted to visit China.
I have the feeling that you are smiling at us from Heaven saying,
"Why are you crying over there? I am already present in China with you!"*

Contents

Foreword vii
Preface xiii
Acknowledgments xvii
Introduction xix

1. **Dialectic of Harmony in Dialogue with Trinitarian Relationship** 1
   Harmony in Chinese Culture 3
   Trinitarian Relationship 9
   Possible Contribution of the Chinese Dialectic
      of Harmony to Trinitarian Theology 21

2. **Ecological Civilization and Integral Ecology** 32
   The Relationship between Human Beings and
      Nature in Chinese Culture 34
   The Relationship between Human Beings and
      Nature from the Catholic Perspective 42
   What Has Gone Wrong? 45
   Relational Paradigm 52
   "Integral Ecology" in Relation to "Ecological Civilization" 61

3. **Fraternity and Social Friendship** 79
   The Ideas of Fraternity, Brotherhood, and
      Universal Love in Chinese Culture 80
   The Ideas of Brotherhood in Christianity 91
   Human Fraternity for Peace and Living Together
      as Proposed by Pope Francis 97

      Fraternity Instead of Clash: Relevancy in Christianity,
          Islam, and China 102
      Fratelli Tutti on Fraternity and Social Friendship
          Consonant with Chinese Culture. 109

4. **Poverty Alleviation and a New Economic Model** 117
      Poverty Alleviation in China 119
      Can China's Poverty Alleviation Be a Contribution
          to a New Economic Paradigm? 126
      The Threat of Materialism, Spiritual Poverty,
          and the Culture of Indifference. 130
      Catholic Social Services, a Witness to
          Spiritual Poverty Alleviation 134
      Simple Lifestyle Consonant with Asian Values and
          with the Spirit of the Economy of Francesco 138

5. **Freedom of Religion and the Golden Rule of Reciprocity.** 151
      Dialogue between the Holy See and Chinese Authorities 152
      Inculturation or Sinicization 155
      Interculturality, a Two-Way Process, Instead of
          Unidirectional Inculturation or Sinicization 163
      Moral Courage beyond Trauma 166
      Mary, Mother of Hope and Tenderness 176

Conclusion 178
Bibliography 199
Index 217

Foreword

Today the future of humanity can no longer be thought of without China, as if this had ever been possible. A civilization that is present on the stage of history is an example of arrogant and extraordinary human performance for all to see. Not only because of its population size and the relevance of its millenary civilization, but also because of the irrepressible and vital creativity that it currently manifests. China has put the Western world on the defensive, in terms of political and economic strategy, often pushing it to adopt the ancient and now unthinkable dialectical model of the "clash of civilizations."

And yet, another path is now ideally possible and realistic, a path of "the culture of encounter." Pope Francis defined the culture of encounter as the budding of a civilization marked by constructive encounter between different cultures that embraces all of humanity. This prophetic path will only succeed with great difficulty. It is the sprouting of a civilization, in the shared experience, from the bowels of what is most authentically human that has been generated and kept, in the breath of the Spirit of God, by different cultures, purified of their dross and deviations and open to each other in reciprocity in the search for truth, the common good, in the practice of justice, and fraternity.

The path of culture of encounter is a viable way, in truth, not discovered today. The encounter between Chinese culture and the message of the Gospel of Christ was, for one example, the bright and promising strategy followed by Matteo Ricci. And is also the strategy which, with the prudent exercise of patience and perseverance, marks the ongoing process of official relations between the Catholic Church and the People's Republic of China.

The proposal outlined in the pages of this suggestive and timely book by Chiaretto Yan moves convincingly and in a well-argued way from this perspective. The author defines it as a "dream": in the sense that it is an ideal gaze nourished by hope. And yet it is not a simple utopia, because it draws, on the one hand, from the promised advent of the Kingdom of God, a kingdom of justice and peace among all peoples. This promise became the leaven of history with the Gospel of Jesus; and which, on the other hand, is grafted into the seeds of expectation and hope present in all cultures and that have taken shape in the great civilizations.

It is a matter of bringing together the understanding of these two realities: the Gospel of God in Jesus and the cultures of humanity. This involves discerning what is most proper and universal in the Gospel, with respect to what has been its inculturation in the West: with its unmissable gains, but also its particularity that calls for enrichment and integration. Isn't this, ultimately, the beating heart of the Christian message: the unity of love that arises from the free encounter of one with the other? Rightly, then, Chiaretto Yan grasps in the message of a God who is Love, therefore, Unity in the Trinity, the horizon within which the historical significance of the Gospel is effectively inscribed in today's humanity. The specific "culture of unity" in the freedom that emanates from it, at the service of promoting an enriching diversity in reciprocity, is capable of capturing the deepest demands and the promises that are present in the "culture of harmony" born from the Chinese genius.

Therefore, it is not only a question of looking at Chinese culture as a providential and necessary factor of integration and rebalancing of the dominant culture in the West today: as, for example, François Julien cleverly proposes to do. Yan looks into the bowels of Christianity to grasp what is vital today and what cultural tradition has nourished it up to now with mixed success, over the course of the centuries. So that the encounter with the living heart of Chinese culture can be the encounter between two living realities: indeed, with the mutual support and fertilization of two living branches of the single trunk of God's history with humanity.

In the Christian sphere, Yan grasps two great signs of this path which, despite everything that seems to say the opposite, is opening up in hearts, minds, and initiatives: First of all, in the wake of the magisterium of the Second Vatican Council, which presents the Church as the sign and instrument of union with God and of the unity of all mankind starting from the Gospel of Jesus, the works of Pope Francis programmatically expressed in the light of the spiritual impulse of *Evangelii Gaudium*, and on a sociocultural level, in *Laudato Si'* and *Fratelli Tutti*. Then, at the same time, Yan incorporates insights of the evangelical performance arising from the impulse of the charism of unity from Jesus's prayer to the Father: "May all be one," as interpreted in the thought and work of Chiara Lubich and the Focolare Movement.

The fresco, documented and timely, and at the same time agile and fresh, that the author offers us sketches the decisive coordinates of this *kairós*. He reads and expresses its main resonances and original declinations through the prism of the experience of a son of China who lives with passion and responsibility the joy and commitment of making what is most proper to the Gospel sprout from the womb of the Chinese culture. That it may shine, in all its beauty, this indispensable and shining color in the rainbow of unity.

Piero Coda
Secretary General,
Pontifical International Theological Commission
Former President, Sophia University Institute, Italy

* * *

In *Fratelli Tutti*, where Pope Francis depicts vividly the threat to our contemporary time with "dark clouds over a closed world," he first described the reality of "shattered dreams." While "for decades, it seemed that the world had learned a lesson from its many wars and disasters and was slowly moving towards various forms of integration," in fact "ancient conflicts thought long buried are breaking out anew while instances of a myopic, extremist, resentful and aggressive nationalism are on the rise" (10–11).

Chiaretto is now boldly presenting his dream with broad strokes of movement between the ideas, concepts. and phenomena of Chinese and Christian civilizations. Raising the curtain on his dream(s) in the preface of the book, he outlines his basic approach: "I am inviting readers to consider two questions at the back of my mind that guide me during my writing: Why do I choose to write about this topic? What is new that I want to share?" He continues thus: "Unlike natural sciences where empirical evidence can be measured, my approach is mostly experiential, first-person, dealing with the 'subject' directly, but it has also come from the privilege of frank, candid, and open exchanges with friends from different nationalities and political persuasions."

In his thirty years of service in China, Chiaretto has also tried to realize his dream in his own ways. Separately we have developed different understandings of Chinese and Christian civilizations. As a professional academic trained in comparative and intercultural studies of Chinese and European civilizations, I have looked closely at how the two civilizations may be compared. In a recent article on the interreligious dialogue between Confucianism and Christianity concerning the theology of mission, I traced the evolution of the dialogue from the 1950s and 1960s to the World Congress of Philosophy in Beijing in

2019, which adopted one of the main axioms of Confucianism as its theme. My concluding remarks from that review were that "from a macro-historical perspective, one can see how the intellectual community of both China and Cultural China has been reshaping and designing a new paradigm for dialogue with the West. On this note, one may further extend the application of the themes of contextualization and methodology to the intellectual movement that has reshaped world history in the last two centuries, which in turn, may reveal the deeper significance of these two themes."[1]

The themes of contextualization and methodology are relevant to a fuller understanding and appreciation of the work of Chiaretto, who takes a macro approach reflecting on the two age-old civilizations. He adopts a transdisciplinary and interdisciplinary approach bringing together areas of theology, philosophy, ecology, politics, economics, and cultural-religious dialogue. Each of these areas offers an immense treasure of specialized knowledge and deep analysis.

Lastly, Chiaretto's effort of macro analysis creates an important perspective for understanding Pope Francis's pontificate. In my guest-edited special issue on *Fratelli Tutti* in *Tripod*, to which Chiaretto and I both contributed, I interpreted Pope Francis's pontificate as an evolving spiritual and ecclesiological mapping of the global church. Taking this as a cornerstone and guiding stick, I described how "Pope Francis's new theological and ecclesiological vision may reconstruct a new paradigm for intercultural and interreligious dialogue in which the Chinese cultural tradition may interact with Christianity under the polyhedral model and integral human development. This envisions an integral approach

---

[1] Edmund Kwok, "Review of *Confucianism and Christianity: Interreligious Dialogue on the Theology of Mission*," edited by Edmund Kee-Fook Chia, in *Tripod*, no. 200 (Hong Kong: Holy Spirit Study Centre, 2022): 209–217.

to reflect on the local and global significance of the encyclical."[2] Chiaretto's book shows, on the one hand, the potential paths of the culture of encounter and dialogue, and on the other hand, the need to treat each culture with the appropriate recognition of the uniqueness of different civilizations—in this case, Chinese and Christian.

The scope of Chiaretto's knowledge is wide-reaching, and his ability to bring different topics and areas into encounter and interdisciplinary dialogue provides the reader with broad understanding of the intercultural and interreligious dialogue between Chinese and Christian civilization, past, present, and future. A convincing illustration of microhistory, his book demonstrates positively the motto of Sima Qian, the Great Historian of China, a motto that has guided me in my decades of historical studies: "To explore the relationship between the Way of Heaven and the Way of Man, have a thorough understanding of the course of historical development and the changes therein, expound my own opinion of events of the past and present my own system of analysis."

Siu-tong Edmund Kwok
Professor Emeritus of Comparative History
Former Dean of Faculty of Arts, Chinese University of Hong Kong

---

[2] Edmund Kwok, "Epilogue: From Fraternity to Integrality—An Integral Reflection on *Fratelli Tutti*," in *Intercultural and Interreligious Reflection on* Fratelli Tutti, edited by Edmund Kwok, in *Tripod*, no. 201 (Hong Kong: Holy Spirit Study Centre, 2022), 209–236.

Preface

I dream of a world of fewer wars and conflicts, less hunger and indifference, the reduction of poverty and greed. I dream of a world of more fraternity, with new relationships of understanding, trust, and respect between persons and among nations. We have developed speed, technology, and businesses that give abundance, but have left us in need of friendship. Social media and instant information have left us more alienated and feeling lonely. More than wealth, we need sharing of goods. More than technocracy, we need human heartedness. More than competition, we need collaboration. More than wit, we need tenderness. Without these values we will turn violent, but with them, the gift of peace bestowed, we can hope again. I dream of respectful dialogues among people of different cultures, faiths, and convictions, recognizing that diversity in harmony can be a gift for one another. I dream of a world, a common home for all, for generations to come, with fresh air to breathe, and for young people to travel freely for exchanges and appreciation of each other's history, culture, art, and literature.

As a follower of the Focolare Movement founded by Chiara Lubich in 1943, I believe in the charism of unity, building a united world beyond all borders. To understand better and appreciate this book, I am inviting readers to consider two questions at the back of my mind that guide me during my writing: Why do I choose to write about this topic? What is new that I want to share?

I was born in China, raised in Hong Kong, and spent long years abroad—particularly in Italy where I did my philosophical and theological studies, including my first doctoral degree at the Gregorian University in Rome and my second doctorate at the Sophia University Institute in Florence.

I have been living in China for thirty years, with the advantage of firsthand experiences from a Chinese perspective, and with regular visits overseas. Despite the travel restrictions due to the COVID-19 pandemic in past years, I was able to visit the United States and Europe. I was invited to participate in a series of conferences on China with the background of the ongoing tension between China and the United States, with unimaginable consequences not just for the two countries but for the whole world, should there be a miscalculation on either side.

From my participation in the conferences, I was more convinced than before of the lack of understanding and bias of each side toward the other, all conditioned by the propaganda, either state-sponsored or the so-called free press with a "hidden agenda." To a great extent, this attitude holds true between the East and the West. Sad to say, even people of goodwill who promote solidarity fall into this trap.

There is an ongoing strategic competition between China and the United States. The strategic ambiguity of US diplomacy is now clear: China should be contained at all costs—hence, trade and technological war, military alliances to isolate China, not to mention the narratives, true or false, pervasive in the Western media, to cast China in a bad light.

China, on the other hand, continues to carry the historical baggage of "a hundred years of humiliation" caused by Western powers, about which people in the West know very little if anything. Until the opening-up policy was implemented, the usual mantra in the West was that the Chinese people are "brainwashed," like elsewhere where brainwashing takes other, more elegant forms: mass media being one of them, not to mention PR firms and lobbyists. Now with the opening-up policy, millions of Chinese tourists "invade the whole world," prior to the pandemic, that is; they now know the West better than the West knows the East. This newfound knowledge is nevertheless not free from the old mindset.

With increasing tensions between China and the West, the United States in particular, the byproduct is a sharp rise in nationalism, especially among Chinese youth. It's a "shot in the arm" for the "national rejuvenation" campaign espoused by President Xi Jinping, with even wider grassroots support. At this critical and dangerous point in time, with so much at stake for the whole world, a new and mutual knowledge is badly, truly needed.

This book intends to be a humble contribution to help readers in both the West and China to know each other in the most important issues at stake, a new knowledge that has consequential geopolitical implications. Unlike natural sciences, where empirical evidence can be measured, my approach is mostly experiential, first-person, dealing with the "subject" directly, but it has also come from the privilege of frank, candid, and open exchanges with friends from different nationalities and political persuasions.

I have opted to focus my attention on the two oldest and existing institutions: the Catholic Church and Chinese culture, whose relationship can well be the game-changer. A cautionary note: Pondering the intercultural and interreligious relationship of these major institutions inevitably risks making broad statements generally accepted by the academic and religious communities, with due respect for contrasting or polarizing opinions. Due to the breadth of the study, I may be repetitive at times. I beg to raise *Repetita Iuvant,* a core Athenian concept picked up by the Romans, who turned it into a proverb: *Repetitio mater studiorum* (Repetition is the mother of all learning). The apparent repetition serves to clarify the analytical complexity basic to this genre of study.

It is commonly stated that the 2008 Beijing Olympics signaled a coming-out party for China. Two years later, China hosted another international event, the 2010 Shanghai Expo, gaining recognition again as a country committed to exchanges and friendship. At the Beijing Horticultural Expo 2019, the Holy See had a pavilion despite China and the Vatican having no diplomatic relations. Beijing did it again quite successfully with the 2022 Winter Olympics. In spite of these "successes," if the Chinese leadership invites and receives the Holy Father, it will really be a cherished event, not only for Chinese Catholics or Catholics worldwide, but a celebrated event, a real surprise in the history of the world.

For those who are interested in Christianity in China, the purpose of this book is to inform and empower engaged readers who may find here and there topics that may make you wonder: How to engage in a fruitful exchange about Chinese wisdom and Christian theology? How can Christians and all people of goodwill work together for the flourishing of our common home? Why should we learn to appreciate more profoundly each other's civilizations? How can we have better politics and international relations for world peace? What can be learned from the Chinese experience of economic development and poverty alleviation? How do urban migration and demographic changes affect the life of the Catholic communities? What are today's Chinese young people looking for? What are the challenges for the clergy and for the formation of the laity? What challenges does the Church in China face in sinicization, inculturation, and interculturality? Why is it important to engage China in Sino-Christian dialogue today? Where is China-Vatican dialogue now and where is it going?

It is my sincere hope that this book may offer a small contribution toward helping to realize the testament of Jesus: "That all may be one" (John 17:21). And at the same time, China can be closer to fulfilling the dream it has had since the dawn of its civilization: "that under the sky we are one family."

Acknowledgments

With grateful heart, I thank Piero Coda and Bernhard Callebaut, advisers at the Sophia University Institute (Instituto Universitario Sophia [IUS]) for my dissertation, which has become the present book. I am thankful for the IUS environment as a center of research and education—and at the same time, a school of life, a meeting place between experience and thought, where different cultures and academic disciplines come together in a strongly relational context, one that seeks to base the interactions between people (among peoples from all over the world) on wisdom and as a gift for one another.

I am privileged to have two distinguished professors to write the foreword: Piero Coda (from the West) and Edmund Kwok (from the East), a foretaste of what's to come in the book.

A special thanks for the support of Thomas McGuire, who proofread and helped edit the book. I also thank Chun Boc Tay, Roberto Catalano, Philipp Hu, Sergio Rondinara, Anthonio Baggio, Luigino Bruni, and Benedetto Gui for their invaluable insights during my conversations with them in the course of writing this book.

Introduction

Why Did I Write This Book?

This book is a continuation of a previous one, titled *Evangelization in China: Challenges and Prospects*, based on my original doctoral dissertation at the Gregorian Pontifical University. The novelty of this present research is broader, taking an integral approach, dialoguing on values between Christianity, represented by the Catholic Church, and China, in five fields: philosophy, ecology, politics, economics, and cultural-religious dialogue.

My dissertation in 2012 was timely, for there was talk at the time of excommunicating some bishops in the Church in China—a step that would have posed, without exaggeration, the danger of a third Great Schism. Instead, my thesis emphasized dialogue. With the election of Pope Francis, the scenario changed, making possible a reopening of dialogue and a historical agreement with China in 2018 on the nomination of Chinese bishops.

The present research is mainly about dialogue between the Catholic Church and China. It is essential to know the present context, where this relationship is being articulated. For this reason, it is necessary to explore the broader dimensions of East-West relations in general, and of China-US. relations in particular. At the present time, the US policy to contain China is more than obvious, with military and economic alliances all motivated by geopolitics. Underneath what is obvious, there are countless hidden initiatives to undermine the rise of China. The 2019–2021 social movement and unrest in Hong Kong, the present wars in Gaza and Ukraine, all point to the fact that the world is facing challenges and dangerous times ahead. The cold war may very well turn into a hot one.

For me, these dialogues are not two-term but three-term relationships, with the gospel message on top. My point of departure is the conviction that revelation is a light that enters into all cultures. Inculturation of the gospel message at one point took place in the West; now, at this propitious time after Vatican II, it is taking place within Eastern culture, with Chinese culture as my focus here.

Another new feature of this research is its transdisciplinary nature, with the charism of unity as the throughline connecting the five fields and disciplines.[1]

Review of a Theological Foundation for Dialogue

The Principle of Revelation

Vatican II affirmed that revelation per se is an event that God communicates, present in all religious and cultural traditions of humanity, which reached its full manifestation in Jesus Christ, on the basis of the tradition of the people of Israel, where Jesus is the Word of God made flesh.[2] It teaches that "those religious truths which are by their nature accessible to human reason can be known by all men with ease, with solid certitude and with

---

[1] Pope Francis emphasizes that the fundamental criteria for a renewal of ecclesiastical studies are to experience the Church as a mystery rooted in the Trinity and of living together, to engage in wide-ranging dialogue at 360 degrees, and in interdisciplinary and cross-disciplinary approaches carried out with wisdom and creativity in the light of revelation, according to the vital intellectual principle of the unity in difference of knowledge and respect for its multiple, correlated, and convergent expressions. Cf. Francis, *Veritatis Gaudium, Apostolic Constitution on Ecclesiastical Universities and Faculties*, January 29, 2018, 4.

[2] Second Vatican Council, *Dei Verbum, Dogmatic Constitution on Divine Revelation*, 1965, 4.

no trace of error, even in this present state of the human race."³ This means that, from the theological and cultural point of view, revelation is the point of reference for all cultures, whether they are Greek and Latin cultures of the West, in which Christianity has already been inculturated in the first centuries, or other cultures of the East, such as Chinese and Indian, for example, where the Christian faith is in the process of inculturation.

The relationship between East and West is not a two-term but a three-term relationship. Revelation is the beginning, which is somehow the criterion of discernment and evaluation of the different inculturations, even between East and West. Revelation is also the source of this dynamism and the bridge. Therefore, it is not simply a direct relationship between East and West.

The approach to the transcendence of revelation, which has been manifested historically, goes to the Scriptures. The Old Testament was originally written in Hebrew; the New Testament, in Greek. This points to the novelty of revelation, which is conditioned by the culture and language through which it is expressed. When we receive revelation through a mediation, we also need to have a direct contact somehow with Jesus. We always have to compare and consult with the sources. The mediating culture is a means to arrive at the source—and is not absolute. It is a mistake for the West to make its interpretation absolute.

The Gospel Message Is for All Cultures

The reality of revelation involves capturing, knowing, and expressing the presence of God within a culture. Though the reality of revelation is thereby expressed, the expressions are not exhaustive because the reality is something bigger. For example, the Christian dogma was formulated in Greek terms in the fourth century, and the whole Church still recites this today. However, the significance

---

³ Ibid., 6.

of the reality of this formulation is something greater, and people of other cultures, such as Chinese, Indian, or African, can grasp meanings and richness that did not arise in the Western world.

Again, this is a relationship not of two, but of three. The reference point is always revelation. Inculturation in the Greek world is not the only one. There can be other inculturations, whether in India or China, for example. In the encyclical *Fides et Ratio*, John Paul II dedicated a chapter to the question of the relationship between revelation and the various cultures. He gives some criteria: "No one culture can ever become the criterion of judgement, much less the ultimate criterion of truth with regard to God's Revelation. The Gospel is not opposed to any culture," He continues,

> On the contrary, the message which believers bring to the world and to cultures is a genuine liberation from all the disorders caused by sin and is, at the same time, a call to the fullness of truth. Cultures are not only not diminished by this encounter; rather, they are prompted to open themselves to the newness of the Gospel's truth and to be stirred by this truth to develop in new ways.[4]

It happened in China with the case of Matteo Ricci. He intuited that Christianity should be inculturated and can be expressed in the language and culture of the Chinese, but the Rites Controversy[5] hampered the effort. Now the Church has enriched its conscience in a sense with inculturation.

---

[4] Pope John Paul II, *Fides et Ratio*, Encyclical on the Relationship between Faith and Reason, 1998, 71.

[5] The Chinese Rites controversy was a dispute among missionaries over the religiosity of Confucianism and Chinese rituals of honoring family ancestors during the seventeenth and eighteenth centuries. The Jesuits argued that these Chinese Rites were compatible with Christianity and should thus be tolerated, but the Dominicans and Franciscans disagreed and reported the issue to Rome. Rome banned Chinese Catholics from the rites, and consequentially Christian missions were banned and suffered a setback in China.

Trinitarian Logic Today Favors China-Christianity Dialogue

Today, what favors a greater possibility of inculturation of Christianity and of revelation in the thought and practice of Chinese traditions is the evolution of the Christian theology of God understood as Trinity. In the early centuries of Christianity—particularly in the fourth and fifth centuries, when the dogmas were formulated in councils such as Nicaea, Constantinople, and Chalcedon—the Trinitarian nature of God was affirmed; the Christian concept speaks about one God in three divine Persons. It is a great reality with regards to God, but the impact on the world of these insights remained rather limited. Although great thinkers such as Bonaventure and Thomas Aquinas said there is an image of the Trinity in the world, this insight did not emerge as a strong living reality in social relationships.[6] As Piero Coda, head of the International Theological Commission, points out, the lack of a strong living image of the Trinity produced a radical crisis in the course of modernity, especially in Europe. There was a conflictual separation of philosophy (reason and freedom) and theology (faith and tradition).[7] Meanwhile, propitiated by the

---

[6] In the Middle Ages, on the basis of giving new meaning to the "sense of Being/being" with an attempt at synthesizing and reciprocally enriching the Patristics, and the philosophical research of Greek origin (Plato, Aristotle, and Plotinus, handed down also through the mediation of Islamic culture), the experience of the gospel in the journey of the Church was lived in a decisive way by Francis of Assisi, and transmitted by the theological intelligence of Thomas Aquinas and Bonaventure. And yet the concept of the Trinity has failed to generate that place of experiencing and of thinking beyond the gains propitiated by the matrix of Greek metaphysics, although reshaped in its encounter with the intelligence of the revelation. One can say that the great Trinitarian theology of those centuries was not entirely able, at its root and in all its anthropological expressions, to emerge beyond the exercise of thought. See P. Coda et al., *Manifesto, Dizionario dinamico di Ontologia Trinitaria* (Roma: Città Nuova, 2021), 141–147.

[7] Ibid., 153–156.

discovery of the positive ontological meaning of creation by virtue of the Word made flesh, new and promising forms of knowledge (natural, humanistic, and social sciences) stood out, but on the cultural scenario also appears the religious wisdom of the East.[8]

In the twentieth century, the Trinitarian logic emerged with force in the Catholic Church, thanks to the renewed relationship with the traditions of the Orthodox Church. It emerged that the Trinity is the grammar of all reality, not only of the mystery of God, but also of the creation, the world, and man. This becomes a new point of departure for a renovation of Christian thinking. Certain classical interpretations of Greek metaphysics, which emphasized substance and separation of God from the world, had become stiff and were not able to grasp the novelty. Coda points out that through great theologians like Karl Rahner, Hans Urs von Balthasar, and those at the Second Vatican Council, the promise of a new thought with a Trinitarian perspective set in.[9] This Trinitarian vision is more dynamic and relational, closer to Chinese traditional thought, especially to the theme of harmony. Today, there are more propitious conditions for this dialogue of Chinese thought with the revelation, and with the tradition of theological thought in the West.[10]

---

[8] Coda et al., *Manifesto,* 149–150.

[9] Ibid., 188–189.

[10] The conditions for propitious dialogue with Chinese tradition and culture are shown by many studies conducted and offer a path for further deepening and exploration. See P. Coda, *Il logos e il nulla. Trinità religioni mistica* (Roma: Città Nuova, 2003), part 3; Coda, *La rivelazione e il segreto del Nulla* [The revelation and the secret of nothingness], Lectio Magistralis on the occasion of the conferment of an honorary doctorate in interreligious dialogue at the Dharma Drum University, Taiwan, 2019; Philipp K. T. Hu, "The Creation of the Universe from Nothingness by Laozi from the Perspective of Nothingness in the Christian Tradition," *Sophia* 13, no. 1 (2021): 75–92; Donald W. Mitchell and James Wiseman, *Transforming Suffering: Reflections on Finding Peace in Troubled Times* (New York: Lantern Books, 2010).

Introduction

This Trinitarian Vision Is Also the Heart of the "Charism of Unity"

The twentieth century saw new movements and communities rise within the Catholic Church, each with its own specificities. One of them, known as the Focolare Movement, gives particular attention to the unity of the human family as contained in Jesus's prayer: "May they all be one." Throughout the history of the movement, members have tried to incarnate the "charism of unity," contributing to the efforts of the Catholic Church for unity. Pope Francis described this charism with the following words:

> The charism of unity is a providential stimulus and a powerful support for experiencing this evangelical mystic of "the we," that is, walking together in the history of the men and women of our time as of one heart and soul, discovering and loving concretely those members of one another. Jesus prayed to the Father for this: "that they may all be one as you and I are one," and in himself he showed us the way, up to the complete gift of all in the abyssal emptying of the cross.[11]

The dynamic rhythm of the Trinitarian vision at the heart of the charism of unity is open to dialogue with all cultures. Openness to dialogue makes possible a response to profound needs in every culture. If the Trinitarian vision expressed partakes only of Western culture, it would be difficult for a Chinese person to find a connection to it. The charism of unity explores the Trinitarian light in different disciplines, a light before all disciplinary mediations that illuminates all, and therefore is transdisciplinary and universal. At the same time, it is also

---

[11] Pope Francis, "Address at the Pastoral Visit to Loppiano, the International Center of the Focolare Movement," May 10, 2018.

interdisciplinary because it relates disciplines, various areas of human knowledges, and activities to each other. The charism of unity is the leitmotif in this research.

Review of the Culture of Unity and the Culture of Harmony

Due to historical circumstances, after Matteo Ricci, it seems that much is still to be done in dialogue between Christianity and Chinese culture. This research investigates the possibility of dialogue between Chinese and Christian culture, concentrating more on cultural roots and the recent developments in the relational prospects of Trinitarian ontology in the West.

Some of the most valuable insights and explications of Trinitarian relationship I adopt here are inspired by the charism of Chiara Lubich, who proposed the "culture of unity" and the mystery of love, "Jesus crucified and forsaken," which could be a pivotal key to reading the Chinese reality and providing original insights.

Unity basically sums up the whole Chinese culture, though the Chinese love to use the term "harmony" rather than "unity": harmony of relations between people as emphasized in Confucianism, and harmony between man and nature as emphasized in Daoism. To achieve this harmony of relationships, Confucianism stresses the importance of one's role so as to regulate one's relationships in the family, and in society as a consequence. This is a vision that corresponds in some way to the idea of little pieces of stone in a mosaic. Daoism instead emphasizes the relationship of man with the Dao, and therefore unity with the fundamental nature of the universe. The two systems of thought, complementary to one another, are the fundamentals of Chinese culture, aiming at total harmony, a cosmic unity, the fruit of the interplay between *yin* and *yang*, the two vital forces of the universe. Archbishop Angelo Fernandes of India said, "The fundamental similarity between the Christian tradition and the Confucian concept of harmony could serve as a common ground for significant and fruitful dialogue."[12]

On the general theme of "Theology of Dialogue," the Federation of Asian Bishops Conference (FABC) issued back in 1988 a document titled *Theology of Harmony*[13] that highlighted precisely the importance of the concept of harmony in interreligious dialogue. It issued several documents in this regard: *Religions in the Service of Universal Harmony* (1988), and under the central theme "Working Together in Harmony in the World Today," the federation has made a series of comparisons and detailed studies between Christianity and some major religions on the concept of harmony: with Islam in 1992, with Buddhism in 1994, and with Hinduism in 1995. This emphasis now encompasses humankind's right relationship with nature and ecology.

Jim Gallagher, in his book on the story of the Focolare Movement and its founder, *A Woman's Work*, describes it this way: "The Ideal was to build unity, or maybe a better way to describe it would be the word 'harmony.'"[14] In synthesis, unity means

---

[12] The Pontifical Council for Interreligious Dialogue (PCID) has organized serious Christian-Daoist Colloquiums with different themes: "Seeking the Truth Together" in 2016 in Taipei, "Christian and Daoist Ethics in Dialogue" in 2018 in Singapore, and "Cultivating a Harmonious Society through Interreligious Dialogue" in 2024 in Hong Kong. There is an earnest effort to dialogue on the concept of harmony between Christianity and Chinese culture, and it is pertinent to start with Daoism. As for Confucianism, it is often characterized as a system of social and ethical philosophy rather than a religion; however, Confucianism was built on ancient religious foundations and values that greatly influenced the way of life of Chinese people from ancient times until now.

[13] Federation of Asian Bishops' Conferences, *Theology of Dialogue*, Tagaytay City, Philippines, 1988.

[14] Jim Gallagher, *Woman's Work: Story of the Focolare Movement and Its Founder* (New York: New City Press, 1998), 21.

harmony of relationships. What Pope Francis said in response to Eugenio Scalfari in 2013 is striking insofar as relationships are concerned: "I would not speak about 'absolute' truths, even for believers, in the sense that absolute is that which is disconnected and bereft of all relationship. Truth, according to the Christian faith, is the love of God for us in Jesus Christ. Therefore, truth is a relationship."[15]

It could also be said that relationship is at the heart of Asian cultures. A concept that follows is reciprocity. Just think of the famous Golden Rule: "Do not do to others what you would not want done to you." It was Confucius who expressed it verbatim as we find it in the Gospel, while in other religions there is something similar but with different words. Tu Weiming, Chinese Confucian scholar, worked together with Hans Küng and Leonard Swidler to advocate the Golden Rule and interreligious dialogue, culminating later in the organization of the last World Congress of Philosophy, in Beijing in 2019, with the conference theme grounded in Confucianism.[16]

Some economists forecast China to become the world's largest economy in the near future. Nevertheless, it faces great challenges at home and abroad in fields such as politics, the economy, and social and environmental issues. Since the time of Ricci, Chinese society, despite official caution, has never been as open to Christianity as it is today. There is much interest in the study of Christianity in the Chinese context, particularly oriented to the social aspect.

---

[15] Pope Francis, Letter to a Non-believer: Pope Francis Responds to Dr. Eugenio Scalfari, Journalist of the Italian Newspaper *La Repubblica*, September 4, 2013.

[16] Edmund Kwok, "Humanism of the Third Generation Confucianism," in *Anthology of Celebrative Essays of Mr. Tu Weiming's 80th Birthday*, ed. Chen Lai (Beijing: People's Press, 2019), 601–603.

Introduction

Present research reads Chinese narratives in light of the culture of unity from different perspectives: politics aimed at fraternity, an economy aimed at happiness, and technological development oriented toward a sustainable environment. Each area presents possible contributions to fulfilling the "Chinese dream." Needless to say, I do not repeat the usual notions—positive or negative, right or wrong—that are favorite topics of the Western media, but take an active attitude in dialogue rather than being pessimistic and passive.

Jesus prays for unity, "That all may be one" (John 17:21). However, the idea of a united world is not foreign to the Chinese, though the Chinese love to use the term "harmony" rather than "unity." Confucius, five hundred years before Christ, said, "Under the sky we are one family." He did not speak of a nation, a people, or a particular race, but always used the term "under the sky" (*tianxia*), which means the entire human race.

Another related main idea in Confucianism is the notion of being "harmonious while diversified [*he er butong*]," that is, diversity in unity. This concept recognizes that although people have differences in opinions, interests, preferences, profiles, and so on, they need first to keep peace and to live in harmony with each other while maintaining their diversity.

The East and West have common values but with distinct characteristics. China emphasizes that the pursuit of these values or goals is a gradual process, without instant solutions. Chinese policymakers are keen to maintain social stability while introducing reforms in different fields in ways that are compatible with existing national conditions. This is an important part of the collective Chinese psyche: do anything to avoid chaos (*luan*) as experienced during the political campaigns of the Great Leap Forward (1958–1960) and the infamous Cultural Revolution (1966–1976).

Some Open Questions

The Chinese dream is an open concept and can be said to be the common aspirations of the Chinese people to have a better tomorrow, to revive their culture so as to gain their rightful place in the world and in history. At this historical time with the present stage of sociocultural development, China is receptive and proposes to pursue core values such as harmony, friendship, civility, prosperity, justice, freedom, equality, and fraternity.

This research aims to encourage East-West as well as China-Christianity dialogue, to facilitate Holy See–China relationships, to promote understandings rather than prejudices and the consciousness that diversity is richness, with the objective of securing world peace. Starting a process, as Pope Francis said, is more important than occupying spaces or achieving short-term goals. More specifically, this investigation attempts to answer the following questions: Is Chinese culture compatible with the gospel? In the spirit of inculturation, how can we dialogue between the culture of unity in Christianity and the culture of harmony in China? What could the Christian contributions be to China and in turn China to the world in the fields of politics, economics, ecology, and world peace? Do the core values of the Chinese dream as defined by Xi Jinping correspond to my aspiration as a Chinese Christian?

Methodology

The present investigation concentrates on some core values of the Chinese dream: "harmony" as an overall value for dialogue and world peace, the value of "fraternity and social friendship" for the field of politics, and "prosperity and alleviation of poverty" in the field of economics. China is also giving much attention to the so-called ecologic civilization; this book also touches on issues of ecology, as well as social justice and religious freedom.

Introduction

The desire of recent pontiffs to bring about a rapprochement with China has been consistent. In order to deepen the understanding of social phenomena in China, it is necessary to approach them from several complementary disciplinary directions and analytical frameworks: philosophy, ecology, politics, and economics.

Pope Francis emphasized in *Veritatis Gaudium* that fundamental criteria for a renewal of ecclesiastical studies are to experience Church as "a mystery rooted in the Trinity" and of living together, to engage in "wide-ranging dialogue" at 360 degrees, and an "interdisciplinary and cross-disciplinary[17] (trans-disciplinary) approach carried out with "wisdom and creativity in the light of Revelation," according to "the vital intellectual principle of the unity in difference of knowledge and respect for its multiple, correlated and convergent expressions."[18]

Since the 1920s, philosophy, politics, and economics (PPE) as a combined degree has long been offered at Oxford University, and in recent decades has been duplicated in other universities worldwide. These courses produce a significant number of notable graduates, but the multidisciplinary approach leads to mostly generalists over specialists. The present research methodology attempts to employ not only an interdisciplinary but also a transdisciplinary approach to confront contrasting situations and conflicting issues in a value-based dialogue between Christianity and Chinese culture.

This research is designed in such a way that value-based dialogue is a method for resolving conflicts and crises by building trust

---

[17] While the term "cross-disciplinary" is used in the English edition of the Apostolic Constitution, the term "trans-disciplinary" is used in the original Italian edition. In some cases, the two terms may be interchangeable, but I prefer to use the term "trans-disciplinary" in the present work, for I am about to speak of a charism that enters into all disciplines.

[18] Pope Francis, *Veritatis Gaudium, Apostolic Constitution on Ecclesiastical Universities and Faculties*, January 29, 2018, 4.

and commitment between big institutions with great histories and contemporary relevance, such as the universal Church and China, between Christianity and Chinese culture. This approach has not been emphasized enough in the contemporary world political context. Pope Francis in his encyclicals *Laudato Si'* and *Fratelli Tutti* encourages the view of the human and ecological crisis through an integral approach, as a way to work together for world peace.

This research starts from a historical and cultural perspective. The later part of the text is more analytical and critical of social phenomena. My approach starts from mostly experiential, first-person reflection, dealing with the subject directly, and then addressing the subject matter with the help of experts and studies. The first chapter deals with the Trinitarian relationship in Christianity and the dialectics of harmony in Chinese culture. The philosophical tools of chapter 1 are used as a leitmotif and pivotal point to provide real insights and tackle other categories in the following chapters of different disciplinary fields: ecology, politics, economics, and religion.

1

Dialectic of Harmony in Dialogue with Trinitarian Relationship

While Matteo Ricci inaugurated a fruitful dialogue between Christianity and Confucianism, dialogue today has to take into account the whole of Chinese culture—namely Confucianism, Daoism, and Chinese Buddhism—including the influence of Western ideology such as Marxism or socialism with Chinese characteristics. Church Fathers such as St. Augustine of Hippo made contributions to theology coming from his profound experience of God and from the encounter between Christianity and Latin culture that has its roots in Greek philosophy. In this chapter, I attempt to read the mystery of the Trinity with categories of Chinese thought. Chiara Lubich developed a spirituality centered on "Jesus abandoned, the key of unity."[1] *This central figure of the forsaken Jesus in the Trinity is pivotal to the understanding of the dialectic relationship of love within the Trinity and of God with man and the world. I find the Daoist concepts of the dialectic of harmony containing many elements helpful for the understanding of the Trinitarian relationship. This will also serve as a key for the dialogue in the field of politics, economics, and ecology to be explored in the following chapters.*

---

[1] Chiara Lubich, *Unity and Jesus Forsaken* (New York: New City Press, 1985), 37.

The Jubilee Year of 2000 was celebrated worldwide, and Beijing's Millennium Tower was built for the occasion. In the center of this millennium monument, there is a circular mural decorated with multicolored stone carvings and a huge relief featuring five thousand years of Chinese cultural history. Among many great figures in Chinese history, Matteo Ricci (1552–1610), who introduced the West and Christianity to China and promoted cultural exchange,[2] is recognized for his unique contribution to China. In 2010, the Catholic Diocese of Shanghai also initiated the cause of beatification for Xu Guangqi (1562–1633), the great Catholic scientist and chancellor of China. The beatification of Xu together with Ricci would be a gratifying event in China and very significant for the Church, considering how China's and the Church's lives have been intertwined. As an outstanding representative of the Western culture of his times, Ricci inaugurated a fruitful dialogue between Christianity and Confucianism. While the Church today affirms the correctness of Ricci's attitude and approach to China, this dialogue today must also consider the whole of Chinese culture. To this precise task, I offer this contribution.

---

[2] Ricci published with his collaborators many works in Chinese, among which are the *Treatise on Friendship*, *Ten Paradoxes*, the first six volumes of *Elements of Euclid*, the *Handbook of Epictetus*, and great *Map of World*, and a short *Catechism*. The most enduring work of all, *The True Meaning of the Lord of Heaven*, is a synthesis of traditional Chinese thought and the fundamental doctrines of Christianity. Matteo Ricci, *The True Meaning of the Lord of Heaven*, ed. E. J. Malatesta (Taipei: Ricci Institute, 1985). Other sources of his life and works can be found in Matteo Ricci and P. M. d'Elia, ed., *Fonti Ricciane*, 3 vols. (Roma: Libreria dello Stato, 1942–1949).

Harmony in Chinese Culture

Confucianism, Daoism, and Buddhism: Complementary to One Another in China

A prominent theme of Chinese culture is the desire for total harmony and cosmic unity, a result of the interplay between the *yin* and the *yang*, the two vital forces of the universe. Harmony between heaven and earth is also a basic theme of Chinese culture, and is the foundation of much religious activity. To achieve this harmony of relationships, Confucianism stresses the importance of one's role in relationship to the family and to society. Daoism emphasizes the relationship of the human with the Dao, and the relationship between humanity and the cosmos. The neo-Confucianist Zhang Zai, of the Song dynasty (960–1279), stressed that heaven and humanity are one.[3]

Confucianism, Daoism, and Buddhism have unceasingly enriched one another in the course of Chinese history and cultural tradition. For most Chinese, the three schools of thought are complementary and contribute to the happiness and harmony of daily life. The mainstream belief of the Chinese across the ages was Confucianism, a humanistic political and moral philosophy with focus on present-worldliness. It is complemented by the otherworldliness of Daoism. Furthermore, the lack of emphasis on transcendence in Confucianism left space for later developments. When Buddhism arrived in China by way of India, with a more precise religious view and spirituality, it supplemented this lack. Daoism with its metaphysical elements interacted readily with Buddhism. In later developments, the

---

[3] In his work *Western Inscription*, Zhang Zai (1020–1077) stressed the unity of heaven, earth, and all beings. Heaven and humanity are one. All people are brothers and sisters because everyone is birthed by heaven.

Buddha was deified in some Mahayana sects. China thereupon promoted Mahayana Buddhism, which then spread to Korea, Japan, and Vietnam.

Ultimate Reality of the Dao, Mysterious and Ineffable

The opening chapter of *Daodejing* (the Book of *Dao* and *De*), states, "The Dao that can be defined is not the constant Dao; the name that can be named is not the constant name."[4] In this same chapter, two other terms—*miao* and *xuan*—were employed to express the mysterious nature of the Dao, though they are translated respectively as "subtle" and "profound."[5] In another chapter, Laozi (Lao-tzu, fl. 6th century BCE) gives three attributes of the Dao: the invisible, the inaudible, and the formless.[6]

Chinese philosophy in this way contrasts with philosophy in the West. Philosophy in the West focuses more on ontology, with emphasis on the study of "being" in order to grasp reality and give it a name. On the other hand, Chinese thought is often viewed from the phenomenological perspective, concentrated

---

[4] The translations of the *Daodejing* in this book are mine, after consulting several recent translations, including Joseph H. Wong, "*Logos* and *Tao*: Johannine Christology and a Taoist Perspective," *Path: Pontificia Academia Theologica* 2 (2003); Chan Wing-tsit, ed., *A Source Book in Chinese Philosophy* (Princeton, NJ: Princeton University Press, 1963), 136–176. In the translation of the first two verses of *Daodejing* here, Joseph Wong used the term "the constant Dao" while Chan instead translated it as "the eternal *Dao*."

[5] Chan Wing-tsit indicated that the translation of *miao* could be "mystery," but Wang Bi preferred "subtlety." Chan, *A Source Book in Chinese Philosophy*, 139.

[6] *Daodejing*, chapter 14: "We look at it and so not see it; Its name is The Invisible. We listen to it and do not hear it; Its name is The Inaudible. We touch it and do not find it; Its name is The Subtle (formless). These three cannot be further inquired into (unfathomable), And hence merge into one." See Chan, *A Source Book in Chinese Philosophy*.

more on social issues, although metaphysical issues have also been addressed since ancient times. As suggested in the opening lines of *Daodejing*, the Dao can neither be described nor given a name; one may start with observation first without giving it a specific name, in order to avoid giving a limited description of the phenomena and of the guiding principles.

Where do we come from? Who are we? Where are we going? These are the basic questions in life. To the Chinese, God is beyond the rational understanding of man. We use the term *laisheng* to refer to the afterlife, ultimate reality, and the transcendent. So, God is above all a mystery. In this mindset, theology as a science of God actually surprises the Chinese mind. In fact, there are still arguments on whether Confucianism and Daoism are religions or not, though for many Chinese, religion, philosophy, and culture are seen as one.

Precisely since God's identity is seen as unknown, Daoism and especially Confucianism focused on humanity and the world around it, and therefore developed a sophisticated ethical and social system. One may say that both are moral and ethical systems. Yet they are also religious in nature, though not explicitly so, because they teach a way of life for here and now. However, this way of life is oriented toward fulfilling humanity's role in the cosmos, and heaven is intended as the destination of the human journey.

Humble and Intuitive Nature of Chinese Philosophy

Confucius was once asked what he thought of life after death, and his reply was explicit: "We do not know the mysteries even of this life; how can we know about the future life?"[7] A quote of

---

[7] Ji Lu asked about serving the gods and spirits. Confucius replied, "You are not able to serve man well. How can you talk about serving gods and spirits?" Ji Lu asked again: "May I ask about death?" Confucius replied,

Laozi in the *Daodejing* goes like this: "He who knows does not speak; he who speaks does not know."[8] The knowledge here refers to knowing the transcendent that is indescribable and ineffable.

When a person says, "I see," in English, it can mean, "I understand." In Chinese, the expression for understanding is *ming*. The term means to be illuminated—to be given the light to understand. As Carmine di Sante writes, in Greek culture the emphasis is on actively "seeing," while the Jewish Christian tradition instead focuses on "listening" (to the words of God).[9] It is interesting to note that in Chinese, one has to be illuminated (*ming*), that is, one must first have the light to see in order to understand. This shows a basic attitude of receptiveness and humility in the understanding of reality. One cannot "see" or "understand" only by using the senses or reason. One has to be illuminated.

The following sentence appears twice in the *Daodejing*: "To know the constant [*chang*] [Dao] is called enlightenment [*ming*]." This means that enlightenment derives from knowing the underlying constant principle or the principle of changes, the eternal Dao that is the source of true enlightenment. In the humility of not knowing through one's own efforts, there can arise an intuition of the Dao. In chapter 6, Laozi makes use of metaphors to indicate the features of an intuition of the Dao: "It is called the root of heaven and earth." One can gain an intuition of the Dao by silently observing all things in their rising from and returning to their root. From this humble intuition, the Dao is understood as the ultimate principle of

---

"You do not understand even life. How can you understand death?" See James J. Legge, ed. and trans., *The Analects by Confucius* (Oxford: Clarendon Press, 1893), Book 11.

[8] *Daodejing,* chapter 56.

[9] Carmine di Sante, *Responsabilità: L'io-per-l'altro* (Roma: Edizioni Lavoro-Esperienze, 1996), 11–44.

the universe, the source and destination of everything: "It is continuous, and seems to always exist. Use it and you will never wear it out."[10] As far as time is concerned, one understands that the Dao is eternal. From the perspective of space, the Dao is everywhere and its effects are endless.

Dialectic of Simplicity

Looking deeper into this continuity, chapter 16 of the *Daodejing* says, "Expand to extreme vacuity" and "Contract to utmost quietude." There is a continuous dynamic, from vacuity (*xu*) through extreme expansion, while quietude (*jing*) contracts to the utmost, which presents a dialectical way of understanding. Chapter 2 begins with these verses:

> When people of the world all know beauty as beauty, there arises the recognition of ugliness. When they all know the good as good, there arises the recognition of evil. Therefore, being [*you*] and nothingness [*wu*] "give relational existence." Difficult [*nan*] and easy [*yi*] complete each other; long [*chang*] and short [*duan*] contrast each other; high [*gao*] and low [*di*] distinguish each other; voice [*sheng*] and tone [*yin*] harmonize with each other; front [*qian*] and back [*hou*] follow each other.

In all these verses, the pairs of opposites, such as being and nothingness, difficult and easy, long and short, high and low, voice and tone, front and back, arise in a dialectic of harmony. It is the method of *yin* and *yang*.

In this way, Laozi described the relationship of interdependence (connection and functioning) of all things in the world, affirming the harmonizing, eternal, and universal principles. As Chan

---

[10] *Daodejing*, chapter 6.

Wing-tsit has pointed out, with a humble intuition of this interrelated process of the changing cosmos, Laozi explicated the superiority of non-action (*wu-wei*) over action and the idea of teaching without words.[11] This does not mean to be passive, but to be an active subject without forcing nature. Ren Jiyu writes that, like exemplary persons, it means to make a change without forcing the situation. One is always in harmony while contributing to that harmony. This dialectical principle guides people in their social life.[12]

The dialectical principle of Laozi is distinctively different from the dialectical method of Hegel. Western logic, codified in the rigid laws of scholastic argumentation, is based on the principle of contradiction and operates by means of subtle distinctions aimed at proving the invalidity of adverse positions. The Chinese tradition instead aims not to refute but to reconcile contradictions. Opposites are the two extremes of the one truth. Different points of view are not mutually exclusive. Reasoning above and beyond concrete realities is considered futile argumentation based on abstract concepts.

Hegel gave this example: "The bud disappears as the blossom bursts forth, and one could say that the former is refuted by the latter. In the same way, the fruit declares the blossom to be a false existence of the plant. These forms do not only differ, they also displace each other because they are incompatible."[13] He saw the progressive development of an organic whole by way of the dialectical method. A thesis gives rise to its reaction, an antithesis, which contradicts or negates the thesis, and the tension between

---

[11] Chan indicated that in this passage of *Daodejing*, Laozi actually anticipated the Buddhist tradition of silent transmission of the mystic doctrine, especially in the Zen School. Chan, *A Source Book in Chinese Philosophy*, 140.

[12] Ren Jiyu, "The Dialectic of Simplicity," *Teaching and Research*, no. 2 (1962): 17–18.

[13] Georg Wilhelm Friedrich Hegel, *The Phenomenology of Spirit: Volume 1*, trans. J. B. Baillie (New York: Cosimo Classics, 2005), 68.

the two is resolved by means of a synthesis. While the Hegelian method is based on refutation and displacement, Laozi's method is based on a dialectical principle of change that blends the contrasts such that they achieve a state of balance in a harmonious way. One refutes contradictions while the other reconciles contradictions. According to Laozi, the created universe carries the pervading principles of the *yin* and the *yang*; through their union it reaches harmony (this passage of *Daodejing* chapter 42 is further explained and elaborated later). There are many examples in the Chinese classics of this dialectical method,[14] which may be called the "dialectic of harmony."

Trinitarian Relationship

The Imprint of One and Three in All Things

How might one interpret the following Daoist passage "All things under heaven come from being [*you*]; Being [*you*] comes from non-being [*wu*]"?[15] First of all, the concept of *you* and *wu* is to be

---

[14] Another example of the dialectic of harmony and simplicity is the following passage in the Book of Changes. See Chen Guying, "Appended Remarks," in *The Translation and Review of Laozi*, book 2, chapter 5 (Hong Kong: Chunghua Book, 2012), 268: "After the Sun goes, the moon comes. After the moon goes, the sun comes. The sun and the moon push each other in their course and thus light appears. After the winter goes, the summer comes. After the summer goes, the winter comes. The winter and the summer push each other and thus the year is completed. To go means to contract and to come means to expand. Contraction and expansion act on each other and thus advantages are produced. The looper caterpillar coils itself up in order to stretch. Dragons and snakes hibernate (contract) in order to stretch out (expand). Investigate the principles of things and refinement until we enter into their spirit, for then their application can be extended, and utilize that application and secure personal peace, for then our virtue will be exalted. What goes beyond this is something we can hardly know. To investigate spirit to the utmost and to understand transformation is the height of virtue."

[15] *Daodejing*, chapter 40.

understood in term of their *you-wu* dialectic co-relation. In fact, they have been translated as "being" and "non-being," "presence" and "absence," "with" and "without," as in the case of *you-ming* (with name) and *wu-ming* (without name).

According to Chen Guying,[16] there have been various interpretations of the following verse in the beginning chapter of the *Daodejing*. For Wang Bi (226–249),[17] *wu-ming* and *you-ming* mean "without name" and "with name," respectively. Therefore, the verse goes: "The nameless is the origin of heaven and earth; the named is the mother of ten thousand things." For Wang Anshi (1021–1086)[18] instead, *ming* is used as a verb, "to name," and *wu* and *you* are nouns that mean "non-being" and "being." Therefore, the verse would go like this: "Non-being names the origin of heaven and earth; being names the mother of ten thousand things."

Contemporary scholars such as Feng Youlan[19] have the following explanation about the terms *you* and *wu*: The *you* in the verse "all things under heaven come from *you*" refers to something material and to physical things: "the materiality of being." The *wu* in the verse "*you* comes from *wu*" refers to something immaterial and metaphysical: "nothingness," which is close to if not identical to "pure act without form and matter." The *you* and *wu* referred to here, in chapter 40, have the same meaning as those of chapter 1, where *you-ming* (with-name) is the mother of all things, and *wu-ming* (nameless) is the origin of heaven and earth. However, the *you-wu* in chapter 1 and chapter 40 is different from that of

---

[16] See Chen, *The Translation and Review of Laozi*, 90.

[17] Wang Bi is regarded as one of the most important interpreters of the *Daodejing* before the discovery of the Mawangdui manuscript in 1973. *Stanford Encyclopedia of Philosophy*, 2013.

[18] Wang Anshi was a Song dynasty (960–1279) scholar and politician who made interpretations to the philosophical Laozi commentaries.

[19] Feng Youlan, *Collection of Discussions on the Philosophy of Laozi* (Beijing: Zhonghua Book Company, 1959), 41. Chinese edition.

Dialectic of Harmony in Dialogue

chapter 2, where it states. "*you* and *wu* [being and non-being] therefore give rise to each other." This passage expresses the mutual relation of *you-wu* as the twofold aspect of Dao. The co-relation of this *you-wu* is like that of *yin-yang*. This *you-wu* refers to the transcendent and metaphysical Dao.

However, the *Daodejing* does not stop with this duality. Rather, Laozi discusses a third dimension that surpasses simple duality. This third dimension is *sheng*. According to Chinese tradition, the term *sheng* has the following meanings: to generate or to arise, to form, to transform, or to manifest. Given this third element, one might analyze chapter 42 of the *Daodejing* verse by verse in the following way:

> Dao manifests itself as One: Dao is being One, absoluteness, and unity.
>
> One becomes two: one composed of two, non-uniformity within unity. Dao by itself contains the *yin* and *yang*, therefore two.
>
> Two becomes three: the third is the relation between the two. The third is the *qi*, the flow and the vital force, and there are the vital forces of *yin* and of *yang*.
>
> Three generates the ten thousand things: relation within and without. These three factors interact to reach an appropriate state, and all things are generated in this state.
>
> The ten thousand things carry the *yin* and embrace the *yang*: all things carry the imprint of *yin* and *yang*.
>
> Blending of their *qi* achieves *he*: *qi* is the vital force, and *he* means harmony as well as totality.

Laozi used "one" as a numerical representation of the Dao as the absolute. "Two" refers to *yin* and *yang*, the two that the Dao contains. The *qi* of the *yin* and of the *yang* is contained in the one Dao, and *qi* is the relationship between the two in the one, making *qi* the third. The final verse of the paragraph says, "The ten thousand things carry the *yin* and embrace the *yang*, the blending of their *qi* achieves harmony." Therefore, we can say that *qi* is the vital force of the two: *yin* and *yang*. The equilibrium of the two achieves harmony. *Yin-yang* is also a process of harmonization that ensures a constant, dynamic balance of all things.[20] The interaction of the *qi* of *yin* and *yang* establishes *he* (harmony), so it gives birth to all things in the cosmos. Harmony is the relationship of "mutually transforming" *yin* and *yang* in the one Dao. It generates new and harmonious life that includes all things. All things have the imprint of "one" and "three."

Here, Daoism provides a terrain for comparison, and we find seeds for dialogue with Christians concerning the Trinitarian relationship. For example, in his encyclical letter *Laudato Si'*, Pope Francis wrote about the "divine principle" of the Trinity and the relationship between creatures: "For Christians, believing in one God who is Trinitarian communion suggests that the Trinity has left its mark on all creation." Humans going out from themselves enter into relationships, "to live in communion with God, with others and with all creatures. In this way, they make their own the Trinitarian dynamism that God imprinted in them when they were created. Everything is interconnected, and this invites us to develop a spirituality of a global solidarity that flows from the mystery of the Trinity."[21]

---

[20] Robin R. Wang, "Yinyang (Yin-yang)," *Internet Encyclopedia of Philosophy*, 2006.
[21] Pope Francis, *Laudato Si'*, Encyclical Letter on Care for Our Common Home, May 24, 2015, 238–240.

The Prologue of the Gospel of John and Experiences of Some Saints

Before attempting to read the mystery of Trinitarian relationships through categories of Chinese thought and, in particular, in light of the Daoist vision outlined above, one must first examine some verses from the Prologue of the Gospel of John, written originally in Greek:

> 1:1 In the beginning was the Word (λόγος): the Word was with (προς) God and the Word was God.
>
> 1:2–3 Through him all things came into being (γίγνομαι), not one thing came into being (γίγνομαι) except through (δια) him.
>
> 1:14 And (καί) the Word became flesh (σὰρξ ἐγένετο), he lived among us, and we saw his glory, the glory that he has from the Father as only Son of the Father, full of grace and truth.
>
> 1:18 No one has ever seen God; it is the only Son, who is close to the Father's heart, who has made him known.

In these verses, the term λόγος (*Logos*)[22] in Greek and *Dabar* in Hebrew is translated as "the Word" and has the meaning of "words" and "expressions." The term προς (*pros*) is translated

---

[22] Although the Gospel of John has been transmitted to us in Greek, John the Evangelist, being a Jew, wrote in Greek using the term *Logos* but was also thinking of the Hebrew term *Dabar*. Anna Pelli affirmed that the philosophical *logos* in the Greek tradition was insufficient to express the reality of the universal *Logos* of God become man in history. A richer meaning was then taken over by Christianity. Cf. Anna Pelli, "Verità e dialogo: la dinamica relazionale del conoscere," Sophia University Institute, Florence, 2013–2014, 18–19; Giustino, *Apology*, 2, 13, 4.

as "with" or "toward" as in the phrase "was toward God" (*pros ton theon*). It indicates dynamism imprinted in the verb "to be." Therefore, it means that the Word is always directed toward someone, living and creating relationship; the Being of the Word is movement so to speak. The Word is not only God but is with God and always dynamically toward God. The terms γίγνομαι (*gignomai*), translated "came into being," and δια (*dia*), translated as "through" as in the verse "all things came into being through him," shows that the Word was not only God and with and toward God but also played a creative and ordering role in forming the creation of all things. The phrase "in the beginning" means that the Word was with God eternally from the perspective of time. As the renowned exegete Rudolf Schnackenburg has pointed out, the term καί (*kai*) indicates a moment when and where the Word "became flesh" (εγένετο, *egeneto*), which the Word until then had not been.[23] The phrase "he lived among us" indicates that the Word entered in time, space, and human history through Jesus Christ.

The opening verses of the Prologue of John's Gospel powerfully express the eternal relationship between God and the Word, the reality of God in God (you in me and I in you). They also present the Word as the focus, the converging point, where God made the otherness of Him come to be. Verses 14 and 18 point out to us that the Word showed us God. The Word glorified God and vice versa. The only Son (the Word) has manifested God and opened his relationship with God to us.

This calls to mind an episode of the Old Testament. "I AM THAT I AM" was the response God used when Moses asked for his name (Exod. 3:14).[24] It is very difficult to translate this verse

---

[23] Rudolf Schnackenburg, *The Johannine Epistle: A Commentary* (New York: Crossroad, 1992), 267; see also Thomas L. Brodie, *The Gospel according to John* (New York: Oxford University Press, 1993), 142.

[24] See Exod. 3:14:

of the Bible. It is revelation of the ineffable name of God. That God alone IS. God's self-revelation has been promised from above as people strive to know God. According to Piero Coda, through this giving of "I Am," of the IS, God enters time and space and creates a relation: "'I Am' is the name of God which can be translated as 'I am always *with* you.'"[25] In the Prologue, God's Word is not just spoken as it was to Moses, but in Jesus it entered into human history to be with us concretely, forever. At the end of John's Gospel, the Holy Spirit is given to bind all to God and together in harmony. The One gives Two, and Two gives Three—the very Three that binds in love One and Two.

In his autobiography, *The Confessions*, Augustine described his encounter with God: "When I first knew thee, thou didst lift me up [*et vestrum sollevasti*]. And thou didst cry to me from afar, 'I am that I am [*Ego sum qui sum*].' And I heard this, as things are heard in the heart, and there was no room for doubt."[26] Coda affirms that, for Augustine, therefore, it is not just with human effort that one can grasp and understand who God is; rather it is God who lowered himself to elevate people to a "being with" God.[27] The first move to tell the Being of God is

---

> Moses said to God, "Who am I to go to Pharaoh and bring the Israelites out of Egypt?" "I shall be with you," God said, "and this is the sign by which you will know that I was the one who sent you. After you have led the people out of Egypt, you will worship God on this mountain." Moses then said to God, "Look, if I go to the Israelites and say to them, 'The God of your ancestors has sent me to you,' and they say to me, 'What is his name?' what am I to tell them?" God said to Moses, "I am he who is." And he said, "This is what you are to say to the Israelites, 'I am has sent me to you.'"

[25] Piero Coda, *La Trinità, quando il racconto di Dio diventa il racconto dell'uomo* (Rome: Marcianum Press, 2015), 16–21.

[26] Augustine, *Confessions* 7.10.16.

[27] Piero Coda observes that the expression "When I first knew thee" indicates a precise event and a living experience for St. Augustine, wherein he emphasized that God "elevated him" to see who God IS—precisely that

not from bottom up, for this attempt is always out of reach, but from top down.

St. Thérèse of Lisieux too found the "elevator" for which she was searching: "It is your arms, Jesus, which are the lift to carry me to heaven, and so there is no need for me to grow up. In fact, just the opposite: I must stay little and become less and less."[28] The "little way" of St. Thérèse is centered on the infinite mercy of God and recognizes that everything is a grace and Providence is in control from moment to moment when one embraces the will of God. She observed, "Jesus is doing all in me, and I am doing nothing." Since everything is a grace, she came to realize that God has no need of one's works. However, the "little way" is not an invitation to do nothing. One has to prove one's love by works, but works without love count for nothing.

This is very much in tune with Laozi's concept of *wu-wei* (non-doing). It refers to the cultivation of the highest state of being in non-doing. It is a kind of paradoxical "action of non-action." A kind of "going with the flow" characterized by living in harmony with the ultimate nature (*ziran*) in response to the world surrounding us. A practical example is what athletes experience when they do something so often that its movements are natural and no thought is needed to act correctly in the right time and place. It is simply done effortlessly, cleanly and in harmony with everything around it. However, it requires endless practice beforehand.

In comparison to the concept of *wu-wei*, in some religious traditions one experiences union with God (mysticism) after a

---

Being that Augustine could well see in a strong ontological sense. See Piero Coda, *Sul luogo della Trinità. Rileggendo il De Trinitate di Agostino* (Roma: Città Nuova, 2008), 30–31.

[28] Thérèse of Lisieux, *The Story of a Soul* (New York: Doubleday, 2001), 113.

long period of mortification (asceticism). In Christian terms, one could call it a state of grace where one opens oneself fully to the gifts of God and partakes in the divine nature of God.

Jesus Christ and Trinitarian Relationship

As mentioned above, the Word is the converging focus in the creation of all things. The Word is also said to be "life" and "light" and is incarnated as Jesus. As narrated later in the Gospel of John, when the hour had come before leaving this world, Jesus prayed to the Father: "I have given them the glory you gave to me, that they may be one as we are one" (17:22). One might interpret this priestly prayer of Jesus on three levels.

First, there is the level of the relationship of love between Jesus and the Father: "All I have is yours and all you have is mine" (John 17:10). It is this relationship of total giving that makes God Father and Jesus Son. Jesus doing the will of God becomes truly the Son, and God letting the Son fulfill his plan becomes truly the Father. Second, there is the level of Jesus's prayer to the Father: "Keep those you have given me true to your name, so that they may be one like us" (John 17:11). This prayer refers to the relationship among Christians of total giving that is one of unity and love. Third, there is the level of Jesus's prayer for his disciples: "May they all be one, just as, Father, you are in me and I am in you, so that they also may be in us, so that the world may believe it was you who sent me" (John 17:21). Only by witnessing this relationship of unity and communion among Christians can others[29] believe in the message of love that Jesus brought.

---

[29] As an additional note here, Donald Mitchell, a professor of comparative religion, finds that there is a mutual indwelling relationship that echoes Chinese Huayan Buddhism. See Donald W. Mitchell, "Dazzling Darkness,

During the Last Supper, Jesus gave the disciples a new commandment: "Love one another, as I have loved you. No one has greater love than this, to lay down one's life for one's friends" (John 15:12–13). In the Gospel of Matthew, at the climax of his passion, echoing Psalm 22, Jesus cried out, "My God, my God, why have you forsaken me?" (Matt. 27:46). And he passed away. The veil of the temple is said to have split in two from top to bottom. This action is reminiscent of the scene of Jesus's baptism when the heavens opened and the Holy Spirit descended as a dove upon Jesus.[30] Indeed, Scripture states that in seeing this total self-emptying lived by Jesus on the cross, a centurion standing in front of him came to believe in the message of love of Jesus's death and said, "Indeed this man was the son of God" (Mark 15:34–39).

With a powerful spiritual experience that occurred in 1944, Chiara Lubich intuited that there is a strong relationship between the abandonment of Jesus on the cross and the prayer of Jesus to the Father that all men be one. The story of Jesus's death on the cross, in loneliness and abandonment, is a profound story of love between the Son and the Father. In this story the cry of abandonment is paradoxically the apex of unity between Jesus and his God.[31] Chiara then started a way of life, which became a worldwide movement committed to living a spirituality of unity.

Buddhism and Chiara Lubich's Mystical Writings," *Claritas: Journal of Dialogue and Culture* 6, no. 2 (October 2017): 6–13. Huayan Buddhism is a school of Buddhism that flourished in China in the seventh century CE. It teaches that not only is Buddha-nature with its Nirvanic essence within all beings, but also all beings exist such that they "mutually penetrate" each other and "mutually indwell" in each other. The metaphor used by Master Fazang is a mirror containing the reflections of other mirrors. Although further comparison could be interesting, I do not want to delve into Buddhism here that may divert from the main content of this section.

[30] See Mark 1:10.

[31] Gerard Rosse, "Il grido del crocifisso, approccio biblico," Sophia University Institute, 2010, 45.

I find the following passage of Lubich about the Trinitarian relationship and the dialectic of love very inspiring in relation to the above:

> Three form the Trinity, yet they are one, because love is and is not at the same time. Even when love is not, it is, because it is love. In fact, if I renounce a particular possession of mine and give it away (I deprive myself of it; it is not) out of love, I have love, therefore it is.[32]

Lubich emphasizes that it is more important "to be love" than to be "doing things for love." One may think, for example, of someone believing to be doing[33] a great service to a sick friend, while the friend finds the service annoying.

Trinitarian Relationship from an Anthropomorphic Point of View

How can this life of self-emptying and self-giving love be lived by people? The relationship of "love" necessitates at least two parties. Piero Coda provides an insightful definition of the Trinitarian relationship: "I am if you are; I am so that you would be."[34] That is, I am my true self only in relation to you, and you are your true self if I am who I am. My fulfillment is the condition for your fulfillment, and vice versa. I find the reason of my existence

---

[32] Judith M. Povilus, *United in His Name: Jesus in Our Midst in the Experience and Thought of Chiara Lubich* (New York: New City Press, 1992), 66.

[33] It calls to my mind the dialectic of harmony in Daoism with regard to one of the most important concepts in Daoism, "doing" and "non-doing" (*wu-wei*), which emphasizes the importance of being rather than doing. In other words, being is in non-doing. I elaborate in more detail later in this book the concept of *wu-wei*.

[34] Piero Coda, "Trinitarian Ontology," lecture, Sophia University Institute, Figline and Incisa Valdarno, Italy, March 11, 2014.

in relation to the other, and in relation to me the other finds the reason of his or her existence. Again, as in the relationship between the Father and the Son, a father is a father because he has a son. The son is a son because of the father. The identity of the two arises in a mutually dependent relationship. It is not a dialectical relationship of negating or denying the other but of fulfilling each other in this relationship.

The relationship between Jesus and God the Father is such: the Son felt abandoned by the Father and died on the cross. At that moment he fully identified with all humankind in their suffering existence, thus he accomplished the will of the Father. At the same time, the Father glorified the Son. Between the Father and the Son is the relationship of "love," the Holy Spirit. The forsaken Jesus completely emptied himself (*kenosis*) to be one with humankind through kenotic love. When he totally denied himself in a loving relationship with humankind, he fulfilled his identity as the Son of God. This brought about a universal Trinitarian relation with all humankind, namely, the Word of God that created the world re-creates humanity and the cosmos in the Son.

Given this vision, how should Christians look at and relate to the world and society? Paul said, "Who has ever known the mind of the Lord? But we are those who have the mind of Christ" (1 Cor 2:16). The "mind of Christ" present in the Christian sees and knows the world through its essence: Love and Unity. It is as if the pupil of the eye of a Christian allows the Light and Love from the mind of Christ to enter within, enabling him or her to be a source of "intuitiveness" and "harmony." While Christians see the negative things around themselves, they are moved from within to seek unity and harmony through the love also found within. This is the source of the "humility" of Christianity and its service to humanity, society, and the cosmos. This attitude brings about positive energy in the world.

Possible Contribution of the Chinese Dialectic of Harmony to Trinitarian Theology

The Second Axial Age and Effort at Inculturation

In *The Origin and Goal of History*, Karl Jaspers pioneered the idea of the Axial Age (800 to 200 BCE).[35] According to Jaspers. human history has gone through four ages: the Neolithic age, the age of the earliest civilizations, the axial age, and the modern age. The so-called axial age is "pivotal," characterizing the period in which new ways of thinking appeared. Many of the great philosophers and religious leaders flourished at roughly the same time, as if something parallel was happening in the world. People were unaware that similar or complementary ideas were being developed simultaneously elsewhere. In Greece, there were Socrates, Plato, and Aristotle; in China, Confucius, Laozi, and Mozi; in India, the Upanishads and the Buddha; and Palestine witnessed several of the greatest prophets. People became conscious of themselves, their limitations, and their potential. Their view of the world and their position in the world changed. They sought the supremely and eternally "real" that lay beyond the world of the senses, and in so doing they created what Jasper called "fundamental ideas" that have defined the modern age through the centuries. Since the 1900s, scholars such as Ewert Cousins and Karen Armstrong say that the gaze of human beings has shifted in such a way that one might call this the Second Axial Period, which could likewise shape the horizon of consciousness for future centuries.[36] This consciousness is global, collective, interreligious, dialogical, experiential, and ecological.

---

[35] Karl Jaspers, *Origin and Goal of History* (New Haven, CT: Yale University Press, 1953), 1–27.

[36] Ewert Cousins, *Christ of the 21st Century* (New York: Continuum, 1998), 7–10.

Globalization has become a reality for the first time in history, and awareness of climate change has birthed the ecological movement, which continues to grow. In the Catholic Church, Pope Francis wrote the encyclicals *Laudato Si'* and *Fratelli Tutti* for the whole world. Because of Vatican II and the work of Saint John Paul II, the Catholic Church, with its universal apostolic nature, has been engaging in the process of interreligious dialogue and inculturation. Vatican II has also called for all people in the Church to experience "sanctity." The lay movements in the Church today are taking spirituality and the experiential dimension of religion beyond the walls of convents and monasteries to the people. This change is not just individual but collective, since the Church sees its role today as caring for all humanity, bringing harmony among the rich diversity of humankind with its many cultures and religions.

Just as the Church Fathers expressed the content of the Jewish Christian religion in the Greek and Roman cultural context, in the past century, people have tried to present the message of the Gospels from the milieu and perspective of Chinese culture. The well-known jurist and philosopher John Wu Ching-hsiung attempted to translate the Prologue of the Gospel of John using the term Dao. The Shanghai diocese made similar efforts through their translations. They translated the original term "Logos" as Dao. Therefore, in the Prologue we read: "In the beginning was the Dao: the Dao was with God and the Dao was God," and "The Dao became flesh, he lived among us." More classical Chinese expressions were also employed in the translation. Today, the expression of incarnation, "The Dao became flesh," is often employed in translations by Protestant Christian churches. However, in the Catholic translation of the text, the expression "the Word" is considered more prudent, until we fully understand the connotation of the word Dao in Chinese culture.

Since people today live in a cross-cultural environment, when carrying out the project of inculturation it is important to understand different articulations and categories of thinking in the East and the West. What method should Asian scholars use to approach Christian studies given the realities of our present age? First, as philosopher Jacques Maritain said, one should begin with an "existential epistemology."[37] That is, one needs to start with the actual religious experience of the encounter with Jesus Christ. Second, one should use "phenomenology" to comprehend the profound nature of the experience of Jesus Christ. These two steps are important to both the West and the East in considering the words of important religious texts.

Third, relationality is critical for both the Christian Trinitarian viewpoint and the Chinese cultural viewpoint, but with different emphases. In the West, for example, relationship with others is emphasized as I-Thou. The approach is to define ontologically who I am and my relationship with others. In the East, the emphasis is on my relationship with the whole—I with the totality. The relationship between the self and another person is seen in the larger context of the True Self and Totality. Fourth, for the West, careful analysis is important in defining the realities discussed in a text as a basis for living. In the East, it is more important to intuit the realities presented in the text as a basis for living. By drawing on similarities and differences and by combining the strengths of East and West, one might discover new hermeneutics in textual interpretation.[38]

---

[37] Jacques Maritain, *Existence and the Existent* (Mahwah, NJ: Paulist Press, 2015).

[38] This project is larger than what I am attempting here. However, in searching for a new hermeneutics, I would refer to Italian theologian Piero Coda, who writes about "Teor-etica." See Piero Coda, *Il logos e il nulla. Trinità religioni mistica* (Roma: Città Nuova, 2003), 28–29; 109–112; 133–136. In Italian "teor-etica" means theory and ethics; there is a continuous

Understanding the Trinity from the Perspective of Chinese Culture

In Chinese culture, the concepts of Dao, *de* and *qi*, and *he* (harmony) have rich connotations. To interpret and understand the Trinitarian relationship from the perspective of a "dialectic of harmony," I propose the following interpretations:

- This is an interpretation of the relationship between the Word and God with the principle of the dialectic of harmony. The relationship could be expressed in these phrases of *Daodejing*: "Being and non-being give rise to each other,"[39] and they are in a "reciprocally transforming" relationship. God exists in eternity. God is the Trinity, three united as one. In Daoist cosmology, "Dao generates one" means Dao is being one, the absolute.
- Two of the Persons in the Trinity are God the Father and Christ the Son. In an expression of the *Daodejing*, two comes from one or "one generates two,"[40] in which the two are *yin* and *yang* or *wu* and *you*. God eternally generates the Son in total giving, making God Father. The Son completely empties himself (*kenosis*), making him the eternal manifestation (*epiphaneia*) of the Father.
- The third Person of the Trinity is the relationship of love, the Holy Spirit (*pneuma*). It could be expressed by the Chinese term *qi* insofar as "the blending of the *qi* of *yin*

---

circle from intelligence to experience, and vice versa. Ontology, as Coda sees it, is never an abstract intelligence but always at the same time practical, because moving knowledge moved freedom, and moving freedom moved knowledge.

[39] *Daodejing* chapter 42 (translation and interpretation of these passages of chapter 42 of *Daodejing* are mine).

[40] Ibid.

and the *qi* of *yang* achieves the *qi* of harmony." *Qi* is the flow and the relationship of love, harmony, and mutual giving. Mutual giving of the "two becomes three."
- This relationship of love is imprinted in all things, as shown in the statement "The three generates the ten thousand things. The ten thousand things carry the *yin* and embrace the *yang*, and through the blending of their *qi* they achieve harmony." In Chinese culture, the generating principle of all things is based on the two elements of *yin* and *yang*, and the third element that is symbolized by the *qi*. All things generated are the result of the blending of the *qi* to achieve harmony within the Totality.

I do not mean that certain ideas found in the *Daodejing* express Christian concepts of the Trinity, but it is necessary to express Christian thoughts from a Chinese perspective just as the early Church Fathers did in the Greek and Roman cultural context. Inculturation is a process that requires time and patience. Vatican II affirms that culture is a human creation and needs to be "cleansed, raised up and perfected."[41] If only more Chinese Christians would put into practice the gospel message—in the process, their faith expressions would gradually be accepted.

In the final analysis, the early Church Fathers did use Greek language and philosophy to express Christian thought. To describe the relationship within the Trinity, they used the term *perichoresis*. It means "dancing around," (flowing) freely, obeying the movement of one another. In Trinitarian language it refers to the dynamic mutual indwelling among the three Persons. I think the concepts of "*yin-yang* harmonizing" and "mutually transforming" might appropriately interpret the Trinitarian

---

[41] Second Vatican Council, *Lumen Gentium*, *Dogmatic Constitution on the Church*, 1964, 17.

relationship. From the early Church Fathers to recent times, *perichoresis* has been applied in three contexts: the relationship between the divine nature and the human nature of Jesus Christ, the relationship among the three Persons of the Trinity, and other interpersonal relationships and God's presence in human affairs. In this last meaning, we see links to human relations and society that are so important in Chinese culture, wherein all things and actions are generated by the flowing and harmonizing of the vital energy (*qi*) of *yin* and *yang*.

The Contribution of Chinese Thought to Trinitarian Relationships

To do theology in the context of Chinese culture,[42] it could be helpful, as we have seen, to translate the term "*Logos*" as "Dao" and to use the expression "the Dao became flesh." However, "*Logos*" simply translated as "Dao" might not be enough. The relationship between Dao and *De* should also be explored, since in Chinese culture the two are linked, both in the texts of Daoism and in the Chinese way of thought. As mentioned earlier, *Daodejing* literally means the Book of *Dao* and *De*. What does this connection between Dao and *De* contribute to our understanding of the relationship between God and the Word?

Contemporary scholars such as Philip Ivanhoe and Roger Ames point out that the Daoist concept of *De* has been "severely undervalued," both in later commentary and in present understandings of Daoism.[43] An understanding of

---

[42] Theological studies are not limited to the aspect of gaining knowledge and of understanding with the head; they require living practices and understanding with the heart. See Yong Lina, "Research on Theological Education in the Church of China," *Conference Proceedings of the Fourth Academic Conference on the Role and Impact of Christianity on Modern Chinese Society* (Hebei: Faith Institute for Cultural Studies, November 18–19, 2014), 25.

[43] Roger T. Ames, "Putting the *Te* Back into Taoism," in *Nature in Asian*

De is indispensable for a full appreciation of the philosophy presented in the text.[44] The word *De* itself can be translated as either "virtue" or "power." In the text of the *Daodejing*, there is a distinction between the expressions of the Upper *De* and the Lower *De*. According to Laozi, the Upper *De* is a power and virtue fully in accordance with the spirit of the Dao. Laozi also uses the expressions Supreme *De*, Great *De*, and Constant *De* to express the infinite nature of the Upper *De*. The Upper *De* has a metaphysical meaning that is foundational for the refined ethical meaning in the sense that for Laozi the Upper *De* emphasizes the ideas of "return to the nature" and *wu-wei* (non-action). The Lower *De*, on the other hand, has a purely ethical meaning that is close to the moral teachings of Confucianism, even paying attention to the concept of propriety (*li*).

Catholic scholar Bernard Li Chien-Chiu writes that while in Confucianism Dao signifies the way of heaven or humans, in Daoism it acquires a metaphysical meaning. Dao is the ultimate reality as well as the first principle underlying form, substance, being, and change.[45] Therefore the connotation of Dao in Daoism is different from its connotation in Confucianism. It is the same with *De*, whose connotation in Daoism is different from its connotation in Confucianism. So, how should the relationship between Dao and the Upper *De* be understood in Daoism?

Traditions of Thought, ed. J. Baird Callicott and Roger T. Ames (Albany: State University of New York Press, 1989), 123. Wade-Giles Romanization of Chinese terms (*te, tao*) in the article have been altered to pinyin (*De, Dao*) for consistency.

[44] Philip J. Ivanhoe, "The Concept of *De* ('Virtue') in the *Laozi*," in *Religious and Philosophical Aspects of the Laozi*, ed. Mark Csikszentmihalyi and Philip J. Ivanhoe (Albany: State University of New York Press, 1999), 239.

[45] Bernard Chien-Chiu Li, "Dao-Logos: Lao Zi and Philo," *Euntes Docente* 1 / Anno LXII (2009), 1.

Laozi said, "The all-embracing quality of the Great *De* is alone derived from the Dao." The Great *De* comes from the Dao. It is the power and virtue of the Dao, and follows only the Dao in all its actions.[46] This means that the Great *De* is the embodiment of the spirit of the Dao and the concretization of the Dao itself. That is, Dao in itself is invisible, and *De* manifests its power and the nature of its action. With the term *De*, Laozi expresses how the Dao takes up power and virtue in creative action and how it returns to the original natural state.

The term *De* as expressed in the *Daodejing* connotes the manifestation of the Dao, whereby it takes up human factors such as virtue and yet returns to the original natural state. "In this natural state," Ding Yuanzhi writes, "*you* and *wu*, with and without, being and non-being, Dao and *De* are interrelated."[47] Here we see that the ontological natures of the Dao and of the Upper *De* are defined in relational terms, rather than in singular terms, as entities in themselves. They have to be analyzed as relational structures, as expressed in the *I Jing* (Book of Changes): "What is called the Dao is in the metaphysical realm while the actualization is in the physical realm." Also, Daoist scholar Chen Kuying writes that when the Dao is in the state of potentiality and not actuality, it is not perceivable by the senses. When the metaphysical Dao concretizes itself at the human level, it is called the *De*. Laozi made use of the development of the body and its functions to explain the relationship between Dao and *De*. Dao in its original state is formless, and its manifestation is the *De*.[48]

With reference to some attempts mentioned earlier, if we simply use the term Dao for *Logos* to explain the relationship

---

[46] *Daodejing*, chapter 21.

[47] Ding Yuanzhi, *Guodianzhujian Interpretation and Research on Laozi* (Taipei: Wanjuanlou Publishing, 1999), 144.

[48] Chen Guying, *The Interpretation and Translation of Laozi Today* (Beijing: Beijing Commercial, 2006).

between the Word and God, it would not be enough. I suggest that the term *De*, especially with emphasis on its metaphysical meaning, could be used in the place of *Logos*—that is, to reflect on *De* in the place of *Logos* and Dao in the place of God. From the perspective of Trinitarian relationship, one might make use of the relationship between Dao and *De* or *You* and *Wu* to interpret the relationship between God and the Word. I argue that this would be more comprehensive and appropriate.

It is a modest spur to induce scholars in this field to ponder on the mystery of the Trinity from the point of view of relationality. It is also an invitation for Chinese Christians to live the gospel so that life experiences become genuine expressions of faith and authentically Chinese. In this regard, it seems that the Chinese dialectical relationship of harmony will make a valuable contribution to Christian theology as it develops in China. The benefit will not only be theological but would also have ethical and social benefits for the development of Chinese culture today.

In conclusion, the concept of non-action in Daoism is understood in Chinese culture in relation to the concept of "making a difference" in Confucianism. Confucianism and Daoism are complementary and in constant interaction in a dialectic of harmony. The cultures of East and West can also have a dialectical relationship that is not conflicting. With the inculturation of Christianity in China, and understanding Trinitarian theology in light of Chinese categories of thought, this relationship can be transformed into a dialectic of harmony for the benefit and enrichment of both East and West.

Some Living Examples and Conclusions

As mentioned before, Christ gave himself completely to fulfill the plan of God the Father. In this way Christ becomes truly himself in his own identity. Throughout Chinese history there have been many well-respected figures—such as Yue Fei (1103–1142), Wen Tianxiang (1236–1283), and Xu Guangqi (1562–1633), just to mention a few—who were exemplary and inspirational to the people for generations. They were able "to lay down one's own life for a just cause,"[49] fulfilling the spirit of "sacrificing one's own self for the good of the bigger Self."

The *Gita*, a book of Hindu Scriptures that reportedly influenced Mahatma Gandhi's life, is a narrative of a dialogue between Prince Arjuna and the charioteer Lord Krishna in front of a battlefield in ancient India. Krishna counseled Arjuna how to defuse the crisis, to fulfill his duty as a warrior and establish Dharma, and to not look at the result of going to war or not, to be or not to be fighting his enemy. It explores the relations between Atman and Brahman, between the I and the totality, the relationship between the self and the greater self, between the soul and God.

During Xi Jinping's state visit to the United Kingdom at the end of 2015, the president of China cited Shakespeare's famous quote, which caused much delight for his hosts. He said: "'To be or not to be, that is the question.' This line from *Hamlet* has left a lasting impression on me." Such a line has become a world classic, not simply because it describes the dilemma of Hamlet in front of the abrupt death of his father, the throne usurped by his uncle who married his mother. It is a state of mental torment, a matter of choice between risking or giving up, acting or not acting. More importantly, it is a greater question about the meaning of life and the values of human existence. The question is "to be or not to be," about being or non-being, *you* or *wu*, the love of total giving or total emptying. These universal values, whether in the East or the West, always strike a chord and bring about resonance.

---

[49] "So, I like life, and I also like righteousness. If I cannot keep the two together, I will let life go, and choose righteousness." Mencius, "Gaozi I," 10. See James Legge, ed. and trans., *The Works of Mencius* (Oxford: Clarendon Press, 1895).

The great scientist Albert Einstein, in an unedited letter to his daughter Lieserl that was published two decades after his death, wrote, "When I proposed the theory of relativity, very few understood me, and what I will reveal now to transmit to mankind will also collide with the misunderstanding and prejudice in the world." He continued, "There is an extremely powerful force that, so far, science has not found a formal explanation to. It is a force that includes and governs all others, and is even behind any phenomenon operating in the universe and has not yet been identified by us. This universal force is LOVE."[50]

---

[50] In the late 1980s, Lieserl, the daughter of the famous genius, donated fourteen hundred letters written by Albert Einstein to the Hebrew University, with orders not to publish their contents until two decades after his death. This is one of them, written to Lieserl. See R. Manjunath, *Understanding the Universe: Quarks, Leptons and the Big Bang* (Bangalore, 2020), 191.

2

Ecological Civilization and Integral Ecology

In this chapter, I investigate the relationship between humankind and nature from the perspective of Chinese culture and Christian theology. Empirical data have shown humankind's negative effects on the environment, which is causing worldwide concern for the ecosystem. My experience at the Beijing Expo 2019 put me in direct contact with two perspectives, "integral ecology" as proposed by the Catholic Church and "ecological civilization" by China. This research seeks to advance a relational paradigm to address the root cause of the crisis.

In 2019 the Pontifical Council for Culture of the Holy See assigned me to be coordinator of the Holy See Pavilion in Beijing at the International Horticultural Exhibition—part of the Beijing Expo 2019, held from April 29 to October 9. It was a once-in-a-lifetime experience. As there are no diplomatic relations between China and the Holy See, this was the first time the Holy See participated successfully in such a high-level international event in China. It was based on a subtle relationship, the situation being delicate, the presence symbolic, the event all the more significant.

The Beijing Expo 2019 theme, "Live Green, Live Better," aimed to promote respect for nature and a better life in harmony with nature. The Holy See Pavilion highlighted the theme contained in the Encyclical Letter *Laudato Si'* of Pope Francis "On Care for Our Common Home." It was a very appropriate platform for cultural exchange, especially in a country like China, officially atheist, where the religiously unaffiliated represent the largest share of the population. During the 162-day run of the expo, the Holy See Pavilion featured the Vatican Gardens by recreating their lawns, fountains, trees, and winding stairs in an area of two hundred square meters. It received an estimated four million visitors from all walks of life and backgrounds. Most of the visitors were from China but also many from abroad.

There were two significant works of art among other displays presented in the pavilion. One work exhibited was an installation of a five-hundred-year-old gilded olive tree bearing a quotation from Pope Francis's encyclical: "Whether believers or not, we are agreed today that the earth is essentially a shared inheritance, whose fruits are meant to benefit everyone" (*LS* 93). A similar message reverberated in the speech of President Xi Jinping at the opening ceremony of the expo: "All humans live in a community with a shared future in the face of eco-environmental challenges. Only through collaboration can we effectively tackle global environmental issues and achieve the United Nations 2030 Agenda for Sustainable Development Goals."[1]

Another artwork among the exhibits was an eighteenth-century painting by Peter Wenzel, *Adam and Eve in the Garden of Eden*. The painting captured the act of Eve handing the forbidden fruit to Adam when they are about to fall into temptation as symbolized by a snake that lurks nearby. This scene from Genesis depicts the earthly paradise the way God intended it to be before the fall of humans. It shows how humans and animals lived together in harmony. The painting conveys the harmonious relationships in creation between human beings, man and woman, nature and humankind, and God and human beings.

---

[1] Xi Jinping, "Highlights of Xi's Speech at Beijing Horticultural Expo Opening Ceremony," *China Global Television Network*, April 28, 2019, https://news.cgtn.com/news/3d3d674e774d7a4d34457a6333566d54/index.html.

World leaders nowadays have to realize and reach a consensus that the world is our common home and we have a shared responsibility to tackle environmental issues together so as to safeguard the future for generations to come. In this chapter, I would like to investigate how to retrieve the original significance of the relationship between nature and humankind from the Christian perspective as well as from that of Chinese culture. The damaging effects of human activities on the environment in the last few decades have almost reached a point of no return, with the potential collapse of the ecosystem. What has gone wrong, and what is the rightful relationship between humans and nature? I also explore some concrete examples or initiatives to reverse this trend and work toward an ecological civilization.

The Relationship between Human Beings and Nature in Chinese Culture

As mentioned before, a prominent theme of Chinese culture is the desire for harmony. The lack of emphasis on transcendence in Confucianism, however, left space for later developments of Daoism and Buddhism. When Buddhism arrived in China by way of India, with a more precise religious view and spirituality, it supplemented this void. In fact, the Buddha was immediately deified in Chinese popular religion. China thereupon adhered to Mahayana Buddhism, which then spread to Korea, Japan, and Vietnam.[2] In the Chinese cultural tradition, Confucianism, Daoism, and Buddhism have unceasingly enriched one another. They are complementary in a sense, and the three schools of thought have expressed important concepts on ecology and nature.

---

[2] Yan Kin Sheung Chiaretto, *Evangelization in China: Challenges and Prospects* (Maryknoll, NY: Orbis Books, 2014), 4–5.

The Chinese term *ziran* means "nature," but also "naturalness." *Naturalness* refers to the primordial state of things, unaffected by the various meanings imposed on it by human beings. We may look at it from three perspectives. In daily language, the term *ziran* refers to the physical world, which is independent of human interference, as opposed to human society. In philosophy, the concept of *ziran*, "naturalness," is different from that of nature in the ordinary sense. It is a natural state of man and of society, which is nevertheless connected to the Dao. In political philosophy, "naturalness" specifically applies to the natural state enjoyed by ordinary people free from the intervention of government supervision and artificial codes of behavior. Daoist political philosophy holds that in governance a monarch should conform to the natural state of the people.[3]

There are three expressions that are quite representative of traditional Chinese thoughts on the relationship between human beings and nature. The Confucian expression *tianren heyi* signifies that heaven and humans are united as one; the Daoist expression *dao fa ziran* in which Dao follows self-so (the state of naturalness); and a Buddhist expression *zhongsheng pingdeng*, which means that all sentient beings are equal. Although these three expressions are not exhaustive in explaining the original concepts, they are particularly significant representations in articulating the relationship between human beings and nature in Chinese culture.

The Relationship between Human Beings and Nature in the Daoist School of Thought

The expression "Dao follows self-so" (*dao fa ziran*) means that Dao operates in accordance with the natural conditions of all things. The meaning is deep and hard to express in simple English

---

[3] Key Concepts in Chinese Thought and Culture, 1999–2019, http://chinesethought.cn/EN.

terms; it means that the Dao develops itself naturally. This idea first appeared in the *Daodejing*, according to which "nature" or "naturalness" means the natural state of things. Dao creates and nurtures everything, yet it does not command anything.[4] Laozi said in the famous lines of the *Daodejing*, chapter 25:

> Man patterns himself on the operation of the earth [*ren fa di*];
> the earth patterns itself on the operation of heaven [*di fa tian*];
> heaven patterns itself on the operation of Dao [*tian fa dao*];
> Dao patterns itself on the laws of "self-so" [*dao fa ziran*].[5]

According to Hans-Georg Moeller, the notion of *ziran* and the notion of *dao* are closely connected. While human beings act according to the laws of earth, heaven, and the *dao*, each tending toward a higher level, the notion of *ziran* breaks this quasi-causal pattern. The *dao* operates simply "self-so"; there is no ultimate cause, "immovable mover," or divine demiurge behind it.[6] For me, not only the notions of *ziran* and *dao* are closely connected, the last line actually describes the Dao as self-so (as *ziran*), naturalness. *Ziran* literally means "self-so," and simply describes the Dao. The Dao is self-so: the final cause, and the "immovable mover" in the terminology of Aristotle and subsequently of Aquinas.

---

[4] See Laozi, *Daodejing*, chapter 51: "It is *Dao* that gives them life. It is *De* that nurses them.... *Dao* gives them life but does not take possession of them."

[5] Laozi, *Daodejing*, chapter 25, translation from Key Concepts in Chinese Thought and Culture.

[6] See Hans-Georg Moeller, "Basic Aspects of Daoist Philosophy," *International Communication of Chinese Culture* 2 (2015): 105; see also R. T. Ames and D. Hall, *Anticipating China: Thinking Through the Narratives of Chinese and Western Culture* (Albany: State University of New York Press, 1995), 184.

In order to grasp the holistic meaning of the *Daodejing* passage above, it is not a matter of making many levels of division—humans, earth, heaven, the Dao, and the *ziran*—but to distinguish the realm of human artifacts and that of the Dao. *Ziran* can be taken as a description of the Dao. What is important is to understand the proper relationship between human beings and the Dao. Human beings follow and observe the laws of the earth (natural sciences) and the laws of heaven (metaphysics). They all follow the Dao, the principle of everything, the law of all laws. The proper relationship between human beings and the Dao implies the harmonious relationship among human beings, nature, and the Dao as such.

The relationship between the Dao and natural things, in political philosophy, implies that the rulers in their relationship with the people should follow the natural requirements of the Dao, which places limits on their power, and governs by means of noninterference to allow the people and affairs to take their own natural course.

The Relationship between Human Beings and Nature in Confucianism

The expression "Heaven and man are united as one" (*tianren heyi*)[7] represents a world outlook and a way of thinking in Confucianism, although it may have a different meaning in Daoism as I have just elaborated above, depending on a different understanding of heaven and man. In Confucianism, the expression holds that heaven, human beings, and nature are interconnected. This world outlook emphasizes the integration and inherent relationship between human beings and nature. It highlights the fundamental significance of nature to man or

---

[7] See Zhang Zai, *Enlightenment through Confucian Teachings*, translation from Key Concepts in Chinese Thought and Culture.

human affairs, and describes the endeavor of human beings to pursue life, order, and values through interaction with nature.

This concept has been expressed in different ways through history. Mencius (372–289 BCE), often described as the second Confucian sage, believed that through mental reflection one could gain understanding of human nature and heaven, emphasizing the unity of mind, human nature, and heaven. Dong Zhongshu (179–104 BCE) said, "In terms of integration of categories, heaven and man are one."[8] Therefore, heaven and human beings are of the same category, sharing the same vital energy or the same principles. Later on, Confucian scholars of the Song dynasty sought to connect the principles of heaven, human nature, and the human mind. Neo-Confucian scholar Zhang Zai (1020–1077) in his famous work "Western Inscription" (*Xi Ming*), writes,

> Heaven is my father, and earth is my mother,
> and even such a small creature as I find an intimate place in their midst.
> Therefore, that which fills the universe I regard as my body
> and that which directs the universe I consider as my nature.
> All people are my brothers and sisters, and all things are my companions.[9]

According to him, a Confucian scholar is sincere because of his understanding, and he achieves understanding because of his sincerity. That is why heaven and human beings are united as one. One can become a sage through studies, and master heaven's law without losing understanding of human law.[10]

---

[8] Dong Zhongshu, "Luxuriant Gems," in *The Spring and Autumn Annals*, translation from Key Concepts in Chinese Thought and Culture.

[9] Chan Wing-tsit, *Source Book in Chinese Philosophy* (Princeton, NJ: Princeton University Press, 1963), 497.

[10] Zhang, *Enlightenment through Confucian Teachings*. See Key Concepts

In an article on Confucianism, Panchiu Lai explains that human beings, heaven, and earth form a trio as one. Human beings and heaven are not only united in the virtue of *ren*, but also in their activities on earth in the universe.[11] *The Doctrine of the Mean* (*Zhong Yong*) in chapter 22 highlights the Confucian conception of the relationship between human beings and nature, and the duty humans have toward nature:

> Only those who are absolutely sincere can fully develop their nature. If they can fully develop their nature, they can then fully develop the nature of others. If they can fully develop the nature of others, they can then fully develop the nature of things. If they can fully develop the nature of things, they can then assist in the transforming and nourishing process of Heaven and Earth. If they can assist in the transforming and nourishing process of Heaven and Earth, they can thus form a trio with Heaven and Earth.[12]

The *Zhong Yong* further suggests that human beings, with human morality and spirituality, can and should play an active role in the process of achieving harmony in nature and the ultimate cosmic harmony. The way of Heaven is embedded in the way of humanity. Therefore, with reference to the idea presented in the *Zhong Yong*, according to Lai Panchiu and Oliver Leaman, human beings are like co-creators of the cosmos.[13]

---

in Chinese Thought and Culture, https://chinesethought.cn/EN/shuyu_show.aspx?shuyu_id=2299.

[11] Lai Panchiu, "God of Life and Ecological Theology: A Chinese Christian Perspective," *Ecumenical Review* 65, no. 1 (March 2013): 67–82.

[12] Chan, *Source Book in Chinese Philosophy*, 107–108.

[13] Lai, "God of Life and Ecological Theology."

The Relationship between Human Beings and Nature in Chinese Buddhism

From the Buddhist perspective, there is the expression "equality for all sentient beings." The Sanskrit term *sama* is translated in Chinese as *pingdeng*, which means the same level with no difference. As a fundamental concept of Buddhism, it originally meant that there was no difference between the various castes. Buddhism then adapted to the Chinese conditions called Mahayana Buddhism with different schools developed.

Buddhism arrived in north China from India in the first century CE, had a strong influence, and was established in the whole of China after a few centuries. The Tiantai school emphasized the skillful guidance (*upaya*) and teachings contained in the Lotus Sutra, showing how the Buddha adapted his teaching to the abilities of his hearers, and how different periods of Buddha's life produced different messages for different audiences. The most characteristic view is that everything already possesses Buddha nature, so enlightenment is a matter of rediscovering what we already are.[14]

Another school of Mahayana Buddhism is called Chan Buddhism or Zen in Japanese. Master Huineng (638–713), the sixth Patriarch of Chan Buddhism, said, "As far as their essence is concerned, there is no difference between all sentient beings. They are all buddhas,"[15] which means they all share the same Buddha nature. It teaches that enlightenment is achieved only through meditation and insight, and not from reason. It promotes prin-

---

[14] Oliver Leaman, *Key Concepts in Eastern Philosophy* (New York: Routledge, 1999), 45–47.

[15] Hui Neng, *Teachings of Sakyamuni Master Huineng, the Sixth Patriarch of Zen Buddhism*, translation from Key Concepts in Chinese Thought and Culture.

ciples of beauty, simplicity, and profundity, finding the meaning of life in ordinary things. Song dynasty poet Liu Kezhuang (1187–1269) said, "I have universal love and equal respect for all, irrespective of closeness of relationship. I recite freely all ancient melodies, without constraint."[16]

Buddhism stresses the value of equality in several respects, of which the most important one is equality for all sentient beings. While the Western concept of equality in modern times is more about having the same opportunities and rights in social relations and activities as a member of society, the Buddhist concept of *pingdeng* is generally considered to mean equality for all living things.

To summarize synthetically, the characteristic views of Chinese traditional culture on ecology and on the relationship between human beings and nature are as follows:

- Heaven, human beings, and earth are interconnected.
- There is an inherent relationship between human beings and nature, and human beings are an integral part of nature.
- There are two approaches in life. Confucianism emphasizes the role of human endeavor in social interactions and interaction with nature, while Daoism emphasizes less interference with nature.
- The balance is to follow the law of nature. One has to pursue life, order, and values. There is equality in all living things, and one needs to respect all living things.

---

[16] Liu Kezhuang, "The Tenth Poem," in *Ten Six-Character-per-Line Poems* (English translation is mine).

The Relationship between Human Beings and Nature from the Catholic Perspective

The Creation Account in Genesis

From the Christian perspective, the relationship between humankind and nature is described in the biblical story of creation. God made humans in his image and likeness. He blessed Adam and Eve and said to them, "Be fertile and multiply; fill the earth and subdue it. Have dominion over the fish of the sea, the birds of the air, and all the living things that crawl on the earth" (Gen. 1:26–28).

God entrusted two basic tasks to the human race. One is to fill the earth and to "subdue" it, which is to take possession of the God-given territory and multiply. The other task is to "have dominion" over all living things with God's blessing, as human beings are made in the image and likeness of God. They are to act on behalf of God to manage all living things. After the creation of man and woman, "God looked at everything he had made, and found it very good" (Gen. 1:31). God was very pleased, and human beings were given the task of cultivating the earth garden. "The LORD God then took the man and settled him in the Garden of Eden, to cultivate and care for it" (Gen. 2:15). Humans are meant to be stewards of the earth.

Therefore, the relationship between human beings and nature is that of stewardship, based on the opening chapters of Genesis (in particular, 1:26–28, 31; 2:15).[17] God has given humans this task with dignity, being uniquely created in the image and likeness of God, to take care of the earth and all living things. God blessed them. It is their unique relationship with God that gives meaning to this relationship of stewardship of nature.

---

[17] Richard Bauckham, *Bible and Ecology* (London: DLT, 2010), 11–12.

However, remember that this original plan of God in the creation account happened before Adam and Eve had fallen into temptation. According to the Genesis narrative, God forbids them to eat fruit from the tree of knowledge of good and evil. The serpent tempted Eve to eat fruit from the forbidden tree, which she shared with Adam. Then the eyes of both were opened, and they became immediately ashamed of their nakedness (Gen. 3:17). Humans had gone astray from the original plan of God and were shut out from the state of innocence. Subsequently, God expelled them from the Garden of Eden. They had to labor and plow the ground in order to make a living, and they must return to the ground out of which they were made. In other words, they would have *to die* (Gen. 3:19).

Person-Nature Relationship in the Light of Original Sin and the "New" Adam

Getting back to the painting *Adam and Eve in the Garden of Eden* displayed at the Holy See Pavilion at the Beijing Expo 2019, all relationships were harmonious before the fall of human beings. In the moment immediately after this harmonious scene, Adam and Eve disobeyed God and ate the forbidden fruit in the Garden of Eden. They then started to pass off the responsibility to one another (Gen. 3:6–13). The three fundamental and intertwined relationships of human life with God, with neighbor, and with the earth had been broken. According to the Bible, this rupture is sin. Humans presumably took the place of God, refusing to acknowledge their creaturely limitations. As pointed out in the encyclical *Laudato Si'*, this rupture distorted the original human mandate to "have dominion" over the earth (Gen. 1:28) and to "till it and keep it" (Gen. 2:15) as stewards. As a consequence, the originally harmonious relationship between human beings and nature became conflictual (Gen. 3:17–19; see *LS* 66).

The view that humanity was distinct from nature and had a God-given right to use and exploit nature for human benefit is seen nowadays as a wrong interpretation of the Genesis verses. As a matter of fact, the exploitation of nature to the point of damaging the environment can be interpreted as the consequence of the human condition of original sin.

The main structure of the Holy See Pavilion is a monolith designed in such a way as to resemble a baptismal fountain. The monolith contains the Garden of Eden painting. In the background of the painting, one can see a winding river, which Genesis figuratively alludes to as the "source of life." As narrated in Genesis and depicted in the painting, the river breaks into four and waters the rest of the earth. Correspondingly, four strips of water cascade down the curtain wall of the monolith in the form of a cross as inscribed on top, which gives it symbolic meaning. There is also something special on the golden frame of the painting of the Garden of Eden. A layer of soil sample purposely taken from the Garden of Gethsemane is applied over the entire frame. It is to recall the passion of Jesus. The connection between the Garden of Gethsemane and the Garden of Eden intends to symbolize that, through the disobedience of Adam, many were made sinners and will die; with the passion and obedience of Christ to the point of dying on the cross, many will be made righteous and will be brought to life (Rom. 5:19; 1 Cor. 15:21–22). The symbolism is that, through baptism, a person is cleansed of original sin. Jesus, the New Adam, with his death and resurrection, brings human beings back in union with God, which is according to the original design: that all relationships are harmonious. God the Father gave us a great blessing choosing us in Christ before the foundation of the world that we might be holy and blameless before him (Eph. 1:3–6).

Regarding the New Adam, Paul compares the first Adam seen at the origin of humanity as he is in his present condition of mortality and under sin (Rom. 5:12)—therefore, a human condition that awaits a fulfillment according to God's final plan. And this fulfillment took place in Jesus Christ, in his death and resurrection. For this reason, Paul calls him the second Adam (Rom. 5:14): the origin of saved humanity, of the "new creation" that brings the humanity of the first Adam to its fulfillment, to the definitive (eschatological) salvation that can be lived by believers, already in the present, even if the fullness of time is still in the future. This signifies, as it is said, the already in the not-yet of the present time. Just as Adam is the origin of the present humanity, Jesus is at the origin of the new humanity.

What Has Gone Wrong?

The Impact of Human Dominion over Nature

In the preindustrial context when Genesis was written, humans had no idea how modern science and technology would develop and affect planet Earth. People at that time were more concerned about the danger from wild animals and threats posed by nature. The attempt to domesticate animals and to harness nature was therefore a matter of human survival.

It was not until the Age of Enlightenment, at the beginning of the seventeenth century, that the human vocation depicted in the opening chapters of Genesis began to be interpreted in a new way. Among thinkers who gave birth to the dawn of the modern era, Francis Bacon held that the aim of scientific knowledge is not simply to know the secrets of nature, but to conquer and subdue it. Scientific knowledge amounted to power, and modern technology was geared to bend nature for human advantage. In his work *New Atlantis*, Bacon advocated the founding of research institutions and a scientific elite to systematically extend humans' nascent dominion over nature.[18] And René Descartes affirmed that the human person is the master and owner of nature and justified this sovereignty on the basis of the rational uniqueness of humans over other living things. Upon the advent of scientific knowledge and technological developments, humans took the role of domination and control over nature.

It is precisely the human spirit in Western civilization in recent centuries that has experienced the scientific revolution, the Enlightenment, and the industrial revolution. However, the optimism of the Enlightenment shattered in the twentieth century. The horrors of the two world wars and the Holocaust made people painfully aware that humans were capable of terrible evil as well as good. The idea of humanity moving progressively toward a better world seemed idealistic and naïve. The Genesis account certainly had influenced Christian views of humanity's attitudes toward nature. However, the question is, does Christianity lead its members to care for the environment or is Christianity to blame for the present environmental degradation?

Historian Lynn White, among others who hold similar views,[19] has criticized the Christian worldview based on the biblical creation story, which, he argued, supports and encourages humanity's aggressive project to dominate and exploit nature. In his provocative article "The Historical Roots of Our Ecologic Crisis," published in 1967, he raised two points: Christianity insisted that it is God's will that man exploit nature for his proper

---

[18] Marvin Perry, *Western Civilization: A Brief History* (Boston: Wadsworth/Cengage, 2013), 243.

[19] Cf. C. Amery, *Das Ende der Vorsehung. Die gnadenlosen Folgen des Christentums* (Reinbek bei Hamburg: Rowohlt, 1972); U. Galimberti, *Psyche and Techne: Man in the Age of Technology* (Milan: Feltrinelli, 1999), 294–295.

ends; it is possible to exploit nature in a mood of indifference to the feelings of natural objects.[20]

People had previously believed that spirits lived in objects such as trees and so thought that nature was sacred. Christianity instead established a dualism of man and nature. Humanity came to be seen as uniquely made in the image of God and as having "dominion" or control over all the creatures of the earth. According to White, Christianity is "the most anthropocentric religion the world has seen."[21] He concludes that the modern technological conquest of nature has led to the present environmental crisis, and Christianity should bear a huge burden of guilt.[22]

Nevertheless, over the years, the comprehension and the way of interpreting biblical texts has changed. The attitude could also change according to the context. While White accused Christianity, another biblical scholar, Claus Westermann,[23] argued that this "dominion" should be seen as stewardship. Rather than exploitation, it is more like a caring and responsible attitude. The Genesis verses are seen as the kingly role involving care rather than exploitation. According to the ancient view, the king is responsible for those he rules. His rule serves the prosperity and well-being of his subjects. God settled Adam in the Garden of Eden to cultivate it. "To cultivate" is the same verb that the Bible uses for the cult or the worship that priests offer to God in the temple. Under the Old Covenant, priests would offer animal sacrifices as a gesture of atonement for sin, an offering back to God of the good things of his creation.

---

[20] Lynn White Jr., "The Historical Roots of Our Ecologic Crisis," *Science* 155 (1967): 1205.

[21] Ibid.

[22] Ibid., 1206.

[23] Claus Westermann, *Genesis*, trans. David E. Orton (Edinburgh: T&T Clark, 1988), 11.

Today, there are basically two approaches to ethical reflection on the relationship between human beings and nature: the anthropocentric position that put humans at the center of consideration and the physiocentric position that focuses on preserving nature independent of human interests. While some critics blame Christianity for being anthropocentric, or human-centered, in exploiting nature, and thus causing the present-day environmental crisis, Sergio Rondinara distinguishes between what he calls cowboy ethics and moderate anthropocentrism.[24]

Cowboy ethics puts the absolute primacy of human beings over nature, characterized by "strong anthropocentrism." Nature possesses no intrinsic value of its own but only economic value ascribed by humans to satisfy their own needs. In this case, human intervention in nature is considered as something morally indifferent. On the other hand, "moderate anthropocentrism" considers positively the ability of humans to transform the natural world. Nature, with the capacity to bring advantages to human society, has the value to nourish, to provide laboratory information and educational meaning to human beings. Ultimately, it considers the origin of nature as part of God's creation.[25]

Instead of considering a human being as the subject in a Descartes model and nature as the object in the sphere of nonhumans, Rondinara considers that nature should be taken as the totality of the physical world, including human beings. There

---

[24] Sergio Rondinara, "Custodire ciò che è salvato," in *Per un umanesimo degno dell'amore: Il Compendio della Dottrina Sociale della Chiesa*, ed. Paolo Carlotti and Mario Toso (Roma: Editrice LAS, 2005), 434.

[25] See John Passmore, *Man's Responsibility for Nature: Ecological Problems and Western Tradition* (New York: Scribner, 1974); Kristin Shrader-Frechette, *Environmental Ethics* (Pacific Grove, CA: Boxwood Press, 1981); Brian Norton, *Why Preserve Natural Variety?* (Princeton, NJ: Princeton University Press, 1991).

is a recursive relationship between person and nature mutually dependent on one another. In this way, human beings are still at the center of creation, as men and women are made in the image and likeness of God. He suggests a shift from a subject-object dualism to a relational paradigm of humans, nature, and God.[26] Person-nature is a recursive relationship, in the sense that God is lord of nature, and humans have a ministerial role of stewardship in nature.[27]

In recent decades, the scale and consequences of humanity's impact on the natural world have become increasingly apparent. The optimism about human progress has been severely challenged; the question now is whether humanity can act with sufficient speed to limit the negative consequences of industrial pollution and global warming. There is an amplified and defused distortion of social economic systems inspired by the technocratic paradigm.

Therefore, in the ultimate analysis, nature is not to be treated as an object for human beings to use. The fault is not scientific development or industrialization per se, but the lack of rightful relationship between God and human beings. Therefore, with an appropriate relationship among human beings, nature, and God, humans would have a great sense of amazement in front of nature as God's creation.

Pollution and Some Related Problems in China

In China's case, putting blind faith in science, technology, and economic development without deepening reflections on the profound relationship between human beings and nature also

---

[26] Sergio Rondinara, "Relazione persona-natura. Il recupero dei significati," *Nuova Umanità*, no. 224 (2016): 47–59.

[27] See International Theological Commission, *Communion and Stewardship: Human Persons Created in the Image of God* (Rome, 2002), 73.

creates problems. The rapid economic growth of China since the 1980s has resulted in many pressing environmental issues to resolve, new and old. For the purpose of this study, I take up two of them: air pollution and food waste.

Rapid urbanization, building of infrastructure, and increasing heavy traffic all contribute to emissions, and China is highly dependent on coal use for power generation. Industrialization has brought about pollution and major health concerns. A respected CCTV host and investigative reporter, Chai Jing, produced a self-financed documentary on China's environmental problems that shocked the nation in 2015. The film reached 200 million viewers in just four days until it was pulled offline, sparking widespread discussion about environmental policy in China.[28] Many industrial cities in China paid the high price for pollution. Pictures of smoggy Beijing are famous just as once were the misty capitals of London and Milan. Government officials and urban elites breathe the same air as the general public. China is committed to comply with the Paris climate agreement, taking big steps to reduce coal use, double down on the mix of national energy sources, and embrace natural gas. Yes, gas supply and price, on which many Chinese rely for a warm winter, depend a good deal on geopolitics involving big powers like Russia and the United States.

Nevertheless, careful observers note that on this issue of air pollution, whereas China used to dominate the top spots for the most-polluted cities in the world, pollution across China has steadily decreased since a clean-air policy was implemented in 2013.[29] The gradual completion of the China-Russia East-Route

---

[28] Nicola Persico, "Fighting Pollution: What China Can Learn from Britain," *Fortune*, March 10, 2015.

[29] Zhang Qiang et al., "Drivers of Improved PM2.5 Air Quality in China from 2013 to 2017," *Proceedings of National Academy of Science (PNAS)*, December 3, 2019, https://pnas.org/content/116/49/24463.

Natural Gas pipeline in 2020, and the Central Asia–China Gas Pipeline in 2015 also helped ease China's dependency on coal.

The other pressing issue is food waste. Experts say the world indeed faces a food shortage as an aftermath of the pandemics, but for China, the real threat to food security comes not from natural disasters such as epidemic or floods, but more from food wastage. With growing affluence, such waste has become a worrying issue in China, so much so that the government initiated what it calls the "Empty Your Plate Campaign 2.0." This campaign aimed at putting an end to officials' extravagant feasts and receptions. It was subsequently extended to the general public.

The *Global Times* published a detailed report on this issue.[30] "Food wastage is shocking and distressing. It is necessary to further enhance public awareness of the issue, amid the fallout from the pandemic," said President Xi. He launched this Empty Your Plate Campaign and encouraged fostering a social environment where waste is shameful and cultivating the habit of thriftiness. It makes me think of how Pope Francis called for this consciousness that "wasting food is like stealing from the poor."

In June 2020, the United Nations warned that the world is on the verge of the worst food crisis in fifty years. The world's top three grain exporters—the United States, Brazil, and India—were also the three countries most affected by COVID-19. A third of the world's food is wasted every year, with about 1.3 billion tons still edible. At least 820 million of the world's 7.6 billion people are suffering from starvation, said CCTV in a Weibo post, citing UN data. It was once reported that food wasted in China was enough to feed 200 million people a year.

---

[30] Wang Qi, "China Launches Clean Plate Campaign 2.0 as Xi Calls for End to Food Wastage," *Global Times*, August 12, 2020, https://globaltimes.cn/content/1197577.shtml.

Food-security education is important, as is the guidance in forming rational consumption habits, both of which are crucial to reducing food wastage and ensuring food security. President Xi also gave specific requirements for reducing waste in schools and promoting students' awareness and practices. There is now more awareness on this issue, as the *Global Times* cited the example of a waitress saying, "We remind our guests when they order too much food."

Policies during the pandemic, which encouraged separate meals and reduced dining out, proved helpful and positive. Ordering food and groceries by apps on phones or online has since become part of daily life. Shopping online has grown tremendously and transformed people's lives in China. However, those changes resulted in another pressing issue: the excessive use of plastic for home delivery packaging, which poses another threat to the environment. China's efforts to care for the environment, while forceful, may not be swift and efficient enough to resolve all pressing issues. Still, the Earth is our common home, and we have valuable lessons to learn from one another.

Relational Paradigm

What is the attitude toward the relationship between human beings and nature?

Relational Paradigm from the Chinese Perspective

In regard to dialogue between Catholicism and other religions, Stratford Caldecott speaks of "asking the right questions" on fundamental realities, recognizing that different religions have different concerns.[31] My emphasis is on those

---

[31] See Stratford Caldecott, *Catholicism and Other Religions: Introducing Interfaith Dialogue* (London: Catholic Truth Society, 2009), 27–29.

fundamental questions rooted in early civilizations coming from Judeo-Christian, Indian, and Chinese traditions. For this we may turn further back to the Axial Age—the concept described by Karl Jasper, when roughly at the same time more than two thousand years ago around the world, the great intellectual, philosophical, and religious systems emerged that came to shape subsequent human society and culture. They came up with fundamental ideas toward speculation about the fate of humanity, the meaning and principles of life, and human beings' relationship with the cosmos. They also posed answers to questions of ultimate concern, such as, What are we? Where are we going? What is the absolute or ultimate reality? What attitude should we take toward the relationship between human beings and nature?

For the Judeo-Christian tradition, the ultimate reality is God who created heaven and earth and who shaped the destiny of all people. For the Hindu-Buddhist tradition, the ultimate concern is reaching the state of total liberation, the *Moksha* or the *Nirvana*. For the Chinese tradition, the ultimate reality is the Dao, the principle and the way of ultimate reality, of the universe, and of human life.[32]

At the beginning of this chapter, I gave the example of the often-quoted verses in the *Daodejing* chapter 25. The expression *ziran* is not to be misquoted to mean the physical world of nature or even Mother Nature as superior to the Dao. This would elevate nature to such a point of giving rise to animist religions based on the veneration of natural phenomena or objects of nature. There

---

[32] According to H. Smith, there are three meanings or levels of Dao. The Dao, as "the way of ultimate reality," has a religious dimension. As "the way of the universe," it is the law governing the universe, the driving power in all nature, the ordering principle behind all life, and in the midst of life. As "the way of human life," it is the norm guiding the behavior of humans who are encouraged to live well and properly in relationships. Cf. H. Smith, *The World's Religions* (San Francisco: HarperCollins, 1991), 108–109, 206.

are two distinctive realms. One is the realm of human beings. The other is the realm of the Dao, which is the ultimate reality, mysterious, indescribable, and perfect.

Feng Youlan (Fung Yu-Lan) (1895–1990) explained that Daoism considered the Dao and nature to be perfect, while Mohism[33] sought to improve on nature because it valued utility, logic, and definition of things. During the Warring States period, there was rivalry between Confucianists and Mohists. Confucianism, which emphasized virtues and humanism, overshadowed Mohism, which had been ignored and then forgotten for almost two thousand years. Otherwise, according to Feng, China would not have lagged behind in scientific development since Mohists aspired to conquer nature, similar to the Baconian conception and attitude toward nature.[34]

The *Daodejing* chapter 25 starts with human beings at the center of attention, following the laws of heaven and earth, and the Dao. In the realm of the ultimate reality, the Dao is self-so. It would be a distortion to describe the Dao as following the physical world of nature as the highest order, giving rise to some sort of worship of nature. Instead, human beings should ultimately live according to the Dao. Humans with all humility still have an essential role in their relationship with the Dao and nature.

Apart from the *Daodejing* text, at the beginning of this chapter I also quoted from Confucian and Buddhist texts: the

---

[33] Mohism is an ancient Chinese school of thought developed by Mozi (400s-300s BCE), emphasizing universal love, utilitarianism, and a focus on practical solutions to social problems. It presented a significant challenge to Confucianism by advocating for impartial concern for all and a more meritocratic society. I will elaborate more on it in the following chapter on fraternity and social friendship.

[34] See Feng Youlan, "Why China Has No Science," *International Journal of Ethics* 32, no. 3 (1922): 237–263; see also E. J. Machle, *Nature and Heaven in the Xunzi: A Study of the Tian Lun* (Albany: State University of New York Press, 1993).

Confucian expression of "heaven and man are united as one" emphasizes the oneness of humankind and the natural world, and the Buddhist expression of "equality for all sentient beings" emphasizes the equality in all living things and the need to respect all living things. There is a humanistic and anthropological approach, given the attitude in Chinese culture of humility and respect toward nature and in front of the mystery of the Dao. It is a continuously seeking harmony in the relationship among human beings, nature, and the ultimate reality of the Dao, as emphasized in the Chinese cultural tradition.

A Relational Paradigm from the Christian Perspective

It is necessary to place a biblical text in its original historical context. The interpretation is influenced by the concerns of the age in which the interpreter lives. Today, as never before, the environmental issue presents itself as a privileged locus where faith is directly addressed, and where "we are invited to give the reasons for our hope."[35] The title of Pope Francis's encyclical *Laudato Si'* was taken from the canticle of St. Francis, "Praise Be to You," echoing and developing the psalm that speaks of all living things as sharing a common kinship and joining together in praise of God and for his wonderful creation (Ps. 148). This is popularly known as the Canticle of Brother Sun and Sister Moon.

Genesis was written at a time when the Jews were suffering. "When the biblical account of Creation was written, the people of Israel were not going through happy days.... There was no more homeland, no temple, no social and religious life, nothing," said Pope Francis in his catechetical instruction about prayer. "Yet, starting from this story of Creation, someone begins to find reasons for thanksgiving, to praise God for their

---

[35] 1 Pet. 3:15; see Rondinara, "Relazione persona-natura."

existence."[36] Human beings are infinitely small when compared to the size of the universe. There is the feeling of amazement in front of nature; as Pope Francis said, "The relationship with God is the greatness of man: his enthronement. By nature, we are almost nothing, small, but by vocation, by call, we are the children of the great King!"[37] This contemplation leads the person who prays to wonder, *What is man?* Despite humanity's frailty, said the pope, "the human being is the only creature aware of such a profusion of beauty."

The consequences of the fall of Adam and Eve were losing their immortality, having to work for their food, undergoing pain in childbirth, and banishment from the Garden of Eden. "Cursed is the ground because of you! In toil you shall eat its yield all the days of your life.... For you are dust, and to dust you shall return" (Gen. 3:17–18). "You shall return to dust" here means that human beings are now mortal. The punishment affects also the human relationship to the ground, meaning the relationship with nature.

Ren Andao has given the following example.[38] Imagine a celebration and someone has prepared to present you with a bicycle as a gift, yet before the bicycle was given, it was stolen. The bike is now a stolen good.

Because of the fall of Adam and Eve, they are no longer in the I-Thou relationship with God, but in an I-It relationship, using a concept coined by Martin Buber.[39] When the first man

---

[36] Pope Francis, "Catechism on Prayer," General Audience at the Library of the Apostolic Palace, May 20, 2020.

[37] Ibid.

[38] Ren Andao, "A Christian between Tien and Humans," *Fountains Periodical* (Taipei), no. 95, 2018.

[39] Buber characterizes "I-Thou" relations as "dialogical" and "I-It" relations as "monological." The I-Thou relationship is between authentic beings, without objectification. I meet you as you are, and you meet me as who I am.

and woman betrayed this I-Thou relationship of trust and free gift from God, the element of sin took over to establish an I-It relationship. While Buber sees the relationship between God and humans as fundamentally I-Thou, the forbidden fruit episode in the Garden of Eden, where humanity disobeys God, can be interpreted as a shift towards an I-It relationship. This shift occurs because by choosing to disobey, humanity begins to view God as an object of knowledge and control (the fruit) rather than a subject of relationship. From that moment on, humans see others, even God, as objects. The I-Thou becomes an I-It relationship. However, God always maintains a giving-receiving relationship. Even though humans become mortal, God wants to maintain this dynamic and dialogical relationship with humans, just like the relationships among the Persons in the Holy Trinity.

What is the relationship between God and humans after the event of Jesus's coming to earth? Even when they fell, God never gave up on them. God is the creator and redeemer of humans. "I have called you by name: you are mine." He is with humans always, for he said, "I, the LORD, am your God, the Holy One." He is the savior "because you are precious in my eyes and honored, and I love you." He does not give up on them; all are called by name; "I created them for my glory; I formed them, made them" (Isa. 43:1–7).

Chiara Lubich, with her charism of unity, intuits that Christ crucified and risen leads all men and women in the participation

---

An "I-Thou" relation participates in the dynamic living process of an "other" while an "I-It" relation experiences a detached thing, fixed in space and time. The I-It encounter is the opposite of the I-Thou relation. In the I-It relation we relate to another as an object, completely outside of ourselves. See Sarah Scott, "Martin Buber (1878–1965)," *Internet Encyclopedia of Philosophy*, June 9, 2020; see also Maurice S. Friedman, "Martin Buber: The Life of Dialogue," *The Religion*, June 9, 2020, https://religion-online.org/book-chapter/chapter-12-the-eternal-thou.

of the "new creation."⁴⁰ The cry of Jesus, the crucified God, awakens in her a unique understanding and experience of his mystery. Jesus's abysmal suffering gives light and meaning to every human suffering and reveals the secret to uniting all people to God and to one another. In her book *The Cry of Jesus Crucified and Forsaken*, written as a love song to Jesus dying and forsaken on the cross, she defines the forsaken Jesus as "the open window" between God and humans. As Cardinal Paul Poupard comments, "'Father, may they all be one' is the prayer of Christ but also the invocation with which Chiara closes her book and opens the dawn of the third millennium to hope."⁴¹ Poupard wishes that whoever reads the book will make this prayer their own, addressing their love letter to the crucified Lord.

God is the Trinity because the Father gives everything to the Son without reservation, and Jesus gives everything back to the Father without reservation, fulfilling the will of the Father. In this process of giving and receiving, life is generated. It is the Holy Spirit, the bond of love, life of God. Life refers to the exchange of giving and receiving, a subject-to-subject encounter.

As explained in the previous chapter on the Trinitarian relationship, the cry of Jesus crucified and forsaken is the climax

---

⁴⁰ Cf. Piero Coda, "Creation in Christ and the New Creation in the Mysticism of Chiara Lubich," *Claritas: Journal of Dialogue and Culture* 5, no. 1 (2016): article 3. Coda explains in the text that "Jesus, out of love for the Father and for human beings, feeling himself detached from the Father, out of love 'loses' the divine link making him one with the Father, namely, the Holy Spirit. But in this very way not only does he find this link again in himself (in the event of the resurrection where his humanity is also glorified by the Spirit) but he also makes human beings participate in it. Thus, thanks to the gift of the Holy Spirit, Jesus Forsaken makes creation participate in the Being of the Creator."

⁴¹ Chiara Lubich, *The Cry of Jesus Crucified and Forsaken* (New York: New City Press, 2001), foreword by Cardinal Paul Poupard, president emeritus of the Pontifical Council for Culture.

of Jesus's passion. The Trinitarian relationship is from God, not something abstract but a living encounter with humans. Jesus, the New Adam, by being forsaken and dying on the cross, makes a gift of divine love to humanity, redeems all humans from the fall of the First Adam, and leads them back to a relationship of communion with God. Jesus takes upon himself in his abandonment the whole of humankind and reveals the law of love—that is, the gift of self to the other. In this act, he restores the distorted relationship of humans with nature, and among themselves.

The Anthropocentrism of Christ

One may say that the Daoists are the first ecologists because of their concept of being in harmony with nature, blending in with the environment, and doing no harm to nature. In the West, in a similar manner, the non-anthropocentric position, which includes biocentrism and ecocentrism, is focused on preserving nature regardless of human interests. All entities in nature have intrinsic value. Consequently, everything that maintains the ecosystems is morally correct and anything that could harm them is not. According to the deep ecology movement, each individual is also related to other individuals and nonsentient natural entities. For ethical considerations there is no clear demarcation nor clear boundary between humans and the environment, as Sergio Rondinara has pointed out.[42]

The *Compendium of the Social Doctrine of the Church* (CSDC) not only keeps a distance from distorted anthropocentric positions but also from physio-centrism:

---

[42] Sergio Rondinara, "Custodire ciò che è salvato," in Mario Toso, *Per un umanesimo degno dell'amore: Il Compendio della Dottrina Sociale della Chiesa*, ed. Paolo Carlotti and Mario Toso (Roma: Editrice LAS, 2005): 434–436.

> A correct understanding of the environment prevents the utilitarian reduction of nature to a mere object to be manipulated and exploited. At the same time, it must not absolutize nature and place it above the dignity of the human person himself. In this latter case, one can go so far as to divinize nature or the earth.[43]

Although the CSDC did not affirm specifically the kind of Christian environmental ethics regarding the person-nature relationship, it cannot be simply considered as a moderately anthropocentric one, but an anthropocentrism characterized by humans' responsibility for their actions toward the natural habitat. As Rondinara emphasized and concluded, it is an "anthropocentrism of Christ."[44]

As Paul says, "Whoever is in Christ is a new creation: the old things have passed away; behold, new things have come" (2 Cor. 5:17). We are, therefore, new creatures, not only because we were redeemed from the situation of nonlove in which sin had relegated us, but because we are now filled with the Spirit of God and have become the leaven of unity for the entire creation—composed of various expressions of human life (social, political, scientific, and economic) but also of peoples and cultures. Through our work and actions, we prepare for the fulfillment of the cosmos (Rom. 8:19–21).[45] This anthropocentrism of Christ is indeed revolutionary and continues to guide the social teaching of the Catholic Church.

Pope Francis in his encyclical letter *Laudato Si'* invites human persons to experience an ecological conversion, in which they seek to live in harmony with nature rather than dominate it. He

---

[43] Pontifical Council for Justice and Peace, *Compendium of the Social Doctrine of the Church*, 2004, 463; see also Pope John Paul II, Encyclical Letter *Centesimus Annus*, no. 37, 1991.

[44] Rondinara, "Custodire ciò che è salvato," 437.

[45] Ibid., 436–437.

encourages us to develop with an integral approach a spirituality of global solidarity, taking into account all relationships. Even if humans make mistakes and go astray, yet there is hope. "All it takes is one good person to restore hope! The biblical tradition clearly shows that this renewal entails recovering and respecting the rhythms inscribed in nature by the hand of the Creator" (*LS* 71). God does not abandon humans; he never forsakes his loving plan or repents of having created it. Humanity still has the ability to work together in building a common home.

Are Christian teachings and the Chinese traditions compatible on the question of the relationship between human beings and nature? By taking up human responsibility and the positive elements in Chinese culture mentioned earlier—the harmonious relationship of human beings with the Dao, with nature, and with other fellow human beings—not only are they not contradictory, but Chinese traditions could be consonant with Christian teachings. Even on the hot topic of the development of artificial intelligence (AI), it is essential to remember that AI is a human creation. Humans only have a caretaker or stewardship role in nature. As Daoists strive to maintain the harmonious relationship with the Dao, Christians have the responsibility to maintain a right relationship with God by obeying his Word.

"Integral Ecology" in Relation to "Ecological Civilization"

"Integral Ecology" in Laudato Si'

The unbridled exploitation of nature by humankind has had negative effects on the environment. In recent times, damage to the Earth has almost reached a point of no return: the collapse of the ecosystem. As noted, Judeo-Christian thinking has been accused of encouraging the negative effects on the environment, and as a consequence, Western civilization in general has brought humanity to the present situation. However, this is not a correct interpretation of the Bible as understood by the Catholic Church.

Christians have at times incorrectly interpreted the Scriptures. With the encyclical *Laudato Si'*, Pope Francis gave this message: "We are not God. The earth was here before us and it has been given to us.... Nowadays we must forcefully reject the notion that our being created in God's image and given dominion over the earth justifies absolute domination over other creatures." That is indeed a distorted interpretation. The biblical texts tell us to "till and keep" the garden of the world (see Gen. 2:15). "Tilling" refers to cultivating, plowing, or working, while "keeping" means caring for, protecting, overseeing, and preserving. The Holy Father emphasizes relationships, respect, and responsibility toward nature as a way of caring for the needs of future generations. In the encyclical he writes,

> This implies a relationship of mutual responsibility between human beings and nature. Each community can take from the bounty of the earth whatever it needs for subsistence, but it also has the duty to protect the earth and to ensure its fruitfulness for coming generations. (*LS* 67)

The pope uses the story of Cain's murder of Abel to illustrate the connection between justice for people and justice for the environment. God asks Cain, "What have you done? The voice of your brother's blood is crying to me from the ground. And now you are cursed from the ground" (Gen. 4:11). Through this story, God is telling humans: listen to the cry of the earth, as much as you listen to the cry of your poor brothers and sisters. This encyclical has an ecological as well as a social dimension. This narrative in a way reflects the human root of the ecological crisis.

The message of the encyclical *Laudato Si'* is like a wake-up call for the whole of humanity, to believers and nonbelievers, that the earth is our common home, and we are responsible for it and for future generations. Pope Francis gave a fresh analysis of the present situation to make people aware of the destruction that humans are rendering to the environment and other fellow human beings.

The deterioration of the environment affects every aspect of human life. Technological products "create a framework which ends up conditioning lifestyles and shaping social possibilities along the lines dictated by the interests of certain powerful groups" (*LS* 107).

Laudato Si' is not just an encyclical about ecology, green consciousness, or social work for the poor. The Holy Father employs the term "ecology" in the sense of the ecosystem: "Everything is in relation to one another," "everything is interrelated," and "everything is interconnected."

"Integral ecology" is the focus and the perspective on which the encyclical is based. G. Costa and P. Foglizzo say, "Integral ecology is an approach to all complex systems, the understanding of which requires focusing on the relationship of the individual parts to each other and to the whole."[46] It is making ecology interact in its various dimensions: environmental ecology, economic ecology, sociocultural ecology, and human ecology.

Pope Francis affirmed, "A strategy for real change calls for rethinking processes in their entirety, for it is not enough to include a few superficial ecological considerations while failing to question the logic which underlies present-day culture" (*LS* 197).

To illustrate some important points raised in *Laudato Si'*, the Holy Father indicates dialogue is the indispensable way to face the urgent challenges. He calls for an "integral ecology" with concrete lines of action. "Interdependence obliges us to think of

---

[46] G. Costa and P. Foglizzo, "L'ecologia integrale," *Aggiornamenti Sociali*, August–September 2015, https://aggiornamentisociali.it/articoli/l-ecologia-integrale.

one world with a common plan" (*LS* 164). He also calls for a "global ecological conversion" (*LS* 5), which will bring about an "ecological spirituality" (*LS* 216), and to change our self-centered lifestyle, getting rid of a throwaway culture, to have an impact on society (*LS* 208). It is also a matter of "ecological education and spirituality" for the present and future generations (*LS* 202–245). Religions must enter into "dialogue among themselves for the sake of protecting nature, defending the poor, and building networks of respect and fraternity" (*LS* 201).

Pope Francis challenged the values of rampant consumerism, unrestrained faith in technology, blind pursuit of profits, political shortsightedness and the economic inequalities that force the world's poor to bear the brunt of an imbalanced ecosystem.

Initiatives on "Integral Ecology"

Pope Francis spoke of an "integral ecology", as inspired by St. Francis of Assisi, who cared for all that exists and called all creatures his "brothers" and "sisters," who communed with them, inviting them "to praise the Lord, and to approach nature and the environment with openness to awe and wonder" (*LS* 11). St. Francis speaks of the natural world in kinship terms: "brother sun and sister moon; brother wind and sister water."[47] It is a call for an ecological conversion, where one seeks to live in harmony with nature rather than to dominate it, and where all benefit equally from the Earth's resources, including future generations. It is an invitation to change concretely and collectively our personal attitude and lifestyle, responding to the cry of the earth and the cry of our brothers and sisters in society so as to promote a "culture of care."

---

[47] "Canticle of the Creatures," in *Francis of Assisi: Early Documents* (New York: New City Press, 1999), 113–114.

At a grassroots level, for Catholics, even the simple act of receiving Communion at Mass could acquire a new awareness. To accomplish the renewal of the cosmos, Chiara Lubich believes that Jesus also expects people's cooperation in communion with Jesus, who dies and rises again, and is certainly the real cause of the transformation for the cosmos. Paul tells us that through our sufferings we complete "what is lacking in Christ's afflictions" (Col. 1:24), and that nature waits "for the revealing of the children of God" (Rom. 8:19). In a conference on the theme of the Eucharist, Lubich said,

> The Eucharist redeems and makes us God. We, dying, complete with Christ in the transformation of the cosmos; in fact, nature is almost a continuation of the body of Jesus because he, by incarnating himself, assumed human nature, in which all creation flows.[48]

In fact, some Orthodox theologians highlight the idea of humans as the priests of creation, offering it to God.[49]

Pope Francis spoke of integral ecology, ecological conversion, and dialogue. How can Chinese Christians be a resource, and how can Christians worldwide act? The ecological crisis is another face of Jesus forsaken. Moved by the spirituality of unity, and the love for this forsaken Jesus as the secret to fulfill the prayer of Jesus "that all may be one," the Focolare Movement has some initiatives and experiences to share in this field.

The Focolare Movement is an active partner of the Global Catholic Climate Movement and collaborates with associations,

---

[48] Chiara Lubich, "Lubich's Talk on the Theme of the Eucharist to Members of the Focolare," October 10, 1976, Rocca di Papa, Italy; see Chiara Lubich, "A Transforming Power," *Living City*, April 2015, 21.

[49] J. Zizioulas, "Priest of Creation," in *Environmental Stewardship: Critical Perspectives, Past and Present*, ed. R. J. Berry (London: T&T Clark, 2006), 273–290.

organizations, institutions, movements of different churches and various religions, and cultures for the care of the planet. It is a global network of people who are passionate about caring for the planet.

On the fifth anniversary of the encyclical on the environment, Pope Francis proclaimed a Special Year of *Laudato Si'* to develop the encyclical on ecology, leading up to a *Laudato Si'* Week[50] from May 16 to 25, 2021. Focolare's Youth for a United World launched a new campaign for the year 2021–2022: #daretocare for people and planet, which proposed "ecological conversion" through initiatives that involve associations, organizations, and institutions, but also through our simple everyday actions, to break the cycle of violence, exploitation, and selfishness so typical of the culture of waste.

For example, EcoOne is an international cultural initiative promoted by the Focolare Movement with a network of teachers, academics, researchers, and professionals who work in environmental sciences.[51] They strive to enrich their scientific knowledge with a profound humanistic interpretation of contemporary ecological problems. Together with other organizational partners, who

---

[50] In the "*Laudato Si'* Week" of 2021, there were webinars and testimonies to encourage dialogue and the exchange of views and to propose concrete actions for the planet. The theme "For we know that things can change" (*LS* 13) shed light on the hope around the world that something can still be done to turn things around, and to showcase the transformative impact of *Laudato Si'* on global education. The program included the "Songs for Creation" festival, the Global Day of Action, and the launch of the "*Laudato Si'* Platform of Initiatives." Leaders from around the world and world-renowned speakers and authors together with many people came together to celebrate the conclusion of the "Special Year *Laudato Si'*." See Lorenzo Russo, "*Laudato Si'* Week 2021," Focolare Movement, May 16, 2021, https://focolare.org/en/news/2021/05/16/settimana-laudato-si-2021.

[51] EcoOne, "Who We Are," September 28, 2016, http://ecoone.org/en/who-we-are.html.

pursue the goal of "universal destination of goods" and closer interdependence between countries, EcoOne strives to introduce and foster these principles of environmental care into social, political, and economic sectors. EcoOne showcases projects that promote ecologically based ideas and studies.

As one of its initiatives in response to Pope Francis's call for changes in lifestyles, the EarthCube is a motivational tool based on a lifestyle aimed at supporting a healthy and sustainable planet. Members are encouraged to roll a cube like dice, read the message that faces up, and find a way to live it. The six messages on the dice are, (1) We are all connected, (2) Everything is a gift, (3) Only what is needed, (4) Discover amazing things, (5) Smile on the world, and (6) Now is the time. Quite a few members of the movement, kids and adults, try to practice this each day, and they share the results and encourage others to adopt this practice, with the purpose of encouraging a relationship-centered and action-oriented response to the needs of the environment.

Steven Kezamutima is a Burundian youth living in Kenya. He and his friends in 2018 initiated a project called Birthday Tree Planting as a concrete response to the invitation of *Laudato Si'* to help protect the earth, our common home. The idea is to plant a tree or trees on your birthday. The motto is, "Cutting cake and planting trees, a new tradition to celebrate birthdays." This project evolved to become a learning experience for children by accompanying the growth of the tree, to taste the fruit of the care for nature, and to appreciate its beauty. Some also came up with the idea of planting fruit trees and medicinal trees to multiply the goals. This choice of medicinal trees came up in 2020 when the pandemic was hitting the world. While African societies have forgotten the use of medicinal plants, these initiatives have contributed to research and discoveries that could help cure and prevent diseases.[52]

---

[52] Amministrazione del Patrimonio della Sede Apostolica, *Laudato Si'*

Ecological conversion is rooted in a spiritual conversion, leading to increasing ecological awareness and changing one's lifestyle for the present and especially for future generations. Contemplating that everything on earth is in a relationship of love with everything, an authentic spirituality and ecological action can flow. At these times, the cries of the poor and the earth are increasing intensely. It is also very important to dialogue with both the millennial spiritual wisdom (taking into account the example of China in the present study) and the postmodern one, which leads to a more complete and grateful gaze toward nature and one another.

On the occasion of the fiftieth Earth Day celebrated on April 22, 2020, Pope Francis reiterated the need for ecological conversion that can find expression in concrete actions. As a single and interdependent family, we require a common plan in order to avert the threats to our common home. He emphasized the importance of cooperation as an international community for the protection of our common home, urging those in positions of leadership to guide the preparations for the two international conferences of great importance in 2021: the UN biodiversity conference in Kunming, China (COP15), and the UN climate change conference in Glasgow, Great Britain (COP26).[53]

The world needs urgent action to protect our common home; at the same time, it must be said that in past decades, rich countries have already outsourced their carbon dioxide emissions and polluting industries to developing countries. As the Holy Father calls our attention to important conventions, listening to experiences in different parts of world and fostering collaboration will certainly impact the future of the earth and humanity.

Reader: An Alliance of Care for Our Common Home, https://humandevelopment.va/content/dam/sviluppoumano/news/2021-news/laudatosireader/Laudato-si-Reader.pdf.

[53] Pope Francis, "General Audience on the Occasion of the 50th Earth Day," April 22, 2020.

"Ecological Civilization" in the Speech of Xi Jinping

In the opening ceremony of the Beijing International Horticultural Expo on April 28, 2019, President Xi Jinping spoke on the theme of "Working Together for a Green and Better Future for All" to nine hundred delegates, including foreign leaders and special envoys from eleven countries, international exhibitors, and horticulture experts. Present among them were Cardinal Gianfranco Ravasi, president of the Pontifical Council for Culture, and secretary, Bishop Mons. Paul Tighe.

I find in Xi's speech consonance with the spirit of *Laudato Si'*. Xi spoke of the Earth in need of a balanced ecological system and China's effort to accelerate its pace in the construction of an "ecological civilization." He emphasized in particular that "all humans live in a community with a shared future in the face of eco-environmental challenges, and only through collaboration can we effectively tackle global environmental issues."[54]

With regard to the relationship between humans and nature, Xi observed that across the history of human civilizations, "the rise or fall of a society is dependent on its relationship with nature." He also acknowledged that "industrialization, while generating unprecedented material wealth, has incurred serious damage to Mother Nature. . . . Nature punishes those who exploit and plunder it brutally, and rewards those who use and protect it carefully."

The Chinese president sees the necessity of pursuing economic prosperity through sustainable development, calling it "green development," and talks of promoting "a simpler, greener and low-carbon lifestyle." He advocates the value of green development that "reveres and cares for nature" by

---

[54] See "Highlights of Xi's Speech at Beijing Horticultural Expo Opening Ceremony," China Global Television Network (CGTN), April 28, 2019, https://news.cgtn.com/news/3d3d674e774d7a4d34457a6333566d54/index.html.

raising people's "awareness of environmental issues," injecting "ecological conservation into every aspect of social life." The approach is "integral."

With regard to science, he suggests "scientific policies" with meticulous scientific research pursued to create a "harmonious ecosystem" following the laws of nature. "Human wisdom" is essential for ecological conservation to sustain the dynamism of earth, "our common homeland."

Xi promises that China is ready to "work with all other countries," and "only together" with concerted effort can we effectively address climate change, marine pollution, biological conservation, and other global environmental issues and achieve the United Nations 2030 Agenda for Sustainable Development. He also spoke of the responsibility toward future generations. Every generation has its own mission. "Our efforts to conserve the ecosystem will benefit not only this generation but many more to come."[55]

There are many convergent points with the spirit of *Laudato Si'*, such as an integral approach to ecological issues, taking into account the needs of society, the economy, the earth as our common home, the need of a concerted effort from all countries, the need to adopt a simpler lifestyle, and the concern for future generations.

Besides these converging points, however, one major point of difference is present: the concept of nature as God's creation. While Xi speaks of respect for the environment in harmony with nature per se, the Christian viewpoint looks at nature, with respect, as God's creation. In that sense, Christians respect nature

---

[55] See "Xi Jinping's Keynote Speech at the Opening Ceremony of the International Horticultural Exhibition 2019 (Edited Excerpt)," *Beijing Review*, September 3, 2019, http://bjreview.com/Beijing_Review_and_Kings_College_London_Joint_Translation_Project/2019/201909/t20190903_800177587.html.

out of love for God. Yet they rely on the good faith and human wisdom of both believers and nonbelievers for a correct attitude toward ecological conservation, sustenance of nature, and the promotion of a harmonious ecosystem. At the end, as Pope Francis said, "Whether believers or not, we are agreed today that the earth is essentially a shared inheritance, whose fruits are meant to benefit everyone" (*LS* 93). We all must live up to this mission.

Initiatives on "Ecological Civilization"

China has abandoned a lot of spiritual resources in its tradition, lost "respect for the heaven and awe for the Dao," and "harmony with difference,"[56] according to Professor Wang Zhihe and Fan Meijun. In *Second Enlightenment*, they criticize the blind worship of science and reason, and the abandonment of important values in traditional culture. Instead, they suggest a third or a middle way to meet the needs of society—to overcome the dichotomy between urban and rural, modern and traditional, East and West.[57] They criticize the sole pursuit of economic growth, but advocates for people to reevaluate their own traditional ecological wisdom, finding local solutions appropriate to local circumstances.

I have written in my previous book on Chinese youth[58] that they used to think that in a big city, one can get big money and a better life, while those living in the countryside are losers. At present, there are many contradictions in the dual urban-rural system. To solve those contradictions, it is often argued within China that

---

[56] Wang Zhihe and Fan Meijun, "Hope Lies in Change," in *For Our Common Home: Process-Relational Response to Laudato Si'*, ed. J. B. Cobb and I. Castuera (Anoka, MN: Process Century Press, 2015), 341.

[57] Wang Zhihe and Fan Meijun, *Second Enlightenment* (Beijing: Peking University Press, 2011), 478.

[58] Yan Kin Sheung Chiaretto, *Seasons for Relationships: Youth in China and the Mission of the Church* (Macau: Claretian Publications, 2019), 17.

urbanization is the key issue. However, urbanization means not only expanding cities but also developing towns in rural areas. Therefore, integrated urban and rural development is important.

Big cities offer a bigger market, but more competition as well. Wang encourages young people to explore possibilities in smaller cities or towns, citing some inspiring experiences of some well-educated youth returning to the countryside. For example, Zhen Bin created the Pohan rural community covering two towns: forty-three villages with 3,865 members, some of whom are university graduates. They foster organic and ecological agriculture instead of chemical fertilizers, and they are quite successful in this endeavor.

In *Second Enlightenment*, Wang also narrates the revolutionary experience of a well-educated girl who, instead of having a lavish banquet for her wedding (as is common in many Chinese families), proposed to her bridegroom a visit to a home for the aged and an orphanage as events for a truly meaningful wedding. On another note, Wang emphasizes the recent change in performance evaluation by local governments, whereby promotions are no longer based on GDP growth but on the happiness index. He also points out that the countryside, in times of financial crisis, has acted as a buffer zone, for one could always go back to his or her hometown in case of necessity, in order to survive with food and a means of living.

Liao Xiaoyi is a former professor in the Chinese Academy of Social Science, an environmental activist, and founder of the NGO Global Village Beijing. In the aftermath of an earthquake in 2008, she proposed a new sustainable-living approach and founded many rural community projects called LoHo Homelands (short for Happiness and Harmony), in collaboration with provincial officials. She has received awards for her contribution to conserving traditional culture and the ecosystem.

The LoHo Homelands feature farmhouses made of bamboo plywood with several facilities for waste recycling and biomass production, thus creating new low-carbon villages. The NGO also provided support to develop eco-agriculture, ecotourism, and creative crafts achieved in consultation with the local communities. The model was much appreciated, and Liao was asked to replicate it in her hometown.[59] The LoHo communities are consistent with constructive postmodernism and favor Chinese cultural traditions in seeking harmony between body and mind, persons and groups. "Chinese-style environmental protection is a wisdom of operational technology," says Liao. "There are still possibilities in China to establish a complex ecosystem composed of dwellings, industries, health-keeping, native culture, and self-consistency of the rural communities."[60]

Liao rejoices at the encyclical *Laudato Si'* and finds many similarities with the ecological civilization that China has promoted in recent years, and John Cobb, a preeminent American scholar on process philosophy, believes that China has the conditions for and stands a good chance of achieving an ecological civilization.[61]

Cobb, who died in 2024, founded the Institute for Postmodern Development in 2005, and with the help of Wang Zhihe they coordinated twenty-three collaborative centers in China and organized annual conferences on ecological civilization. Cobb also founded the Institute for Ecological Civilization in 2015, which has been active in China.

---

[59] See A. Moriggi, "Chinese Women at the Forefront of Environmental Activism: Wang Yongchen, Liao Xiaoyi and Tian Guirong," *DEP (Deportate, Esuli e Profughe) Journal*, no. 35 (2017): 206–227.

[60] Ibid.

[61] See Cobb and Castuera, *For Our Common Home*, i–vi.

In a recent book titled *China and Ecological Civilization: John B. Cobb, Jr., in Conversation with Andre Vltchek,* Cobb says that as a result of policy changes, in 2016, for the first time, more people moved from cities to countryside than from countryside to cities. Development of villages has been emphasized along with the goal of ecological civilization. It is highly probable that this important shift in Chinese society will endure.[62]

My own research on Chinese youth confirms this reverse trend.[63] There is a movement toward smaller cities and towns, where new development areas offer more opportunity for youth.

Cobb also sees that the markets and financial considerations in the future may play an important but secondary role. He says that Chinese leaders did recognize that simply postponing the work for clear skies and a healthy environment would not work. The nation needed to work on economic growth and a healthy natural environment simultaneously. The central government began to evaluate the success of provincial governments by their achievements in these two distinct realms. Growth goals were set below what would be possible, so that it could be channeled in less environmentally harmful directions. Experiments with eco-villages received encouragement.[64]

It is a good sign that the notion of an ecological civilization has already been written into the Chinese Constitution. China built a solar-powered office building of more than eight hundred thousand square feet in Dezhou, Shandong Province, which opened in November 2009. It was the world's largest such

---

[62] Ibid.

[63] Yan, *Seasons for Relationships,* iv.

[64] John Cobb and Andre Vltchek, *China and Ecological Civilization: John B. Cobb, Jr., in Conversation with Andre Vltchek* (Kindle edition, 2019); Andre Vltchek, "China's Determined March towards the Ecological Civilization," *Investig'Action,* May 12, 2019, https://investigation.net/en/chinas-determined-march-towards-the-ecological-civilization.

structure at that time, built in preparation for constructing the largest solar city. High-speed trains recorded about twenty-four thousand miles at the end of 2020, almost double the distance in 2015, according to the China State Railway Group. The plan is that this will develop further not only in term of total distance, but in environmental friendliness and interconnectivity within China and with neighboring countries, thus pursuing the One Belt One Road Initiative (BRI).[65]

Nevertheless, critics such as Richard Smith note that China remains by far the world's largest consumer of fossil fuels, the leading producer and consumer of steel, and the largest importer of lumber. He does not believe that China could maintain economic growth and create an ecological civilization at the same time.[66] Instead, Jeremy Lent sees that China, having arrived at the level of a developed nation and regaining its status as a world power, might redirect its vitality from continued consumerism into advancing the quality of life for its people. It is like planting the seeds for the vision of an ecological civilization.

Some Reflections

There are different forms of dialogue, including cross-cultural and interreligious. According to recent teachings of the Catholic Church, there are, for example, the *dialogue of life*, where people strive to live in an open and neighborly spirit, sharing their joys and sorrows, their human problems and preoccupations; the *dialogue of action*, in which Christians and others collaborate for

---

[65] See Andrew Benton, "China Releases 2021–2035 Transport Plan," *International Railway Journal*, May 11, 2021, https://railjournal.com/policy/china-releases-2021-2035-transport-plan.

[66] See Richard Smith, "China's Drivers and Planetary Ecological Collapse," *Real-World Economics Review*, no. 82 (2017), http://paecon.net/PAEReview/issue82/Smith82.pdf.

people's integral development and liberation of people; and the *dialogue of shared experience*, where persons rooted in their own religious traditions share their spiritual riches.[67] The initiatives mentioned above, whether in the name of integral ecology or ecological civilization, show concern for our common home and for the good of humanity. All promise hope for the future.

Jeremy Lent sees that while Europeans have pursued a path based on a worldview driven by "conquering nature" that has since become global in scope, traditional Chinese culture was founded on a worldview of "harmony between human beings and nature." Early Chinese philosophers believed the purpose of life was to seek harmony.[68]

Xi Jinping made a point at the US-hosted global climate summit on April 23, 2021, when he said, "To the principle of common but differentiated responsibilities, developed countries should increase their ambitions on addressing climate issues, while helping less-developed nations speed up their shift to low-carbon growth in financing, technology, and capacity building."[69] In fact, it was a responsible commitment when Xi pledged at the UN General Assembly in September 2020 that China would reach peak carbon-dioxide emissions by 2030 and achieve carbon neutrality before 2060, which could cut global warming this century by 0.25°C.[70] This happened at a time when

---

[67] Pontifical Council for Interreligious Dialogue, *Dialogue and Proclamation*, 1991, 42.

[68] Jeremy Lent, "Can China Really Lead the Way to an 'Ecological Civilization'?" ENSIA at the University of Minnesota's Institute on the Environment, August 29, 2018, https://ensia.com/voices/ecological-civilization.

[69] Catherine Wong and Sarah Zheng, "China and the US: United on Climate Action but Divided on Responsibility," *South China Morning Post*, April 23, 2021, https://scmp.com/news/china/diplomacy/article/3130788/they-pledged-work-together-china-and-us-disagree-division.

[70] Hector Pollitt, "Analysis: Going Carbon Neutral by 2060 'Will Make

US president Donald Trump had withdrawn from the Paris climate agreement. President Joe Biden subsequently committed the United States once again to the climate agreement. Although President Xi did not attend the COP26 in person, he supports the formal pledges of real action by the Chinese government to achieve net-zero emissions by 2060, and vows to halt new coal plants abroad. In a surprise announcement toward the end of the COP26 summit, China and the United States, the world's two biggest CO_2 emitters, pledged to act in a joint declaration that they will "recall their firm commitment to work together" to achieve the 1.5°C-temperature goal set out in the 2015 Paris Agreement, and agree to boost climate co-operation over the next decade.[71] Unfortunately, at the time of this writing, President Trump in his second term has once again withdrawn the United States from commitment to the agreement, which would signal a significant setback for global climate cooperation, embolden fossil-fuel interests, and strain diplomatic relations.

Another reason for nations to act with shared responsibility and a sense of unity is that developed countries have long been outsourcing their production emissions to China or other developing nations. Therefore, nations need to work together to foster a community of life for man and nature.

At the beginning of this chapter, I quoted a poem by Chinese philosopher Zhang Zai from a thousand years ago: "Heaven is my father, and earth is my mother, and even such a small creature as I find an intimate place in their midst. Therefore, that which fills the universe I regard as my body and that which directs the

---

China Richer'," *Carbon Brief*, September 24, 2020, https://carbonbrief.org/analysis-going-carbon-neutral-by-2060-will-make-china-richer.

[71] BBC News, "COP26: China and U.S. Agree to Boost Climate Co-operation," November 11, 2021, https://bbc.com/news/science-environment-59238869.

universe I consider as my nature. All people are my brothers and sisters, and all things are my companions."[72] One may hope that we recover the significance of this profound recognition of interconnectedness of humans and the universe, rooted in Confucian wisdom, that has been passed down over the centuries. It also reminds me of the "Canticle of the Creatures" by Francis of Assisi. The cry of the earth today finds an echo in the cry of abandonment of Jesus to the Father on the cross. As Lubich said, "The cry of Jesus didn't remain without an answer. He did not remain in the abyss of that infinite separation, but re-abandoned himself to the Father. In this way, he brought human beings back to communion with the Father."[73] In him, all relationships are reconciled: the communion of humans with God, the relationship between humans and nature, and the relationship among human beings, between East and West. In him, we may find the secret for overcoming all difficulties, transforming death to life, darkness to light, and reconciling East and West. Whether working toward an ecological civilization from the Chinese perspective or toward an integral ecology from the Christian perspective, my experience at the Beijing Expo proves that we can meet and collaborate well with peoples from different religions and cultures. We must therefore find ways through dialogue to walk together, making use of our reciprocal riches to build an ecological civilization, and to achieve a civilization of harmony and love.

---

[72] Chan Wing-tsit, *Source Book in Chinese Philosophy* (Princeton, NJ: Princeton University Press, 1963), 497.

[73] Chiara Lubich, "We Answer to Terrorism with the Discovery of Jesus, Perennial Easter," interview on *Holy Week with Zenit*, Rome, April 8, 2004.

3

Fraternity and Social Friendship

Brotherhood in the history of Christianity is intrinsic to a strong spiritual meaning of fraternity in Christ, and thus is manifested in sharing of goods in a community and helping the poor. The notion of brotherhood contributed to the abolition of slavery in society. As the motto of the French Revolution was, "Liberty, equality, and fraternity," the notion of fraternity[1] has since then become a political category. During the greater part of the twentieth century, however, the principles of freedom in liberalism or equality in socialism have been emphasized in one political system or another, but the triptych motto has not been taken altogether as a whole—and fraternity has become a forgotten principle. The concept of fraternity was translated into Chinese as bo'ai (universal love), which, according to some scholars,[2] is influenced by the concept of agape in Christianity. Recent studies in the history of Chinese philosophy show much interest in the teaching

---

[1] The terms "fraternity" and "brotherhood," are synonyms and their uses in this research are interchangeable. The former indicates the quality of being brothers while the latter indicates the state of being brothers. I use the term "fraternity" because it has the same root with the French Revolution motto "Liberté, Egalité, Fraternité." However, the term "brotherhood" is more commonly used in English; today sisterhood is also understood as part of the concept.

[2] Renowned Chinese intellectuals at the turn of the nineteenth century were Sun Yatsen and Kang Youwei, who spread the Chinese term *bo'ai* for fraternity. I quote them and other more recent scholars in this chapter.

*of jian'ai (all-embracing love) of Mohism, also a forgotten principle, overshadowed by Confucianism.*³ *By exploring fraternity in Chinese culture, I intend to explore its significance as a relational term, with special emphasis on relationships and reciprocity. In this chapter, I also explore the relevance of the concept of fraternity in Chinese culture and in Christianity, especially after the signing of the Document on Human Fraternity for World Peace and Living Together and the proclamation of the encyclical Fratelli Tutti by Pope Francis.*

The Ideas of Fraternity, Brotherhood, and Universal Love in Chinese Culture

A Chinese idiomatic expression to describe deep friendship and brotherhood is, "a relationship as close as one's hands and feet." The Bible also uses bone and flesh (Gen. 2:23) to say that husbands ought to love their wives as their own bodies (Eph. 5:28).

From the "Fraternity" Motto to "Universal Love" in the Chinese Language

This notion of fraternity among the triptych motto of the French Revolution has been translated into Chinese as *bo'ai* (universal love). However, literally it should be translated as *xiongdi* (brothers) or *shouzu* (hands and feet). As a matter of fact, Chinese scholar Gao Pengcheng points out that the French Revolution

---

³ Much of Chinese philosophical tradition originates in the Spring and Autumn and Warring States Periods (770–221 BCE), known as the era of "A Hundred Schools of Thought," when significant intellectual development saw the births of major branches of Chinese philosophy: Confucianism, Daoism, legalism, and Mohism. Historically, there were disagreements between Confucians and Mohists, especially during the time of Mencius (372–289 BC). In the later part of this chapter, I elaborate on how the two schools of thought differ and can eventually be reconciled.

never mentioned the "universal love" motto.⁴ According to Gao, modern Chinese intellectuals such as Sun Yatsen (1866–1925) and Kang Youwei (1858–1927) were instrumental in influencing the translation of the term "fraternity" as *bo'ai*, which has a connotation more of universal love. In 1906, Sun and other revolutionaries formulated the Chinese United League's Revolutionary Strategy, which stated, "Everyone in the country has the spirit of *ziyou* [freedom], *pingdeng* [equality], and *bo'ai* [universal love]."⁵ In the same year, Kang Youwei published a couple of articles about the French Revolution in *New People's Daily* mentioning that "the political theory of the Revolution was very high that is in the name of *bo'ai* [universal love]."⁶ These statements were not precise, in the sense that the motto of the French Revolution was fraternity and not universal love.

With the Xinhai Revolution in 1911, which overthrew the Qing dynasty, Sun became the founding father of the Republic of China. His use of *ziyou-pingdeng-bo'ai* gradually became the mainstream of discourse. Zhao Zhengping, however, another member of the United League, noticed that in the context of colonialist aspirations of European countries toward Asia, the concept of "fraternity" they proclaimed was not the Chinese *bo'ai* (universal love).⁷ Sun also once clarified that, in the original French Revolution motto "freedom-equality-fraternity," the

---

⁴ Gao Pengcheng, "The French Revolution Never Mentioned the Motto of *Bo'ai*," *Qinghai Social Science*, no. 2 (2014): 196–201.

⁵ Sun Yatsen, "The Revolutionary Strategy of the Chinese Alliance," in *The Complete Works of Sun Yatsen*, vol. 1 (Beijing: Zhonghua Book Company, 1981), 296.

⁶ See Kang Youwei, "The French Revolution," in *Political Theory of Kang Youwei* (Beijing: Zhonghua Book Company, 1981), 590.

⁷ See Hou Sheng (Zhao Zhengping), "The Philosophy of Universal Love," *Southern Newspaper*, no. 3 (November 1910). For details, see also *Selected Works of the Ten Years before the Revolution of 1911*, vol. 3 (Hong Kong: Sanlian Bookstore, 1960), 749–754.

meaning of the term fraternity is "*xiongdi*" (brothers) or *tongbao* (compatriot). He found a certain narrowness in the term *xiongdi*. He said, "It is the livelihood and happiness of four hundred million people in China at stake." He vigorously promoted the *bo'ai* thinking. Gradually, the term *xiongdi* was replaced with *bo'ai*. Although the term had not been widely used in China until that time, it was originally taken from Chinese classics. He considered the term very appropriate. Since then, the motto "freedom-equality-fraternity" in the Chinese language has been popularized as "*ziyou-pingdeng-bo'ai*."[8]

In the historical context, prior to and after the fall of the Qing dynasty and the nation's repeated defeats by Western powers, there was a Chinese identity crisis. Many intellectuals, including Sun and Kang, attempted to adopt and integrate Western ideals into Chinese cultural values to develop a new cultural and national identity as a way to renew the country.[9] While Kang looked upon the Confucian classics to find an answer to the Western challenge, Sun later converted to Christianity,[10] and his concept of *bo'ai* was somehow influenced by the Christian concept of universal love.

Ren'ai *from the Confucian Tradition*

To trace the development of the Chinese idea of universal brotherhood, I attend here to three concepts of *ai* (love) in the Chinese language and culture. These three concepts of love and

---

[8] Sun Yatsen, "Three People's Principles? Nationalism? Sixth Lecture," March 16, 1924, in *The Complete Works of Sun Yatsen*, vol. 9 (Beijing: Zhonghua Book Company, 1986), 283.

[9] See Li Shi, *History of Thoughts in the Qing Dynasty*, Deep into China Histories series (2019); see also Werner Meissner, "China's Search for Cultural and National Identity from the Nineteenth Century to the Present," *China Perspectives*, no. 68 (2006): 41–54.

[10] Vincent Goossaert. "1898: The Beginning of the End for Chinese Religion?" *Journal of Asian Studies* 65, no. 2 (2006): 311.

loving relationship are *ren'ai*, *jian'ai*, and *bo'ai*, and they are distinct from each other.

First is *ren'ai*, a love defined by a Confucian term, *ren*. Confucius spoke very often about *ren* (human-heartedness).[11] The ideogram *ren* is composed of "person" on the left and "two" on the right, indicating the relationship between two human beings. It has a rich connotation of benevolence, forgiveness, humanity, self-affirmation and the affirmation of others in recognizing the dignity in both oneself and others.

Ren is related to other Confucian concepts: *yi* (righteousness), *li* (propriety), and *zhi* (wisdom). *Yi* has been described as "a categorical imperative."[12] Later in Mencius's relational ethics, *yi* is better defined as norms of "relational appropriateness." They are summarized in the concept of "propriety," which includes the "rectification of names" and the "five basic human relationships" of parent-child, husband-wife, ruler-subject, between friends, and between siblings. Names such as ruler, minister, father, son, and brothers are names of "social responsibilities," and each one must fulfill their responsibilities and duties accordingly.[13] Names are like titles that describe an office and a responsibility. The connotation of "rectification of names" does not refer to the right or wrong of a deed or a person, but rather to one's rightful relationship with others related to one's role.

The practical form of *yi* (righteousness) is *ren*. Human-heartedness emphasizes reciprocity and altruism. Reciprocity is well expressed in the Golden Rule or the ethics of reciprocity: "Do not do to others what you would not want others to do to you."[14] Altruism

---

[11] Feng Youlan (Fung Yu-Lan), *A Short History of Chinese Philosophy* (New York: Macmillan Publishing Company, 1948), 69.

[12] Ibid., 42.

[13] Ibid.

[14] See W. Theodore de Bary, ed., "*Analects* 15:23," in *Sources of Chinese Tradition* (New York: Columbia University Press, 1960); see also *Analects* 12:2.

is well expressed in another verse of the *Analects*: "Now the man of perfect virtue, wishing to build up himself as such, seeks to build up others as well; wishing to enhance himself, seeks also to enhance others").[15]

Contemporary scholar Feng Youlan says that love in Confucianism is based on the principle of gradation. According to Mencius, it is natural to love your kin more than others. However, such love should be extended until it includes distant members of society as well. "Honor the elderly and care for the young in other families as we do to those in our own."[16] It is to practice the principle of *zhongshu* (altruism). As mentioned earlier, that is equivalent to the practice of human-heartedness.[17]

Jian'ai *of the Mohist Tradition*

Mozi, a Chinese philosopher who lived in the fifth century BCE in the generation immediately following Confucius, developed the concept of *jian'ai*. The term is usually translated into English as "all-embracing love."[18] However, contemporary scholars explain it in a variety of terms: impartial concern,[19] or inclusive care.[20] The following is how Mozi presented his argument on *jian'ai*.

Mozi first makes a distinction between partiality and universality by saying that a man holding to the principle of partiality would not care for his friend as himself, or others' parents as his own. A man holding to the principle of universality instead would care for his friends and their parents as his own. Mozi then asks which principle is right. He then uses his "tests of judgment"

---

[15] *Analects* 7:2
[16] *Mencius* 1A7.
[17] Feng, *A Short History of Chinese Philosophy*, 72.
[18] Ibid., 53–55.
[19] See Loy Hui-chieh, "Mozi," in *Internet Encyclopedia of Philosophy*.
[20] Chris Fraser, "Mohism," in *Stanford Encyclopedia of Philosophy*, 2015.

to determine the right principle. The tests are three: "its basis, its verifiability, and its applicability." A right principle should be based on the will of heaven and on the ancient sage-kings, verified by the senses of the common people, and applied by the government to see if it is beneficial to the country and the people. The third test is the standard he uses to determine all values.[21]

He uses this standard to prove the desirability of "all-embracing love": If everyone regards the state of others as he regards his own, the cities of others as his own, and the clans of others as his own, others are regarded like self and he would not assault others. Therefore, instead of harming the world, he benefits the world. If we make an investigation, could there be any benefit coming from detesting others and injuring others? The answer is no: benefits can only come from loving others and benefiting others. If we have to distinguish those loving and benefiting others, certainly they are not partial but universal. That being so, love is the source of the major benefits in the world, so all-embracing love is right.[22]

Mohists advocated undifferentiated all-embracing love, which is Mozi's core teaching. The system of thought is transmitted to us in the work with Mozi's name in fifteen volumes, each with two to seven chapters, including on *jian'ai* (All-embracing love), on *tianzhi* (Will of heaven), and on *feigong* (Condemnation of offensive war). He was committed to the ideal of a harmonious social order and the welfare of "all under heaven." To support his argumentation, he taught the need for individual piety and

---

[21] Feng, *A Short History of Chinese Philosophy*, 53–54.

[22] The translation of this passage of Mozi is my own, but I also take reference from the following translations: W. P. Mei, trans., *Mozi*, 4C2 on Universal Love, Chinese Text Project, https://ctext.org/mozi/book-4/ens; see also Chris Fraser, "Book 16, 'Inclusive care' of Mozi," in "Mohism," *Stanford Encyclopedia of Philosophy*, 2015.

submission to the "will of heaven."[23] He condemned unprovoked military aggression and advocated strong defense to avoid war.

Like Confucius, Mozi made it his task to advise rulers. However, his philosophy and the practice of love without distinction was in direct contrast and challenge to the Confucian moral ideal of benevolence or human-heartedness, which differentiated the special love for one's parents and family. He deplored the Confucian emphasis on rites and ceremonies as a waste of government funds.

Confucians—in particular Mencius, who lived after the time of Mozi—bitterly attacked the Mohist concept of undifferentiated love because Mohism challenged the dominant Confucian ideology. Mencius said, "Mozi's principle of *jian'ai* amounts to making one's father of no account. To have no father and no sovereign is to be like the birds and beasts."[24]

The Forgotten Principle

Mohism emphasized equality in loving others while Confucianism emphasized gradation. Confucius's benevolence pays more attention to morality. Rulers favored Confucianism, which encouraged faithfulness and facilitated stability, rather than Mohism, which was not accepted or promoted. Mohism was not fully appreciated at the time and lost its influence since the Han dynasty in the third century BCE. The proposal of *jian'ai* was

---

[23] Although before Mozi some classic texts in China already spoke about the love of heaven for men, but Mozi was the one who made the basis of his doctrine of universal love the need to imitate heaven and to love all. See Philipp K.T. Hu, "La volontà del cielo nell'antica sapienza cinese introduzione, traduzione e commento dei capitoli 26–28 di Mozi," *Nuova Umanità*, no. 217 (2015): 65–89.

[24] *Mencius* 3B9.

deemed impractical.[25] Confucianism overshadowed Mohism, and *jian'ai* became a forgotten principle.

In the historical period of the Qin and Han dynasties, rulers typically favored Confucians, who came from the aristocratic spectrum of society, and not Mohists, recruited more from the common people to form the *youxia* (knight errants).[26] More recently, Chinese scholars have tried to rehabilitate Mozi as a "philosopher of the people,"[27] highlighting his rational-empirical approach to the world as well as his proletarian background.

While Mozi criticized the ceremonial duties of Confucianism, he did not criticize the Confucian central ideas of *ren* and *yi*. While he spoke of his central idea of *jian'ai*, he indeed also included the qualities of *ren* and *yi*. He encouraged frugality and going to the essential.

There were disagreements historically between Confucians and Mohists. However, it would be fair to say that Mohism was not impractical; in fact, Mozi did care about the practical value of utility.[28] It would also be unfair to say that Confucians just encouraged reciprocating favors, but rather the main intent of Confucianism is reciprocity and altruism. It would also be fair to say that both Confucianism and Mohism have concerns over pragmatism and reciprocity, and in some aspects the two philosophies complement one another.

---

[25] See Hu, "La volontà del cielo nell'antica sapienza cinese introduzione," 85.

[26] See Feng, *A Short History of Chinese Philosophy*, 50.

[27] See Huang Songkang, "The Ultimate Realization of the Confucian Ideal Universal Harmony as Seen by China's Revolutionary Thinker Li Dazhao (1889–1927)," *Ultimate Reality and Meaning* 9, no. 3 (1986): 196. See also Henry Epps, *Ethics Vol. II: Universal Ethics and Morality* (Scotts Valley, CA: Lulu, 2012), 15–16.

[28] Hao Changchi, "Is Mozi a Utilitarian Philosopher?" *Frontiers of Philosophy in China* 1, no. 3 (2006): 383.

Bo'ai, *Universal Love*

In modern times, Mohism was given a fresh analysis. Sun Yatsen advocated "a spirit of common good under the sky or the world as a commonwealth shared by all."[29] He used "universal love" as one of the foundations for his idea of Chinese political theory,[30] although he introduced the term *bo'ai* instead of *jian'ai*. *Bo* in Chinese means broad, extensive, or immense; therefore, *bo'ai* means a love that is immense and extensive. Although the expression *bo'ai* was not as commonly and popularly used in Chinese classics as the expression *ren*, "*bo'ai*" could be traced in classic Chinese literature. The following are some citations:

> Wise rulers in the past discovered that education could change people for the better, so they advocated *bo'ai*, and consequently no people abandoned their parents. They taught people about morality and rules of conduct, and consequently they all acted accordingly. (A quote from the *Classic of Filial Piety* by Confucius [551–479 BCE])

* * *

> The principles of a ruler should be to govern according to natural laws without unduly interfering. He should act with *bo'ai*, and to select the talented and upright for office. (A quote from *Garden of Stories* by Liu Xiang [77–6 BCE])

---

[29] Sun Yatsen quoted the citation "A Public Spirit Will Rule All under the Sky when the Great Way Prevails" from one of the Six Classics, *Liji the Book of Rites*, in ancient China.

[30] One of the major legacies of Sun Yatsen was the creation of his political philosophy of the Three Principles of the People, including the rights of a people (*minquan*), the livelihood of the people (*minsheng*), and democracy (*minzu*).

* * *

Bo'ai is an expression of *ren*, to practice it in a proper manner is righteousness, and the practice of both is to attain the Dao. (A quote from *The Origins of Dao* by Han Yu [768–824])

Although the term *bo'ai* in the ancient texts has the meaning of broad and immense love for all, it was an expression related to the concept of *ren* that is based on human relationships. The term applied basically to a concept of governance for the love and benefit of the people. It also referred to a kind of social morality and personal integrity based on harmonious engagement with others, goodwill, and mutual help.

Intellectuals of the early-twentieth-century Republican period—including Kang Youwei, resilient advocate of Confucianism, or Sun Yatsen, who became Christian—in using the term *bo'ai* held great sensitivity for the Western perspective.[31] From such a perspective, or rather the Christian perspective, *bo'ai* is loving people as oneself, not just loving good people or people who are worthy of being benevolent, but even loving the enemy. Therefore, it has the idea of universal love, very similar to the concept of *agape* in Greek, which the Christians adopted, moving from the realm of human relationships to the supernatural realm.

Although the Confucian concept of love starts from kinship love with an emphasis on faithfulness and forgiveness, it then extends to a more altruistic love of caring for the elderly and the young of others. Similarly, the Golden Rule of Confucius actually expresses the same concept of the reciprocity almost with the same words as Jesus spoke (Luke 3:31) five hundred years later as an expression of universal love.

---

[31] Goossaert, "1898: The Beginning of the End for Chinese Religion?"

In the final analysis, Mohists may have taken the positivist approach toward the reality of universal love, directly linking it to the will of heaven. Confucians instead may have taken the constructivist approach, rationalizing the multiple realities of human nature in order to discover the underlying meaning of universal love. We have also seen universal love from the Christian perspective: a love that is ready to sacrifice oneself for the good of another. Mencius also says, "So, I like life, and I also like righteousness. If I cannot keep both, I will let go life, and choose righteousness."[32] As a matter of fact, we have come across different traditional Chinese schools of thought with regard to the ideas of *ren'ai, jian'ai, bo'ai,* universal love, fraternity, and a relationship described as between one's hands and feet. They all emphasize relationships.

Youshan, *Concrete Expression Nurtured by Distinguished Chinese Tradition*

The time-honored traditional Chinese culture has always emphasized the cultivation of virtues. The values of friendliness and fraternity have been expanded in the practice of human relationship to include social relationships—and relationship also with nature. As mentioned, the concept of universal brotherhood in Chinese has been enriched with the encounter with Western culture, particularly with Christianity. In the official narrative of China's leaders, though continuing to insist on a Marxist theory of historical analysis, the value of friendliness and fraternity are considered an integral part of distinguished traditional Chinese culture and of the core socialist values.

---

[32] Mencius, "Gaozi I," 10. See James Legge, ed. and trans., *The Works of Mencius* (Oxford: Clarendon Press, 1895).

Fraternity and Social Friendship

In the nineteenth National Congress of the Communist Party of China Report delivered on October 18, 2017, Xi Jinping said, "Core socialist values and fine traditional Chinese culture are alive in the people's hearts."³³ He reiterated on many occasions values quoted from the Chinese classics mentioned above. As a matter of fact, he said that the core socialist values should be nurtured by distinguished traditional Chinese culture and should be down to earth.³⁴ One of the twelve socialist core values of the Chinese dream actively promoted recently in China is *youshan* (friendship). As President Xi stressed in a state visit to Great Britain in 2015, "In today's world, no country can afford to pursue development with its door closed. One should open the door, warmly welcome friends and be hospitable to them."³⁵ So this friendship does not apply only at the personal or social level, but also refers to relationships between nations.

The Ideas of Brotherhood in Christianity

Jesus called his disciples brothers after his resurrection: "Go and tell my brethren" (Matt. 28:10; John 20:17). "The disciples of Jesus are brothers not by nature, but by the gift of grace, because that adoptive filiation gains a real share in the life of the only Son, which was fully revealed in his Resurrection."³⁶ According to the *Catechism of the Catholic Church*, this filial relationship is fully

---

³³ Xi Jinping, *The 19th National Congress of the Communist Party of China Report*, Beijing, October 18, 2017.

³⁴ See Zhuo Xinping, "Responsibility of a Scholar and Future of Religious Studies," *Chinese Culture Research*, no. 1 (2018), https://aisixiang.com/data/109310.html.

³⁵ "Exclusive Q&A with Chinese President Xi Jinping," Reuters, October 18, 2015.

³⁶ *Catechism of the Catholic Church*, 654.

revealed in the resurrection. Christians have faith in Christ who is the Son of the Father, who is the firstborn among many brothers. It is striking to see how the New Testament repeats the terms "brother," "brotherhood," and "brotherly love." Italian theologian Piero Coda indicates the Christian origin of the political notion of fraternity as "not referring to an ideal to achieve but to a reality acquired." He notes how in the Gospels the root of fraternity is indicated in the universal fatherhood of God, since the love of God, when received, becomes the most formidable agent of transformation in human existence and relationships with the other.[37]

Brotherhood from the Old Testament

The profound identity of humankind, men and women, with the vocation of being brothers and sisters is well presented in Genesis. God created them "in his image and likeness" (Gen. 1:26). Fraternity is the love of God that human beings can live among themselves. It is only due to linguistic limitation that the masculine expression of "fraternity"[38] is used. It means brotherhood and sisterhood, a relationship that includes men and women.

According to the Old Testament, out of jealousy and sibling rivalries, Cain murdered his brother Abel. They are sons of Adam and Eve born after the fall and continue their parents' failure. This fratricide (Gen. 4:1–8) is a rejection of the vocation and identity, as brothers and sisters, mentioned above.

---

[37] Piero Coda, *Il logos e il nulla: Trinità, religioni, mistica* (Roma: Città Nuova, 2003), 337–338.

[38] Some other languages have no such problem: Spanish, besides the word *fraternidad*, has *hermano* and *hermana*, from which come *hermandad*. German, besides the word *Brüderlichkeit* from *Bruder* (brother), can indicate both *Bruder* and *Schwester* (sister), by the plural *Geschwister*, from which there is *Geschwisterlichkeit* (of brothers and sisters).

However, according to the Old Testament, the covenant with Noah, Abraham, and Moses started history once again from the beginning. This covenant of God with his people provides a premise and creates a human space into which the practice of the ideal of brotherhood becomes possible, and where God has inscribed this ideal since the beginning of human history. In fact, it is written in the Psalms, "Behold, how good and how pleasant it is for brethren to dwell together in unity!" (Ps 133:1).

In the New Testament: Friends and Brothers

One finds passages in the Gospels where Jesus calls his disciples "friends," such as, "This is my commandment, that you love one another as I have loved you. Greater love has no man than this, that a man lay down his life for his friends" (John 15:12).

As the saying goes, you can choose your friends, but you cannot choose the family you were born into. Sibling relationships come by birth naturally as in a family, not by choice. However, once the disciples choose to follow Jesus, they become like brothers in the same family. Jesus describes the brotherly relationship with and among his followers, saying, "One is your Teacher, and you are all brothers" (Matt. 23:8); "Go and be reconciled to your brother and then come and offer your gift" (Matt. 5:24); "For whoever does the will of my Father in heaven is my brother and sister and mother" (Matt. 12:50).

The meaning of this reference to "brothers" became more evident when Jesus revealed himself after the resurrection, saying, "Go to My brethren and say to them, 'I ascend to My Father and your Father, and My God and your God'" (John 20:17). The followers of Jesus are not brothers and sisters by blood, but brethren in Christ as shown in the letters of the apostles, such as John, Peter, and Paul: "We know that we have passed out of death into life, because we love the brethren. He who does not love abides in death" (1 John 3:14).

The life of the early Christian community testifies to brotherhood: "The community of believers were of one heart and mind, and no one claimed that any of his possessions was his own, but they had everything in common.... There was no needy person among them, for extra goods were put at the feet of the apostles and were distributed each according to needs" (Acts 4:32–35).

Jesus Saves Not Only Single Persons but Also the Relationship

Pope Francis affirmed that "God, in Christ, redeems not only the individual person, but also the social relations existing between men."[39] Jesus saves and loves humankind to the point of being cursed by the law of God. St. Paul says, "Christ ransomed us from the curse of the law by becoming a curse for us, for it is written, 'Cursed be everyone who hangs on a tree'" (Gal. 3:13). This is a direct reference to Deuteronomy: "Anyone who is hanged on the tree is a curse of God" (Deut. 21:23), for he should be buried outside the boundary in order not to defile the land the Lord has given. Jesus launches his cry of abandonment on the cross toward God in an extreme act of faith while being cut off from any relationship with the Father and with the brothers. By dying forsaken on the cross, rejected as an outcast, Jesus canceled the boundary between the chosen people and the gentile. He made the two peoples one.

As for the social and political consequences of fraternity, Paul in his letter to the Galatians affirms that, for Christians, "there is neither Jew nor Greek, there is neither slave nor free person,

---

[39] Pope Francis, *Evangelii Gaudium, Apostolic Exhortation on the Proclamation of the Gospel in Today's World*, November 24, 2013, 178.

there is not male and female; for you are all one in Christ Jesus" (Gal. 3:28). The three marked separations of those times were the categories of race and culture, social class, and the distinction between men and women.

The forsaken Jesus started from building fraternity with a preferential love for the poor and marginalized, as indicated in statements such as "Blessed are the poor" (Luke 6:20) and "whatever you did it to one of the least of these brothers and sisters of mine, you did it to me" (Matt. 25:40). Christian fraternity helped abolish slavery and the difference of social class. Another distinguishing mark of Christians is, "Love your enemies! Do good to those who hate you" (Luke 6:27; Matt. 4:44). The forsaken Jesus overcomes—with free determination, once and for all—the category of enemy. With his death and resurrection, Jesus restored the relationship after the fall of Adam and Eve. The covenant with Israel is extended to all people (Gal. 3:28).

The accomplished form of fraternity is in the reciprocal love of *agape* in Christ; in the history of Christian civilization, it presupposes freedom of the individual, who is constitutively open and dedicated to dialogue with those committed in the search of real justice.[40] If Jesus came only to save individual persons, affirms Piero Coda, it would be easy to postpone our yearnings in the hope of life after death. Instead, it is significant that Christians are to take active part in the "coming of the kingdom" of God "already," but at the same time "not yet," seeing it in its glory.

---

[40] Piero Coda, "Per una fondazione teologica della categoria politica della fraternità," in Antonio M. Baggio, *Il principio dimenticato: La fraternità nelllla riflessione politologica contemporanea* (Roma: Città Nuova, 2007), 107–108.

Brotherhood in the History of Christianity

Early Church Father Tertullian told what happened in the early days of Christianity when pagans were converted upon seeing the love that reigned among Christians: "See how they love one another."[41]

The history of the Western world is deeply influenced by Christian culture. Christian brotherhood manifests itself in a vast spectrum of contexts. It starts from the spiritual meaning of fraternity in Christ to the sharing of goods in a community and helping the poor. This help goes from simple almsgiving to the duty of hospitality and care. Monastic fraternity presupposes cohabitation and sharing of goods, as witnessed, among others, by St. Francis of Assisi and his fellow companions.

"In the name of fraternity, hospitals, hospices, and schools were built." As Antonio Baggio relates, "Especially in medieval and modern times, fraternity did not remain closed within a private realm but played a public role. It gave life to a complex world of social solidarity and care for those in need which preceded contemporary systems of welfare."[42] It also contributed to the abolition of slavery in society.

Brotherhood as a Political Category

As the motto of the French Revolution was "Liberty, Equality, and Fraternity," the notion of fraternity has, since then, become a political category, as one of three constitutive principles and ideals of a political project heretofore unseen. And yet, according to historian Mona Ozouf, fraternity belongs to a different sphere from liberty and equality—the realm of moral obligations rather than rights, and community rather than individuality. There were

---

[41] See Tertullian, *Apology*, trans. T. H. Bindley (1890), 39, https://tertullian.org.

[42] Antonio Baggio, "The Forgotten Principle: Fraternity in Its Public Dimension," *Claritas: Journal of Dialogue and Culture* 2, no. 2 (October 2013): 36.

two forms of fraternity: one was identified with a social link as a free pact, the other with a religious link based on Christian brotherhood. There was a "partial" interpretation and "deficit" of political reflection in the conception of fraternity in view of the unresolved problems of democracy.[43]

After this initial proclamation of the French Revolution, fraternity almost immediately disappeared from the public scene. Without fraternity, freedom and equality were inserted into democratic systems; they became two almost antagonistic visions of the world. For most of the twentieth century, however, while the principles of freedom in liberalism or equality in socialism have been emphasized in one political system or another, the triptych motto has not been taken altogether as a whole; fraternity has been a forgotten principle. As Baggio says, the triptych of "freedom, equality, and fraternity" must be taken together like the three legs of a table in order to function.[44]

Human Fraternity for Peace and Living Together as Proposed by Pope Francis

A Significant Testimony and a Pact of Fraternity Today

St. Francis of Assisi met the sultan of Egypt al-Malik al-Kamil in 1219. Already two years before that, he had sent his Franciscan brothers to the Holy Land. It was the time of the Crusades when Christians and Muslims were enemies. At considerable risk, Francis engaged the sultan in a peaceful dialogue. Not only did Sultan al Kamil not kill Francis, he secured for him and his companions

---

[43] Mona Ozouf, "Liberté, Égalité, Fraternité, Stands for Peace, Country and War," in *Lieux de Mémoire*, Tome III, ed. Pierre Nora (Paris: Quarto Gallimard, 1997), 53–89.

[44] Baggio, *Il principio dimenticato: la fraternità nella riflessione politologica contemporanea*, 22.

safe return to the Christian camp with gifts of honor. He even told Francis, "To pray to God for him, that God may reveal to him the law and the faith that is more pleasing to Him."[45]

With the backdrop of this eight hundredth anniversary of St. Francis of Assisi meeting Sultan al-Kamil, Pope Francis made a historic three-day trip to the Arabian Peninsula to become the first pope to visit the birthplace of Islam. On February 4, 2019, in an interreligious meeting at the Founder's Memorial in Abu Dhabi, United Arab Emirates, Francis greeted the head of state, civil and religious dignitaries, and the diplomatic corps. Together with Grand Imam Ahmed el-Tayeb of Egypt, the Holy Father signed a historic joint declaration, "Human Fraternity for World Peace and Living Together." He also delivered an address on the theme of human fraternity.[46]

Main Points of Pope Francis's Address and Commitment in Abu Dhabi

Pope Francis started the address by saying, "I have come here as a brother seeking peace with the brethren. We are here to desire peace, to promote peace, to be instruments of peace." The focus of the talk is on human brotherhood for peace. Seeking common ground with Islam in the narrative of Noah, Pope Francis made use of the allegory of fraternity as the Ark of Noah. To sail the stormy seas of the world today, we need to enter the ark of peace

---

[45] The narrative is reported from St. Bonaventure's *Life of St. Francis* and from Jacques de Vitry, "History of the Orient," in *St. Francis of Assisi, Omnibus of Sources* (Cincinnati: St. Anthony Messenger Press, 2008). See also Jack Wintz, "Franciscans and Muslims: Eight Centuries of Seeking God," Franciscan Media, 2019.

[46] Pope Francis, Interreligious Meeting Address of His Holiness, Apostolic Journey of His Holiness Pope Francis to the United Arab Emirates, Founder's Memorial, Abu Dhabi, February 4, 2019.

as a family. He stressed that no violence is justifiable in the name of the Merciful One. God is the Father of all, and therefore we are all brothers and sisters, forming the great human family in the "harmony of diversity."[47]

There is the urgent task of "building bridges between peoples and cultures," the pope said, and religions should help the human family to deepen the capacity for reconciliation and for the vision of hope, and offer "concrete paths of peace." These paths are education and justice, the two wings of the "dove of peace" that allow it to fly. The Holy Father used the metaphor of a dove, which was the logo of the event.

Pope Francis emphasized education for future generations, which is often influenced by false values fomented by hatred and prejudice. Education about and through reciprocity is important, knowing not only oneself but also others and their cultural values. This generation will be held accountable for the outcome of the education of future generations.

The second wing of peace is justice. Justice should not be limited only to family members, compatriots, and believers of the same faith. True justice has to be universal. The world's religions should keep watch as sentinels of fraternity in the night of conflict, to remind people not to just profit from greed in satisfying immediate demands. They should stand on the side of the poor.

The enemy of fraternity is individualism, yet there's also indifference, which does not care about the dignity of the stranger and the future of children. A purely utilitarian development cannot provide real and lasting progress. Only an integral and cohesive development provides a future worthy of the human person. This kind of development makes the desert flourish.

---

[47] Pope Francis, "Interreligious General Audience on the Occasion of the 50th Anniversary of the Promulgation of the Conciliar Declaration *Nostra Aetate,*" October 28, 2015.

The Holy Father ended the address emphasizing that the world's religions can help the seeds of peace to flourish. God is with those who seek peace. He then blessed those present. By the power of prayer and daily commitment to dialogue, we can oppose war, the monetization of relations, the desertification of altruism, and the gagging of the poor. By being together today, it is a message of trust, an encouragement to all people of goodwill.

Some Concrete Actions as Commitment

The introduction of the document on human fraternity signed by both the pope and the grand imam affirms, "Faith leads a believer to see in the other a brother or sister to be supported and loved." It also invites "all persons who have faith in God and faith in human fraternity to unite and work together."[48]

The document includes some basic concepts. It declares "the adoption of a culture of dialogue as the path; mutual cooperation as the code of conduct; reciprocal understanding as the method and standard." The pope and the grand imam call on world leaders "to work strenuously to spread the culture of tolerance and of living together in peace." They also ask opinion makers "to rediscover the values of peace, justice, goodness, beauty, human fraternity and coexistence," and to promote these values everywhere. They also say that "terrorism is deplorable and threatens the security of people ... but this is not due to religion, even when terrorists instrumentalize it. It is due, rather, to an accumulation of incorrect interpretations of religious texts and to policies linked to hunger, poverty, injustice, oppression and

---

[48] Holy See Press Office, "Document on Human Fraternity for World Peace and Living Together," signed by His Holiness Pope Francis and the Grand Imam of Al-Azhar Ahmed Al-Tayeb, Abu Dhabi, February 4, 2019.

pride." At the end, they ask that the document be studied and deepened, and then be applied concretely.

As a matter of fact, a multifaith committee was formed in August 2019 for achieving the goals contained in the Document on Human Fraternity for World Peace and Living Together. It has members from the United Arab Emirates, Egypt, Spain, and Italy. As a concrete commitment, the committee came up with initiatives such as the proposal to the United Nations to declare a date on February 3, 4, or 5 to be proclaimed a Day of Human Fraternity, and to invite representatives of other religions to join the committee.[49] This first meeting of the higher committee fell coincidentally on September 11, at the end of which each participant prayed according to their own faith for the victims of every act of terrorism.

The pope hopes that similar initiatives may arise in other parts of the world, and in particular with daily commitments. He said, "Although sadly evil, hatred and division often make news, there is a hidden sea of goodness that is growing and leads us to hope in dialogue, reciprocal knowledge and the possibility of building, together with the followers of other religions and all men and women of good will, a world of fraternity and peace."[50] Another public event took place at the New York City Public Library on September 20, 2019, bringing together hundreds of people from different religious and cultural backgrounds.[51]

---

[49] Holy See Press Office, "Press Release No. B0685," *Bollettino*, September 11, 2019.

[50] Holy See Press Office, "Declaration of the Director of the Holy See Press Office," Summary of the Bulletin, August 26, 2019.

[51] Bernadette Mary Reis, "A Celebration on Human Fraternity," *Vatican News*, September 21, 2019.

Fraternity Instead of Clash: Relevancy in Christianity, Islam, and China

It is very significant that Pope Francis presented his address on human fraternity for peace in a pact with Grand Imam Al-Tayeb. They represent Christianity and Islam, the two largest religions in the world, with more than half of the world's population.[52] The pact between the pope and the grand imam is meant to be a testimony of fraternity taking up the responsibility to become instruments of peace.

In an analysis of the papal address, the concept of human fraternity is presented as a common platform for dialogue, not only among world religions, but also with all cultures and peoples in the world. To extend this dialogue with elements of Chinese civilization, I have discerned some points mentioned by Pope Francis about human fraternity that echo Chinese values. They may serve as a bridge for dialogue between Christianity and Chinese culture.

Gradual Approach of Extending Fraternity to Others

The point of departure for Pope Francis was the recognition that fraternity is at the root of our common humanity. All persons in the world are to live as brothers and sisters in the one human family. Faith in God is the starting point of this fraternity, but "the benevolent gaze of God includes each person in the human family." This fraternity is destined to extend to people of all religions and cultures. The "spirit of fraternity," as proclaimed by the Universal Declaration of Human Rights,[53] is a dynamic factor in social cohesion.

---

[52] Christianity makes up 31.5 percent of the world's population and Islam 23.2 percent. Pew Research Center, "The Global Religious Landscape," The Pew Forum on Religion & Public Life, December 18, 2012.

[53] "All human beings are born free and equal in dignity and rights. They are endowed with reason and conscience and should act towards one another in a spirit of brotherhood." See Universal Declaration of Human Rights, Art. 1.

One of the signature lines of President Xi Jinping of China is, "If the people have faith, the nation has hope, and the country has strength."[54] Of course, the faith that he refers to is the faith in an ideal, and not a religious belief. What he means is that people should remain steadfast to their ideal. In the Confucian tradition, the concept of fraternity starts within the family with the emphasis on benevolence (*ren*). Such love should then be extended until it includes distant members of society as well. "Honor the elderly and care for the young in other families as we do for those in our own" (*Mencius* 1A7).

Maintaining Unity in Diversity Nourished with Dialogue

As the pope said, believers are called to commit themselves to the "equal dignity of all," and to seek "fraternity in diversity." There is an urgent task of "building bridges between peoples and cultures," forming the great human family in the "harmony of diversity."

Just as Jesus prays that all may be one (John 17:21), the idea of a united world under heaven is not extraordinary to the Chinese. Confucius says, "Under the sky [*tianxia*] we are one family." One may argue that, in that epoch, "under the sky" referred to what was known to the Chinese, which they considered as the center of the world (middle kingdom). Confucius did not, however, speak of a nation, a people, or a particular race, but *tianxia*, meaning the entire human race. The Chinese traditionally use the term "harmony" to express harmonious relationships between humans and nature in Daoism, and between human beings in Confucianism. Curiously, the use of the term "unity" is quite recent, linked more to the unity of the country (the republic) in contrast to the different warring kingdoms in the past. It is interesting to note that one of the two big slogans at the façade of the Forbidden City facing Tiananmen

---

[54] "Xi Jinping: If the People Have Faith, the Nation Has Hope, and the Country Has Strength," Xinhuanet, February 28, 2015.

Square reads, "Long live the unity of all peoples of the world!" Harmony and unity may be quite similar or different depending on the context in which these two Chinese words are used.

Relating to this, another central idea in Confucianism is the notion of being "harmonious while diversified [*he er butong*]," which is very much in tune with what Pope Francis called "harmony of diversity." It has a better-known equivalent, "unity in diversity"—also the founding motto of modern Indonesia—meaning the country's numerous cultures and ethnicities living together in harmony. This concept recognizes that although people have differences in opinions, interests, preferences, profiles, and so on, they should first keep peace and live in harmony with each other while in their diversity. In this way, tolerance and integration are encouraged.

There is a certain dialectic of harmony in Chinese culture. As quoted in chapter 1, Laozi says in the *Daodejing*, "When people of the world all know beauty as beauty, there arises the recognition of ugliness. When they all know the good as good, there arises the recognition of evil. Therefore, being and non-being give relational existence,"[55] arising in a dialectic of harmony. Daoism emphasizes the advantage of non-action over action and of teaching with deeds over teaching with words—making a change without forcing the situation and aiming at harmony. This principle of the dialectic of harmony guides people in their social life.[56]

The Importance of Relationships and Reciprocity

Pope Francis emphasized the importance of relationships and reciprocity. There is no genuine self-knowledge without the other. He also asks for the "courage of otherness": looking after

---

[55] Laozi, *Daodejing*, chapter 2, 1–2.
[56] Ren Jiyu, "The Dialectic of Simplicity," *Teaching and Research* 2 (1962): 17–18.

the human family through a daily and effective dialogue, keeping one's own identity with full recognition of the other, and seeing in the other truly a brother or sister, a child of one's own humanity.

When a disciple of Confucius asked him if any one word could guide them through life, the master's answer is *shu*, which means reciprocity, mercy, and forgiveness: "Do not do to others what you would not want others to do to you."[57] As mentioned at the beginning of this chapter, Chinese ideograms containing Confucian thoughts have rich connotations. Reciprocity and mutual responsibility are, however, at the core, and are applied to the so-called five basic human relationships. In these relationships the point is not just to differentiate statuses but to establish responsibility between them. Relationships are rectified according to one's role and responsibility toward the other.

These values of reciprocity and rectification of relationships in Chinese culture are applied to interpersonal relationships, in the family and in social relationships. China also operates by these principles in the field of international relations, and references to responsibility in the whole of the world are not absent in public discourse and official narratives.

No Violence Can Be Justified in the Name of Religion

"No violence can be justified" against a brother or a sister in the name of religion, said Pope Francis. "Human fraternity requires of us, as representatives of the world's religions, the duty to reject every nuanced approval of the word 'war.'"

This element of nonviolence was advocated by Mozi already in the fourth century BCE China. He condemned unprovoked military aggression and promoted strong defense to avoid war in his famous treaty called Condemnation of Offensive War (*feigong*). He was committed to the ideal of a harmonious social

---

[57] *Analects* 15:23.

order, teaching the necessity for individual piety and submission to the "Will of Heaven," which formed the basis of his core teaching on universal love (*jian'ai*).

Education

Pope Francis was aware that young people are surrounded by fake news, materialism, hatred, and prejudice, so he encourages investing in education. "They need to learn to defend the rights of others with the same energy with which they defend their own rights."[58] It is noteworthy that in Chinese, individual human rights are closely associated with the rights of the people. In the West, the emphasis is more on individual rights, while in the East, the people's rights take precedence, as individual rights give way to the common good. Education should form the young generation to strike the right balance with peaceful means, and never resort to violence, which may degenerate into vandalism and social turmoil. He reminded us of the importance of reciprocity in education. One day, they will judge well the previous generation if they have provided the foundation for "new encounters of civility." The alternative is for young people to be left with "mirages and the empty prospects of harmful conflicts of incivility."

Chinese culture attaches great importance to education. Confucius was an educator who wanted to develop well-rounded people, *junzi*, who would be useful to the state and to society. As Feng Youlan points out, one major theme of Confucian teachings is harmony in society as an ultimate concern. Confucianism teaches reciprocity and altruism.[59] This is why Confucius is venerated in China as the teacher for all ages.

---

[58] Pope Francis, "Interreligious Meeting Address of His Holiness."
[59] Feng, *A Short History of Chinese Philosophy*, 40.

True Justice and Universal Love

Peace and justice are intrinsically related. "Peace dies when it is divorced from justice, but justice is false if it is not universal," says the Holy Father. "A justice addressed only to family members, compatriots, and believers of the same faith is a limping justice; it is a disguised injustice!"

True justice has to be universal. In Chinese, "justice" has the connotation of righteousness. What is right (just) is relative depending on your point of reference (for me, for the others, for the community . . .). In the Western mindset, what is right and just may be absolute, but in the East, there is more emphasis on relationships. What is right and just at times may not be clear-cut, and relationships are to be promoted. Righteous interpersonal relationship in the Confucian tradition is based on the principle of gradation, but it also extends to include others in society with altruism, honoring the elderly and caring for the young in other families as your own. It is interesting to note that "justice" (*zhengyi*) in the contemporary sense is now actively promoted in China as one of the twelve core socialist values of the Chinese dream; nevertheless, the traditional value of righteousness has to be considered. Testimonies are not lacking throughout Christian history of those who were ready to sacrifice themselves, their careers, and even their lives for a just cause. This Confucian moral value exerts an attitude of positive living and life-guiding principles, which provide ideals and standards for people and encourage them to be loyal to country, filial to parents, respectful to elders, and friendly to friends, fulfilling the spirit of sacrificing one's own self for the good of the bigger Self.

The Holy Father invited world religions to keep watch as "sentinels of fraternity in the night of conflict" and commit to standing against injustice and tragedies in the world. He called us to defend the least of our brothers and sisters and stand by the poor. "Our being together today is a message of trust, an encouragement to all people of good will."[60] The world's religions have the task of reminding people that "greed for profit renders the heart lifeless" and that the current consumerist market system does not benefit encounter, dialogue, or family, which are essential dimensions of life. Christians are called to fulfill the wish of Jesus "that all may be one." Believers are to be united in the name of the Merciful One. Universal brotherhood for peace is the common desire of all people of good will.

As I have shown, the ideas of *ren'ai* in Confucianism and *jian'ai* in Mohism complement each other. Sun Yatsen integrated these ideas of love with fraternity inspired by the concept of universal brotherhood in Christianity and expressed it with the term *bo'ai* (universal love). He advocated "under the sky a public spirit of common good" and used *bo'ai* as one of the foundations for his idea of Chinese political theory. The concept of *bo'ai* denotes a contemporary idea of universal brotherhood, taken from Confucian classics as well as from Christianity; it is applicable to East and West.

Concrete Actions and Paths of Fraternity for Peace Are Necessary

Jesus says that no one has greater love than to lay down one's life for one's friends. Christian fraternity demands that one is ready even to offer his life for the love of others. Mencius speaks of the spirit of letting go of life for the sake of righteousness, sacrificing oneself for the greater good. Historically Mozi's proposal of *jian'ai* was doomed as impractical, and his idea of "universal love" was not fully understood and has been forgotten. Although ancient Chinese philosophers did argue about the origin of things, their concerns ultimately pointed to how society should be organized, how one should act. They were endowed with a strong sense of pragmatism.

---

[60] Pope Francis, "Interreligious Meeting Address of His Holiness."

The pragmatic expression of friendship wants good for others. It is an open invitation to find concrete ways to practice universal brotherhood. Pragmatic friendship is in sharp contrast to what we see around the world nowadays; all the more, concrete initiatives and daily commitments are urgently needed.

As the Holy Father said, "The miserable crudeness of war" in some countries is caused by the logic of armed power, the monetization of relations, the arming of borders, the raising of walls, the gagging of the poor. Let us oppose all this with the "sweet power of prayer" and "daily commitment" to dialogue, finding concrete paths of fraternity for peace. The joint declaration on Human Fraternity for World Peace at Abu Dhabi is a historical document that gives impetus to further concrete initiatives and encourages daily commitments. In order to practice fraternity and put it into concrete actions, the declaration has set an outline of a method, a code of conduct, and a path, and invites further deepening of the document's content.

Fratelli Tutti on Fraternity and Social Friendship Consonant with Chinese Culture

When Francis was elected pope, his very first gesture and words from the balcony of St. Peter's Basilica were to invite the whole Church to embark on "a journey of fraternity." In a crucial moment, when the people and the world were suffering in the midst of the pandemic, he stood alone in front of the vast but empty St. Peter's Square to pray, urging the people to ease their fears through faith and fraternal love. The powerful televised image was imprinted in millions of minds throughout the world. This image had a strong impact also on the people in China. In front of the challenges of the world's ills and fractures, he issued the encyclical *Fratelli Tutti*, calling for change and action in a new vision of fraternity. His message and deeds have been consistent and clear: the world today needs human fraternity and social friendship. I find many expressions of Pope Francis very compatible with Chinese culture.

Promoting the Moral Good of Agathosyne, Benevolentia, and Ren'ai

In *Fratelli Tutti*, the Holy Father talked about promoting integral human development for seeking and pursuing the good of others and of the entire human family. To emphasize the meaning that he wanted to communicate to us, he uses two terms, one in Greek and the other in Latin.

He says that the New Testament uses the Greek word *agathosyne* to describe one fruit of the Holy Spirit (see Gal. 5:22). It means pursuit of the good, striving for excellence and what is best for others—not simply material well-being, but growth in maturity and health. A similar expression exists in Latin, *benevolentia*. It is an attitude that "wills the good" of others. It indicates a yearning for goodness, an inclination toward all that is fine and excellent, a desire to fill the lives of others with what is beautiful, sublime, and edifying (*FT* 112).

I find these two terms used by Pope Francis to be very much in accord with the Confucian term *ren'ai*, which has a rich connotation of benevolence, humanity, and recognizing the dignity in self and others. As a matter of fact, in the official translation of the New Testament in Chinese, the term *ren'ai* is already used to indicate a benevolent and mutual relationship.

From the Love within the Same Nation to the Hearts Embracing Foreigners

Pope Francis in his encyclical *Fratelli Tutti* said that the ancient commandment to "love your neighbor as yourself" (Lev. 19:18), was usually understood in earlier Jewish traditions as referring to relationships within the same nation. However, the hearts of the Jewish people were expanded to embrace foreigners as they themselves had once lived as foreigners in Egypt. Of the command "not to do to others what you would not want them to do to you" (Tob. 4:15), Rabbi Hillel of the first century before Christ stated, "This is the entire Torah. Everything else is commentary." In the New Testament, Hillel's precept was expressed in positive terms: "In everything, do to others as you would have them do to you; for this is the law and the prophets" (Matt. 7:12).[61]

Similar to Rabbi Hillel's expression, the Confucian version of the saying "Do not do to others what you would not want others to do to you" is also expressed in a negative form. The Confucian concept of love, *ren*, started from family or kinship love, but then was developed and extended to a more altruistic love, caring for the elderly and the young of others. Over the history of China, different states and peoples have always come into contact with one another. Confucianism emphasizes the concept of reciprocity and *tianxia* (under the sky). There is this development of love starting from within the family to that of whole world under the sky.

Pope Francis affirmed that man is made for love; therefore, he must go beyond the self toward others to find fuller existence. Love is capable of transcending borders of regions or countries. He says, "The ever-increasing number of interconnections and communications in today's world makes us powerfully aware of the unity and common destiny of the nations" (*FT* 99). Concurrently, in China, President Xi is promoting the initiative of building "a community of common destiny for mankind," which he outlined to the UN Assembly.[62] This is becoming a mantra

---

[61] Pope Francis, *Fratelli Tutti*, Encyclical Letter on Fraternity and Social Friendship, April 3, 2020, 59–60.

[62] See Constitution of the Communist Party of China, revised and adopted at the 19th National Congress of the Communist Party of China, October 24, 2017; see also Xi Jinping, "Working Together to Build a Human

in Xi's rhetoric for two reasons. First of all, China condemns hegemony or a monopolar world order dictated by military prowess. Second, there is a need of promoting a multipolar world order of fairness in which developing countries can emerge to attain their potential within a new economic system. As the ancient Chinese saying goes, "Within the four seas," which refers to the whole world: "We are all brothers." This idea of brothers is not limited to family, nor to interpersonal social relationships, but can also be extended to ethnic and state relations.

Freedom without Fraternity Is Contradictory

As I mentioned earlier, true justice has to be universal. The triptych motto has to be taken as a whole, as freedom without fraternity is contradictory. The Holy Father denounces racism and radical individualism as viruses. He upholds "social friendship" and "universal fraternity" that promotes persons, human dignity, and the common good. "To claim economic freedom while real conditions bar many people from actual access to it" is contradictory doublespeak. He says that "words like freedom, democracy, or fraternity prove meaningless" if our economic and social systems do not take care of the weak and vulnerable (*FT* 110).

Francis emphasizes that the human person, with his or her inalienable rights, is by nature open to relationship. To limit the term "human rights" to individualistic rights is a misuse of the term. Unless the rights of each individual are harmoniously ordered to the greater good, those rights become a source of conflict and violence (*FT* 111).

Community with a Shared Future," speech at the UN Office, Geneva, January 18, 2017, in *On Building a Human Community with a Shared Future* (Beijing: Central Compilation and Translation Press, 2019), 427–440.

I address the negative effects of unchecked freedom in liberal capitalism in the later chapters on economics and freedom. With regard to the issue of excessive emphasis given to certain categories of rights—namely, political and individual rights—many Asian nations stress the importance of a balance between the rights of individuals and the good of the community. Asian culture in general gives more importance to the community, in strong contrast with the West, which traditionally exalts the individual to a much greater degree. The most fundamental of rights, after all, is the right to life—speaking, for example, in the material sense of the right to food and nutrition. For what does a person do with all his or her rights, even the noblest ones, if he or she is dying of hunger? If this right were officially recognized and promoted, perhaps rich nations would not waste incredible amounts of money and resources on armaments.

With his emphatic condemnation of war, Pope Francis in *Fratelli Tutti* stressed solidarity to combat globalized indifference and promote the "universal destination of goods" over the absolute right to private property (*FT* 111). In Chinese culture, which is more communitarian than individualistic, there is a concept not as well known in the West: *minquan* (the rights of a people),[63] which stands alongside *renquan* (the rights of a person). For decades, the Chinese government has strived to improve people's livelihood. The White Paper issued by the State Council "bases the cause of human rights on the endeavors to

---

[63] The Three Principles of the People is a political philosophy by Sun Yatsen that includes the rights of a people (*minquan*), the livelihood of the people (*minsheng*), and democracy (*minzu*). He played an instrumental role in the overthrow of the Qing dynasty during the Xinhai Revolution, was the first provisional president when the Republic of China was founded in 1912, was a uniting figure in post-Imperial China, and remains unique among twentieth-century Chinese politicians for being widely revered among the people on both sides of the Taiwan Strait.

solve the principal contradiction in Chinese society, [and] focuses on people's ever-growing needs for a better life."[64]

As a matter of fact, a central theme of Asian values is the priority of the community and the importance of its stability. Only the stability of individual components can ensure the harmony of the whole, and harmony is the highest value in Asia. Values or virtues being practiced and articulated embrace the sense of collectiveness rather than individualism, the ability to bear suffering, the sense of sacrifice for the greater good, and the sense of respect for others, especially elders and authority, which leads people to be more obedient and cooperative.

A Better Kind of Politics: Love of All Loves

For Pope Francis, "better politics" is to work for the common good in service of the whole people, instead of just attracting popularity or consensus from voters, thus fomenting selfishness. He criticized a politics subject to finance; instead, politics should center on human dignity, with policies not just for the poor but with and of the poor (*FT* 169).

He also emphasized the important role of the United Nations for the family of nations, making use of negotiation, mediation, and arbitration. A better kind of politics is working for the common good and human dignity, which includes eradication of poverty, protection of human rights, and promotion of the force of law rather than the law of force (*FT* 173–175).

Better politics means securing work for people to live a normal social life, and developing a strategy for alleviating poverty. That means tackling, in a radical and integral way,

---

[64] Information Office of the People's Republic of China, "Seeking Happiness for People: 70 Years of Progress on Human Rights in China," white paper issued by the State Council, September 2019.

problems of hunger, drugs, weapons, terrorism, social exclusion, sexual exploitation, slave labor, organized crime, and organ and human trafficking. The pope draws from the social teaching of the Church, the perspective of solidarity and subsidiarity, to which he now adds an emphasis on fraternity (*FT* 187–189).

How can this be a stimulus for ordinary Christians, Western or Chinese? Antonio Baggio took the experience of the Focolare to illustrate how Chiara Lubich with her companions answered this question in the war-torn Italian city of Trent when they started living the gospel and helping the poor. They gradually formed a community that carried the sign of three basic elements needed to create the conditions of political life: liberty, equality, and fraternity.[65] First, the free decision she and her companions made to love; second, to favor the poor who were helped with the goods of the more well-to-do, thus creating bonds of fraternity between the two groups; and third, achieving equality through fraternity.

Lubich's thought on fraternity grew in the context of the new social movement she was founding. She spoke about the forsaken Jesus as the model for politicians at the first congress in 2000 of the Movement for Unity in Politics. She sees Jesus as the model of a politician, not because he is the miracle worker who attracts and feeds the crowd, but because of the greatest love manifested in his abandonment. The forsaken Jesus is the one who embraces all divisions, defeats, and separations present in humanity—and he brings them all back to unity with God.[66]

Politics is the love of all loves for Lubich, and she gives the

---

[65] Antonio M. Baggio, "Love of All Loves: Politics and Fraternity in the Charismatic Vision of Chiara Lubich (Sophia University Institute)," *Claritas: Journal of Dialogue and Culture* 2, no. 2 (October 2013): 53–65.

[66] Chiara Lubich, "The Movement for Unity and a Politics of Communion," Address to the International Conference of the Movement of Unity in Politics, Castel Gandolfo, Italy, June 9, 2000. See Chiara Lubich, *Essential Writings* (New York: New City Press, 2007), 240–244.

following examples: "Politics seen as love creates and preserves those conditions that allow all other types of love to flourish: the love of young people who want to get married and who need a house and employment; the love of those who want to study and who need schools and books; the love of those who run their own business and who need roads and railways, clear and reliable laws."[67]

Lubich made a fundamental contribution to the rediscovery of fraternity, particularly during the last years of her public engagement. Baggio explains that there is a Trinitarian logic of fraternity in her early experience that is on one hand rooted in the religious background of the Christian faith. On the other hand, her proposal of politics as love of all loves grows in the social movements of the present political arena.

With this perspective, fraternity is relevant to all people in its universal human dimension, also outside of any religious affiliation. In this regard, I explore in the next chapter the experience and effort of China on the themes of economics, governance, education, poverty alleviation, and the construction of infrastructure. Although it is a case study of nonreligious efforts, it may offer an opportunity to inspire a new paradigm in economic development for the common good.

---

[67] Chiara Lubich, "A United Europe for a United World," Address to One Thousand Cities for Europe (a conference for European mayors), Innsbruck, Austria, November, 9, 2001. See Lubich, *Essential Writings*, 254–255.

4

Poverty Alleviation and a New Economic Model

Pope Francis called for a change in the current economic paradigm, taking into account integral human development. With the crises of the pandemic and climate change, and of global recession, China is one of the very few countries that registered positive economic growth in 2020. With the sheer size of its economy and its own characteristics, China does not claim that its development model could be an example for other countries. However, there may be something that the China experience could inspire. As the Holy Father says, "There is a scandalous growth of poverty in broad sectors of society throughout our world. Faced with this scenario, we cannot remain passive, much less resigned."[1] *In this chapter, I would like to focus on some points for consideration. Are there elements of the Chinese experience in poverty alleviation that could contribute to a new economic paradigm? I also discuss issues of spiritual poverty and the dilemma of Catholic social services in China. Could there be a possibility of building a consensus view for a new model of economy from the Chinese experience and that of Catholic teachings?*

---

[1] Pope Francis, "Message on First World Day of the Poor," November 19, 2017, 5.

This chapter starts with a historical analysis of different periods of China's experience from the last century to the present. It focuses on the economic transformation of China, the experience of poverty alleviation, and the characteristics of the economic development model. Sometimes Chinese newspaper headlines signal the message: "This country is growing rich, but its citizens are still poor." How has China's development model contributed to the alleviation of poverty? The effort to alleviate poverty and to promote economic development seem to go hand in hand. Yes, as the society becomes more prosperous and materialistic, there emerges a great need for an alleviation of *spiritual* poverty and a growing emphasis on social values as well. In China, an officially atheist country, the role of the Church in society is limited; nevertheless, the Church can still play a realistic role in contributing to the alleviation of spiritual poverty. I present here some concrete initiatives of the Catholic Church in China, particularly in regard to social services, which enhance social values by giving testimony of Christian charity, and the contribution made to a spiritual dimension of daily living.

During the past decades, as a developing country, the process of development in China has concentrated much effort on GDP growth. As mentioned in the previous chapter, the attention of the central government in recent years has shifted to the so-called Green GDP and provincial government performance based on measuring gross ecosystem product (GEP) growth. Aside from aiming to alleviate poverty, China has also set new goals, such as achieving an ecological civilization. It happens to be very timely and in tune with the environmental and social concerns presented in the encyclicals of Pope Francis and his call for a new paradigm of economic systems. The chapter concludes with experiences and initiatives called the Economy of Francesco and Economy of Communion.

Poverty Alleviation in China

From a Historical Perspective

For those who have been to Shanghai or have seen at least images of it, they probably know the Bund (*Waitang*), the historic waterfront of Shanghai. On the opposite side of the river, in contrast, is the ultramodern Pudong, a new area with skyscrapers and a bright, colorful skyline. Along the Bund is an array of buildings in colonial-style architecture. At the southern end is a lighthouse built by the Jesuits more than a century ago. At the other end is the Monument to the People's Heroes, built to remember all the people who contributed to the rejuvenation of China in the last two hundred years.

It always helps to look at China, even on topics such as the alleviation of poverty, from a historical perspective. China was in decline at the turn of the nineteenth century under the Qing dynasty and was called the sick man of Asia. Looking at the timeline of China's last hundred years of modern history, three milestones of change can be traced from 1919 to the present day.

May 4, 1919, marked the beginning of the May Fourth Movement, inspired by a magazine called "New Youth" (*Xinqingnian*) and young Chinese intellectuals who wanted to renew China, a sociopolitical reform movement directed toward national independence, emancipation of the individual, and the rebuilding of society and culture. However, from the year 1919 to 1949, when the People's Republic of China was founded, it was a thirty-year period characterized by turmoil, Japanese occupation, and civil war. The 1949–1979 period was thirty years of emphasis on ideology, specifically the communist ideology. In the period from 1979 to 2009 were thirty years inaugurating the open-door policy, characterized by the pursuit of reform and development.

After China held the 2008 Olympics in Beijing and the Universal Expo of Shanghai in 2010, more and more Chinese have gone abroad for studies or visits, a period characterized by more exchanges with the rest of the world. President Xi declared in 2020 that China had succeeded in the eradication of extreme poverty. Although the thirty-year period ahead cannot yet be defined, in a 2021 article, President Xi stated the concrete objective of "common prosperity" aimed at promoting high-quality economic growth, and advancing the goals of all citizens sharing the opportunity for wealth and welfare.[2] Xi envisions China moving toward a "new era of building a community of shared future for mankind," committed to meeting people's aspirations for a better life.[3]

Economic Reform Factors

In this process of economic transformation, one might ask, what unique features of this process of reform are especially interesting? Bert Hofman, a World Bank official, in his paper at a conference in Shanghai, pinpointed six distinct factors of Chinese

---

[2] After thirty years of reform and opening up, the Chinese government put much emphasis on poverty alleviation in order to achieve eradication of extreme poverty by 2020. It has become increasingly clear, especially with recent statements of President Xi, that the nation's next objective is achieving high-quality growth, represented by the acronym GROW: high-quality **G**rowth, **R**edistribution of wealth, **O**pportunity for all citizens, and **W**elfare. See Xi Jinping, "To Promote Common Prosperity on Solid Ground," *Qiushi Journal*, October 15, 2021. Recent years have seen studies on China's future development path. See, for example, Quan Heng, "Navigating China's Economic Development in the New Era: From High-Speed to High-Quality Growth," *China Quarterly of International Strategic Studies* 4, no. 2 (2018): 177–192.

[3] *People's Daily*, "Build a New Type of International Relations and a Community with a Shared Future for Mankind," October 29, 2019.

transformation: an experimental way, stability, gradual reform, decentralization and incentives, pragmatism and transitional institutions, and institutionalization of reforms.[4]

Experimental way. China applied a gradual, experimental way to reform its economic system, especially in the early stage after Deng Xiaoping announced the open-door policy in 1979. The economic conditions were simply different from those of Eastern Europe and Latin America.[5]

Stability. When central planning was relaxed, competition among regions and their enterprises became possible, but the state and the ruling party remained intact throughout the reforms, so China could focus on the economic and social transition.

Gradual reform. A famous saying coined by Deng, "Crossing the river by feeling the stones," became China's mode of economic reform, implementing partial reforms in an experimental manner, often starting in a few regions and expanding them upon proven success. Four special economic zones—Shenzhen, Zhuhai, and Shantou in Guangdong Province, and Xiamen in Fujian Province—were created in the southern coastal area in 1980. The Pudong New Area in Shanghai was opened to overseas investment only in 1990.

Decentralization and incentives. By decentralizing, China turned the country into a laboratory for reforms. Successful experiments were quickly adopted throughout the country. The fiscal reforms introduced in 1980, with high revenue

---

[4] Bert Hofman, "Reflections on Forty Years of China's Reforms," Keynote Speech at Fudan University's Fanhai School of International Finance, January 2018.

[5] China was poor and predominantly a rural country at the onset of reforms. The Eastern Blocs were too dependent on the Soviet Union, and Latin American countries had comparative advantage only in one or two industries and were economically vulnerable. See Barry Naughton, *Growing Out of the Plan: Chinese Economic Reforms 1978–1993* (Cambridge: Cambridge University Press, 1995).

retention rates for local governments—for example, Guangzhou Province—had strong incentives to pursue growth and promote a market economy.

Pragmatism and transitional institutions. From a planned economy grew a dual-track system allowing for a nonplanned economies, such as Township and Village Enterprises (TVEs), to emerge. (This was taken over later by private and foreign investment enterprises with protection of property rights.)

Institutionalization of reforms.[6] From the China Academy of Social Sciences, a variety of think tanks were developed, such as the Development Research Center (DRC) of the State Council, the Development and Reform Commission (DRC), and the highly influential Systems Reform Commission (SRC).

Achievements in the Poverty Alleviation with Economic Reform Effort

If the main topic under discussion is poverty alleviation, why speak of economic reform and development? It is precisely because economic development and poverty reduction are interconnected; they have to go hand in hand. China has been able to achieve poverty reduction goals by means of steady economic development, undergoing tremendous change over the past four decades. The massive economy continued to expand at a fast pace, with an average of 9.5 percent annual growth since the early 1980s, compared to a world average of 2.9 percent annual global growth in the same period.

China has been putting into practice an age-old saying: "Give a man a fish and he will eat for a day. Teach him how to

---

[6] See Chen Ling and Barry Naughton, "An Institutionalized Policy-Making Mechanism: China's Return to Techno-Industrial Policy," *Research Policy* 45 (2016): 2138–2152.

fish and you feed him for a lifetime." Administered by a secular government, China has achieved remarkable development and poverty reduction in the last forty years—a relatively short span of time. This is unprecedented, accounting for 70 percent of the world's total poverty reduction figure.[7] The country has maintained its social stability over a long period, making it a country that provides a great sense of social safety.

According to some scholars, this remarkable economic progress can also be attributed to certain cultural factors:[8] for example, Chinese people are industrious and frugal with a high saving ratio. Other factors include a large and educated workforce and a political system that allows the pursuit of reforms that are in the long-term interest of the country and the people.

In addition, the rapid economic development has had a significant impact on people's quality of life. The higher education system leads to technological advancement. High-speed trains,[9] mobile payments, the bike sharing system,[10] and online payment systems have changed the daily life of the Chinese.

---

[7] Liu Xinyong, "China Focus: Reform, Opening-Up Create New Wonders in Human History," Xinhua Net, December 17, 2018.

[8] See ibid. Two researchers—Tu Xinquan, a professor at the University of International Business and Economics in China, and Song Luzheng, another Shanghai-based researcher—point out some cultural factors behind China's economic reform success.

[9] China inaugurated its first high-speed train service of about 75 miles between Beijing and Tianjin shortly before the Olympics in 2008. This massive network is currently close to 30,000 miles long—more than the circumference around the Earth's equator, and is expected to reach 60,000 miles by 2030.

[10] The success story of three university students using the bicycle-sharing system is inspiring, as they made a significant transition from a pastime to a big business venture. The convenience of shared bikes like Ofo and Mobike spread the idea of a sharing economy.

A World Bank document[11] even suggested that China has found a poverty alleviation path with its own characteristics—and that the "Chinese experience" could be offered as poverty relief in other countries.

The Chinese government officially adopted its Targeted Poverty Alleviation Strategy (TPAS) in 2014. The government report[12] urges local governments to take targeted measures to ensure that assistance reaches poverty-stricken villages and households. Village work teams were sent to targeted areas to analyze demand, make development plans, and coordinate assistance resources. The government took measures such as encouraging banks to give microloans to farmers and setting up rural cooperatives allowing farmers to pool their resources to raise production. Statistics show that starting from 2012, an average of 1.3 million poor people per year cleared the poverty line. The country had set the goal of wiping out poverty and becoming a moderately prosperous society by 2020.

Paradoxes

The urban population in China has grown from 20 percent to almost 60 percent in the last forty years.[13] Half of its population has moved from the poverty-stricken rural areas to cities that offer

---

[11] "Consensus Reached at the International Forum on Reform and Opening Up and Poverty Reduction in China," International Forum on Reform and Opening Up and Poverty Reduction in China, jointly hosted by the Chinese Government and the World Bank Group, November 5, 2018, worldbank.org.

[12] *South China Morning Post*, "Grinding Poverty in China: Is Xi Jinping's Alleviation Campaign Making Any Difference?" March 25, 2018.

[13] The urban population has grown from about 18.6 percent in 1979 to 57.9 percent in 2017. See "China: Urban Population as a Share of Total Population," *World Data Atlas*, 2018, https://knoema.com/atlas/China/Urban-population.

a decent life. The controversial one-child policy was introduced in 1979, exactly the same year as the inauguration of the economic reform. The rationale was to reduce China's enormous growth in population, which was hard to feed. It brought about social consequences and challenges, such as problems of rural "left-behind" children and urban "single-child" families, resulting overall in an aging population. Since 2013, the controversial policy has gradually been relaxed. China is now stepping up measures and incentives to encourage a rise in the birth rate. Another paradox is the reverse trend now happening among the youth: a movement toward smaller cities and towns, where new development offers more opportunities.

In chapter 2, I mentioned the environmental pollution issues in China brought about by industries, urbanization, traffic congestion, infrastructure building, and dependency on fossil fuels. The dependency of energy consumption on international geopolitics is a complex issue.

Competition led to rapid economic growth but created the problems of pollution, income disparity, and other shortcomings. Many point out that the lifetime income of an average young worker would not be sufficient to purchase an apartment in big cities. Since 2020, the Chinese central government has started to evaluate local government performance in certain provinces, not by the GDP but by gross ecosystem product (GEP) growth, or the rise in the happiness index of the people. This truly is a paradigm shift.

The success in poverty alleviation has also created paradoxes. My intention is to put the one-child policy and the industrial and rapid economic growth policies of the past in context, so as to understand the dilemmas to be solved. It is a reminder that timely corrective measures and continuous reform policies are always necessary—to anticipate, for example, the aging population and pollution problems before it is too late.

Can China's Poverty Alleviation Be a Contribution to a New Economic Paradigm?

As mentioned earlier, China has experienced gradual and continuous economic reform in the last forty years, accomplished in an experimental manner. The country is big, and the size of its economy is huge. In fact, by GDP per capita (according to World Bank data), China is still considered a Global South and developing country. It has created an economic model consonant with its own cultural characteristics and history while maintaining a steady political system.[14] Its development model may not be suitable for other countries; its experience, however, could certainly offer inspiration and contribute to the reflection of a new economic paradigm for poverty alleviation.

Relationship between Developed and Less Developed Regions

Deng Xiaoping once famously said, "To get rich is honorable." That unleashed tremendous potential for economic reform and the opening up of China. More significantly, however, the second part of his quote was often left unnoticed. He said that we permit some people and some regions to become prosperous first, for the purpose of achieving common prosperity. Therefore, common prosperity is the key and the main objective.

---

[14] This can also describe Singapore, Vietnam, and Malaysia: countries that experienced economic growth with more autocratic or centralized systems of government. Political stability is an element of "Asian values" drawn from Confucian ethics, which I discuss in this book. This notion is part of many Asian countries' political philosophy in practice, but has been criticized in the West as an excuse to justify undemocratic regimes. There are many proponents of Asian values among renowned personalities not only in the political field, such as Lee Kuan Yew of Singapore and Mahathir of Malaysia, but in the economic and cultural fields as well.

The Chinese experience of prosperous coastal provinces paired with and helping poor provinces in western China can be shared and proposed at the international level for the assistance and relationship between developed and developing countries. The transfer of clean technologies to developing countries is also the responsibility of developed countries, in order to solve the global environmental crisis and to safeguard our common home for humanity, as is stressed in the *Compendium of Social Doctrine of the Church*.[15] The interprovincial experiences within China could be regarded as a reference, as some countries in the European Union—including Portugal, Spain, and Ireland—have also developed a similar policy.

A few years ago, in a symposium with business leaders, Xi Jinping launched a new "Go West" development plan to counter post-coronavirus geopolitical risks and obstacles posed by US-China decoupling, as reported in an article in the *South China Morning Post*.[16] The idea is to form a new development pattern, a "dual circulation" strategy, with a domestic circulation between the prosperous eastern China and the less-developed western China as the main body, with domestic and international circulations mutually promoting one another.

A New Economic System with Asian Values

Pope Francis spoke of an integral approach to a new economic system, taking into account the relationship with the ecological system, social justice, respect for other cultures, and fraternity. This new paradigm could integrate economic models from the

---

[15] Pontifical Council for Justice and Peace, *Compendium of Social Doctrine of the Church*, 2004, 475.

[16] Frank Tang, "China Launches New Go West Development Drive to Counter Post-coronavirus Geopolitical Risks," *South China Morning Post*, June 22, 2020.

"chopsticks cultural sphere," with Confucian ethics and Asian values such as harmony, diligence, frugality, and a high savings rate.

Chinese scholar and environmental activist Liao Xiaoyi[17] rejoices at the encyclical and finds many similarities with the "ecological civilization" that China has promoted in recent years, and John Cobb, a preeminent American scholar of process philosophy,[18] believes that China has the conditions for and stands a good chance of achieving an ecological civilization.

We have seen how China in the last few decades has attained remarkable achievement in poverty alleviation, combining the practice of age-old wisdom and the Targeted Poverty Alleviation Strategy. Its efforts toward and realization of poverty alleviation offer hope for countries facing common challenges. Above all, China has demonstrated a development model that is consonant with its own culture, taking into consideration the local conditions, its present stages of development, and the international environment.

Endogenous Development: Meritocracy and Wise Governance

Last but not least, a crucial point in the China development model is its particular system of governance and the government's role in guiding sound policy for the nation's common good. Confucianism emphasizes meritocracy and wise governance.

---

[17] Liao Xiaoyi, a former professor at CASS and founder of the Global Village Beijing NGO in the aftermath of the 2008 earthquake, proposed a new sustainable living approach and founded many rural community projects called Happiness and Harmony Homelands in collaboration with provincial officials. She has also received awards for contributions to conserving traditional culture and the ecosystem. See A. Moriggi, "Chinese Women at the Forefront of Environmental Activism," *DEP Journal*, no. 35 (2017): 206–227.

[18] See *For Our Common Home: Process-Relational Response to Laudato Si'*, ed. J. B. Cobb and I. Castuera (Anoka, MN: Process Century Press, 2015), i–vi.

For example, at the beginning of the reform and opening up of China, there were two major factors: active integration in the globalized industrial chain and division of labor. The gradual transition from the early 1980s "three-plus-one trading mix" (encouraging production, processing, and assembly for foreign orders combined with government subsidy)[19] to the current sound industrial system has benefited concretely from globalization. China entered the WTO in 2001.

Although market mechanisms dominate economic development, the government's role is essential in guiding industrial policies in certain key areas such as new energy, high-speed rail manufacturing, and electric vehicles. Without these industrial policies, China's economic development would be uneven and vulnerable, similar to that of certain Latin American and Asian countries with comparative advantage in only one or two industries. These factors are related to sound government industrial policy, and also a diligent and skillful workforce.

China's ability to seize the dividends of globalization is also directly related to its high talent pool. It has effectively invested in education (nine years of free compulsory education and strong state subsidies for universities), the ecological environment, and poverty alleviation. The Chinese government leadership has the ability to take advantage of "endogenous development" (development from within its culture). Over time, the model has proved capable of outperforming the promises of populist leaders from so-called liberal democratic systems, which have proved divisive for their peoples.

China has clear policy programs—for example, the four modernizations in the Deng Xiaoping era, and the "two

---

[19] Chen Xie, "The Other Side of the Global Imbalances: The Politics of Economic Reform in China under the 'New Normal,'" PhD diss., University of York, March 2018, 175–176.

centenaries" goals as proposed by Xi Jinping. China also has to confront the challenge of corruption, especially in the process of transition from a planned to a market economy, and in a system where government officials are appointed with too much power. However, the leadership in recent years has proved steadfast in combating corruption, and national leaders selected by the Central Organization Department have made the Chinese Communist Party, the ruling party, resilient and capable of governing. These internal strengths, apart from integrating with the global economy, have led China to its current successes.

The Threat of Materialism, Spiritual Poverty, and the Culture of Indifference

Spiritual Poverty

Relentless pursuit of economic development has created an abysmal spiritual vacuum in the Chinese people. As some scholars have pointed out, there is a great need for alleviating not only material poverty but spiritual poverty as well. Given their materialistic view of life, are the people happy? As economic development allows society to become more affluent, the younger generation is constantly exposed to consumerism. The trend goes beyond the issues of leisure and free time and is manifested in more malicious forms, such as greed, envy, and the worship of money. The stimulation of voracious appetites has even become an annual ritual. Every November 11 (or 11/11), e-commerce stores offer steep discounts. The date was chosen to represent the status of singles, catering to their loneliness to take advantage of the internet shopping holiday.

Incidents of selfishness and indifference, such as the tragedy of little Yueyue,[20] food safety, and corruption scandals in the early

---

[20] A two-year-old girl was hit by two vehicles and ignored by passers-by

2010s shocked the Chinese national conscience, provoking much public outrage about rampant materialism and the immorality of contemporary Chinese society. Another way of escape from reality is to forget everything and enjoy the development of information technology and the products of a modern economy.

Pressure on Youth

Chinese youth are under tremendous pressure. They have different kinds of challenges to face. They are under pressure in childhood to study and work hard to find a life partner and form a future family. The whole family or clan concentrates its efforts for the single child to pass the *gaokao* (university entrance exam), a tradition that can be traced back to the Confucian state exam during the Han dynasty period (206 BCE–200 CE). Moreover, parents pool their resources to help the young to choose a spouse.

College is a time for academic pursuits, independent thinking, and seeking a meaning for life. In Chinese schools, students are still taught a mainly materialist conception of history, according to Marxist ideology. Nevertheless, Hua Hua of the Shanghai Academy of Social Sciences (SASS) conducted a survey targeting Christian student fellowships[21] and found that, while there is an intense competitive atmosphere in the educational system, some students become Christians because they find harmonious relationships and greater solidarity within these groups.

---

until a scavenger, Chen Xianmei, intervened. The girl eventually died at a hospital in Foshan on October 13, 2011. The images of the tragedy, spread on the internet, inflamed millions of bloggers, who criticized the materialism and immorality of Chinese society. Still, the witness of Xianmei offered some grounds for hope.

[21] Hua Hua, "A Survey on College Students' Christian Belief: Taking Some Shanghai Students as Example," *Youth Studies* (Shanghai) 1 (2008).

In addition, I interviewed Professor Bao Leiping, a senior researcher at the Youth Research Center of the same academy. According to Bao's findings, youth in a metropolis like Beijing or Shanghai—like their counterparts in developed countries—have already entered the postmaterialist age. Yet she calls attention to characteristics different from those highlighted by American scholar Ronald Inglehart, who coined the term "post-materialism."[22] For her, Chinese youth do have their own opinions and self-expressions, but their outlook is not as liberal and individualistic as Inglehart characterized. They treasure stability, but without blindly following things. To a certain extent, they still stick to traditional cultural norms on gender and family, respect for authority and for their parents. The role models for teenagers are not consumerist types, movie stars, or singers, but productive types, such as Ma Yun (Jack Ma) and Ma Huateng (like Bill Gates or Steve Jobs, their counterparts in the United States).[23]

Some years ago, Liang Zhi, a PhD candidate at the elite University of Tsinghua, appeared on a TV program. On one hand he was boastful, showing off his degrees in law, communications, and management, yet he showed distress and sought advice about what job to take. The TV host criticized this egoistic approach to career, and afterwards many netizens also expressed their dismay.

---

[22] Postmaterialist characteristics are an emphasis on self-expression and quality of life, environmental protection, freedom of speech, and gender equality. In contrast, materialist characteristics are economic security and social order—with an emphasis on traditional, cultural, and religious values—and authority of all kinds. The shift involves an intergenerational change of social norms from traditional values to those linked with individual well-being and self-expression. See Ronald Inglehart, "Post-materialism," Encyclopedia Britannica Online, November 16, 2016.

[23] Bao Leiping, "Youth Idols in China since 1949 from the Structural Perspective," *Youth Research* 1 (2009): 67–75.

By contrast, there is an exceptional story that could inspire young people: Three Peking University (PKU) students, by using a bicycle-sharing system, transformed the leisure pastime of cycling for them in 2014 into a long-term business, the Ofo Bicycle covering five hundred campuses in 2016. The project continued to develop, with digital innovations using a smartphone app to unlock bicycles, and turned into a big business venture. As of 2017, the Ofo Company operated over ten million bikes in 180 cities and thirteen countries and was valued at $3 billion.[24] Although it did not survive ferocious competition in the cruel world of business finance, Ofo was replaced in 2019 by Hellobike, backed by Alibaba. The convenience of the bike-sharing system combined with a mobile payment app, along with the concept of a "sharing economy," was further developed in China, harnessing shared resources that have proved beneficial to economic development.[25]

Another challenge for Chinese youth today is the high rate of unemployment, especially following the pandemic. Economist Keyu Jin points out that China's education system traditionally emphasizes college degrees rather than vocational school. It is also a cultural factor that parents always expect their children to attend university, which has led to an oversupply of graduates for white-collar jobs, and a lack of technicians with soft skills to fill the manufacturing sectors. She recommends policy incentives to steer students toward sectors with labor shortages to overcome this educational mismatch. According to her analysis, while China remains politically centralized under the Communist

---

[24] Tao Li, "Parents of Ofo's Bike User Sue Company for Negligence after Accident," *South China Morning Post*, October 27, 2017.

[25] Yan Kin Sheung Chiaretto, *Seasons for Relationships: Youth in China and the Mission of the Church* (Macau: Claretian Publications, 2019), 26–27.

Party, its economic system operates in a radically decentralized manner. Therefore, while politics do not easily reform in China, economic policies could more quickly adapt.[26]

Catholic Social Services, a Witness to Spiritual Poverty Alleviation

Catholic Social Services

Catholics belong to a small minority group in China. Catholic charity projects are just a drop in the bucket compared to many large-scale government projects. However, when they are undertaken out of love, they bear witness to the faith.

The year 2008 was a particularly difficult year for the Chinese nation as a whole. Many parts of South China were hit by snowstorms at the beginning of the year. Just a few months later, an earthquake measuring 7.8 on the Richter scale devastated the Wenchuan area in Sichuan Province.

Facing this disaster, in collaboration with local clergy and laity as well as receiving support from within China and abroad, such as from Caritas, Jinde Charities immediately launched a series of responses, including donations, emergency relief, rescue efforts, and epidemic prevention services. It provided medical and commodity support in the relocation camps, as well as psychological counseling and reconstruction of social institutes in the aftermath. It was an occasion for Catholic organizations like Jinde to witness to Christian faith and charity. It joined hand in hand with civil authorities and the Chinese people to work for the quake victims in their rehabilitation efforts and reconstruction projects.

---

[26] Jin Keyu, *The New China Playbook: Beyond Socialism and Capitalism* (London: Swift Press, 2023), 115–144.

Other social service centers of the Catholic Church are also present in Xi'an with an affiliate of Jinde Charity, and in Shanghai, with the Guanqi Social Service Center. The Guanqi Social Service Center was set up in the Shanghai Diocese in 2005. Since then it has launched many projects and activities, such as scholarships to support kindergartens, aid for orphanages and disabled people, and care for the elderly and for migrants. Other dioceses also offer similar social service–oriented projects catering to the needs of the people.

Jinde Charities was founded in May 1997 in Shijiazhuang. It is the first nonprofit organization (NPO) of the Chinese Catholic Church for social services, registered as Jinde Charities Foundation in 2011. In 2018 it became qualified as a foundation, with crowdfunding permits, to join the 9/9 Philanthropy Day for public fundraising for certain projects.

Witnesses Contributing to Spiritual Poverty Alleviation

In 2014, Pope Francis donated fifty thousand dollars through Jinde in support of the victims at Ludian, Yunnan Province. Besides emergency aid and disaster relief, in recent years Jinde has coordinated the Ricci Volunteer Program, which trains students for short-term volunteer work. It also has engaged in activities such as offering scholarships to subsidize students in need, visiting poor families, caring for the elderly, providing fertilizer and seeds to farmers, holding health seminars, HIV-AIDS prevention, and other social development services and projects. It has been operating a home for the elderly since 2002. As a government official once commented, "With its service to society, Jinde has built up a positive image of the Catholic Church."[27]

---

[27] UCANews, "First Catholic-Run Non-profit Organization Registered with Chinese Government," August 3, 2006.

In the past, some people would always be skeptical about philanthropic works being used for propaganda purposes, whether they came from the government or from the Church. During the peak of the coronavirus outbreak in China in early 2020, there were some concrete reports of sister-nurses providing ambulance services, and laypeople along with clergy and even a bishop doing voluntary work in attending to those in need. A social media group was created by a few sisters from different dioceses, including one from Wuhan, serving people in need of counseling in difficult times. As a Chinese saying goes, "In a crisis there could also be an opportunity." Like a blessing in disguise, all these experiences gave the people a sense of solidarity.

Pope Francis in his message for the World Day of the Poor in 2018 said, "We Christians are inspired by faith and by the imperative of charity, in humility offering our cooperation without seeking the limelight.... The Spirit is the source of our actions that reveal God's closeness.... It is precisely the poor who can break through our indifference.... The cry of the poor is also a cry of hope that reveals the certainty of future liberation."[28]

American political scientist Samuel Huntington foresaw that while the age of ideology had ended, future conflicts in the world would be dominated by the clash of civilizations.[29] Instead of speaking about the clash of civilizations, Pope Francis emphasized "the culture of encounter." He wrote in a letter,

> It is time to combat the culture of indifference, which makes the need of building the culture of encounter ever more urgent. A fruitful encounter gives back to

---

[28] Pope Francis, "Message on World Day of the Poor," November 18, 2018.

[29] Samuel Huntington, *The Clash of Civilizations and the Remaking of World Order* (New York: Simon and Schuster, 1996).

each person dignity as sons of God. If I do not look, if I do not stop, if I do not speak, I cannot make an encounter happen, and I cannot help build the culture of encounter. We must therefore find a way, through dialogue to walk together, making use of the reciprocal richness, historical and cultural, of our civilizations and build a common future of harmony.[30]

Pope Francis's personal witness of humble lifestyle and reaching out to the poor won the sympathy of the Chinese people and the trust of the authorities, leading to a historic agreement between the Holy See and China.

At this point, I would like to share a personal experience. In early 2018, I was surprised to have received an email from Szymon Holownia, a professor from Poland, who is also a journalist. He has two foundations and runs some charity projects in Zambia for orphans, children with AIDS or Down syndrome, and victims of human trafficking. He told me that he had found at the Johannesburg airport my book about China and the challenges and prospects of evangelization, and became interested. I provided him with some information about Catholic charity organizations mentioned in my book. A year later, I met him in person in Shanghai, learned that it was already his second visit to China, and together with Fr. Xue of Yahweh Caritas, he was helping to open a psychological intervention center in Hangzhou. Until a few years ago, China for Szymon was a reality so far away, difficult to understand. Now he is present here with concrete actions. As an age-old saying goes, "It is better to light a candle than to curse the darkness."

---

[30] Pope Francis, personal letter, November 27, 2018, in response to letter from Kin Sheung Chiaretto Yan with a gift of two books by Yan to the Holy Father.

Simple Lifestyle Consonant with Asian Values and with the Spirit of the Economy of Francesco

*Simple Lifestyle Advocated by Pope Francis—
and a Chinese Example*

In his encyclical *Fratelli Tutti*, Pope Francis began to reflect on universal fraternity and calls for a simple lifestyle inspired by St. Francis of Assisi. He ends with the prophetic image of St. Charles de Foucauld. Foucauld gave testimony of total surrender to God, identified with the least and abandoned while living in the depths of the African desert. Pope Francis exhorted us to dream together as a single human family at the beginning (*FT* 8) and repeats at the end of the encyclical that God inspires in each of us the dream that inspired Francis of Assisi and Charles de Foucauld to be a brother of every human being (*FT* 286–287). Pope Francis also highlighted inspiring figures from other Christian denominations, religions, and cultures, such as Martin Luther King Jr., Desmond Tutu, and Mahatma Gandhi. These examples remind me also of Tao Yuanming (365–427), an inspiring figure in Chinese history.

There is a Chinese proverb, "Refuse to bow for five bushels of grain" (*Buwei wudoumi zheyao*), which means refusing to swallow one's dignity for a meager existence. Five bushels of grain refers to the historical salary of a low-ranking official. The quotation comes from Tao Yuanming, a famous poet and politician. As a young man, he was rather idealistic. He thought that if he served as an official and assisted the king, he could make the world a wonderful place. His dream was shattered when he witnessed the rampant corruption and the sordid dealings in court. Feeling disdain and contempt for worldly affairs, he resigned and retreated to the countryside. Apart from his many poems, Tao is best known today for his *Peach Blossom Shangri-la*, a short work with the intriguing depiction of a land hidden from the outside world. The name Peach Blossom Spring (*Tao Hua Yuan*) has since become the standard Chinese term for utopia or paradise on earth.

Tao spent much of his time living simply in the countryside. The following is one of his poems, "Returning to Garden and Fields to Dwell" (*Gui Yuan Tian Ju*):

> I've loathed the madding crowd since I was a boy
> While hills and mountains have filled me with joy.
> By mistake I sought mundane careers
> And got entrapped in them for thirty years.
> Birds in the cage would long for wooded hills;
> Fish in the pond would yearn for flowing rills.
> So I reclaim the land in southern fields
> To suit my bent for reaping farmland yields.
> My farm contains a few acres of ground;
> My cottage has eight or nine rooms around.
> The elm and willow cover backside eaves
> While peach and plum trees shade my yard with leaves.
> The distant village dimly looms somewhere,
> With smoke from chimneys drifting in the air.
> In silent country lanes a stray dog barks;
> Amid the mulberry trees cocks crow with larks.
> My house is free from worldly moil or gloom
> While ease and quiet permeate my private room.
> When I escape from bitter strife with men,
> I live a free and easy life again.[31]

---

[31] Translation taken from Poetry Translation of English Learning, http://kekenet.com/kouyi/201503/363431.shtml.

His poems show a longing for a return to nature, deprecation of artificial limits or restrictions in interpersonal relationships, and the desire for a simple life. He shows perseverance and integrity in his poem, and he has been regarded as the first Chinese poet associated with the fields-and-gardens genre of poetry.[32]

The Economy of Francesco (EoF) and an Economic Paradigm Shift

Just as in *Laudato Si'*, Pope Francis used an integral approach in *Fratelli Tutti*. For him, ecology, politics, the economy, and social problems of the poor are all interconnected. His encyclical *Fratelli Tutti* builds on the parable of the Good Samaritan to show how we have to be intimately involved with those in need who are near us. He explains how we must act at local levels very concretely, and work with others so that our fraternity radiates outward to the ends of the earth.

Fratelli Tutti makes a clear distinction about people, populace, and populism. Pope Francis was very critical of leaders who use the common people for their own advantage instead of "being at the service of the people."[33] The encyclical also criticizes the corruption of political systems that often serve the interests of elites and privileged classes, and undermine the common good. He appealed for concern for the vulnerable, respect for human dignity, and recognition of the rights of migrants, while working to avoid the injustices that cause migration in the first place. Above all, the political sphere should be a place of encounter, of work for the good of the people, and not a place to "hide behind

---

[32] Burton Watson, *Chinese Lyricism: Shih Poetry from the Second to the Twelfth Century* (New York: Columbia University Press, 1971), 79.

[33] Luigino Bruni, *Guida alla lettura dell'Enciclico Fratelli Tutti* [Guide to Reading Fratelli Tutti] (Milano: Paoline Edizioni, 2020), 14.

a populism that exploits them demagogically, or a liberalism that serves the economic interests of the powerful" (*FT* 155).

Pope Francis pointed out that neoliberalism simply reproduces itself by resorting to magic theories of spillover or trickle-down economics,[34] which do not solve social problems such as inequality but instead give rise to new forms of violence threatening the fabric of society. He adds that "the fragility of world systems in the face of the pandemic has demonstrated that not everything can be resolved by market freedom" (*FT* 168). The world therefore needs a new type of politics that promotes dialogue and solidarity, triggering a call for a change in the economic paradigm.

Subsequently, a month and a half after the signing of *Fratelli Tutti*, an international event, The Economy of Francesco (EoF), was held in Assisi from November 19 to 21, 2020, featuring young economists and entrepreneurs from all over the world. In the event, many testimonies were shared. Particularly relevant and one of the main inspirational experiences that led to the EoF process was the initiative of Chiara Lubich, who called for an Economy of Communion (EoC), inaugurated thirty years ago in Brazil.

Pope Francis publicly acknowledged and encouraged the EoC initiative by meeting its members gathered from all over the world in Rome.[35] Since the financial crisis of 2007–2008, popes have spoken openly about the crisis facing the global economy and the urgent need for an alternative economic system. In recent years, the EoC initiative has received official attention. Pope Benedict

---

[34] Spillover or trickle-down theory is the economic proposition that taxes on businesses and the wealthy in society should be reduced as a means to stimulate business investment in the short term and benefit society at large in the long term.

[35] Pope Francis, "Address to Participants in the Meeting 'Economy of Communion,'" sponsored by the Focolare Movement, Rome, February 4, 2017.

XVI in his social encyclical *Caritas in Veritate* refers explicitly to the kind of experiences the EoC brings about.[36]

The EoC was established in 1991 by Chiara Lubich, and the initiative expresses a culture of giving as opposed to a culture of having. The EoC originates from the Focolare Movement, whose spiritual identity is based on striving for communion (or unity) with others. This culture of giving involves a communion (or sharing) of goods among Focolare members as well as helping people who are not members of the movement. Hence, the EoC can be described as a manifestation of the culture of giving in terms of economic activity. Entrepreneurs within the EoC consider it essential to make profits to ensure that their businesses remain viable and expand. They also consider it necessary to distribute their profits to those who are in need and to promote social development. Lubich elaborates on how profits are used in this economic model.

One part of these profits would be used to help the business grow; a second part would be used to help those who are in need, giving them the possibility of living a dignified life while looking for work or by offering them work in the business itself. Finally, a third part would be used to develop educational structures for the formation of men and women motivated by a culture of giving. The goal would be the formation of "new people," which means business leaders, entrepreneurs, workers, and students with a new mentality of communion. Without such new people, it is not possible to build a new society.[37]

The idea of the EoC came about when Lubich visited Brazil in 1991. She noticed where she was staying the enormous circle

---

[36] Pope Benedict XVI, *Caritas in Veritate*, June 29, 2009, 39, 46.

[37] Chiara Lubich, "The Experience of the 'Economy of Communion': A Proposal of Economic Action from the Spirituality of Unity," in *The Economy of Communion: Toward a Multi-dimensional Economic Culture*, ed. Luigino Bruni (New York: New City Press, 2002), 15–16.

of slums (*favelas*) that seemed to her to be a "crown of thorns" around the city of São Paulo, a vibrant economic hub of Brazil. In her diary for May 15, 1991, Lubich reaffirmed that poverty constituted one of the biggest and most tragic problems on earth. She prayed to God for a new insight on how to act. A few days later, an idea emerged. She reasoned that it was not enough to exercise acts of charity, works of mercy, or the communion of goods between individual persons. She was addressing a group of entrepreneurs, people capable of managing profitable companies efficiently. The innovation she proposed was that the profits be put in common according to the three parts mentioned above. The actual amount to each of the three would depend on the needs of the company. In this way, Lubich's proposal addressed not only a social problem of the poor and marginalized, but went directly to the heart of the question of economics.

Bernhard Callebaut recalls his conversation in Petropolis, Brazil, in 1988 with Leonardo Boff, the famous author of many works on liberation theology, and also a keen observer and participant in the project of ecclesial base communities (*communicado ecclesia de base*; CEB). Boff said that a reason for the relative lack of real impact of liberation theology and the CEBs on Brazilian society came from their failure to engage the middle class.[38]

The dream that Chiara sought to realize is equality in the evangelical sense, where all are sons and daughters of God. The EoC was created for this end, and the Latin American church has taken to heart the preferential option for the poor. Lubich recognized the big gap in Brazilian society between the rich and poor. She saw a need not only to free the poor but also to free

---

[38] Bernhard Callebaut, "Economy of Communion: A Sociological Inquiry on a Contemporary Charismatic Inspiration in Economic and Social Life," *Claritas: Journal of Dialogue & Culture* 1, no. 1 (March 2012): 80.

the rich, with the idea that true liberty is found in real social relationships. As Callebaut points out, "Her initiative brought together two functions of society: the economic and the social, symbolically represented by the figures of the entrepreneur and the poor." He sees it as a "prophetic economy," in Max Weber's terms, linking the preferential option for the poor of the Latin American church and the birth of new ecclesial movements.[39]

Fratelli Tutti affirms the principle that the right to private property is secondary to the universal destination of goods. Luigino Bruni points out that the Church has recalled this principle since the times of the early Church Fathers, that the right to the private ownership of goods is subordinate to a more fundamental principle, that "the goods we possess are a gift." This principle is rooted in a biblical humanism where "the earth belongs to Yahweh" and we are only tenants of the land that is always promised and given.[40] Related to this priority, the encyclical also speaks of the role of an entrepreneur:

> Business activity is essentially "a noble vocation, directed to producing wealth and improving our world." God encourages us to develop the talents he gave us, and he has made our universe one of immense potential. In God's plan, each individual is called to promote his or her own development, and this includes finding the best economic and technological means of multiplying goods and increasing wealth. Business abilities, which are a gift from God, should always be clearly directed to the development of others and to eliminating poverty, especially through the creation of diversified work opportunities. (*FT* 123)

---

[39] Ibid., 71–82.
[40] Bruni, *Guida alla lettura dell'Enciclico Fratelli Tutti*, 10–11.

For Edmond Eh, the EoC is an alternative model of subsidiarity economics that addresses the weaknesses of both the market economy and the centralized economy. Businesses under this model have to operate efficiently so as to survive and remain competitive in the context of the free market. As well, they are self-regulating by nature and do not require governmental interference in order to behave in an ethical manner. "On an Aristotelian analysis, businesses of the EoC practise *oikonomia* which promotes well-being for all instead of *chrematistike* which leads to the accumulation of private wealth." He says, "It is a significant model of common good entrepreneurship that integrates spirituality with business practices in a manner that promotes fairness and solidarity for all."[41]

Since 1991, hundreds of enterprises have participated in the EoC initiatives in Brazil and worldwide. As Lubich intended, it has become not only a personal but a collective lifestyle, a culture called the "culture of giving." They are initiatives that do not oppose the free market system, but work in favor of the poor. It is a new way of thinking about business and social justice, and therefore to develop educational projects to foster a culture of giving. When Pope Francis called for the Economy of Francesco (EoF) event and a new economic paradigm, there were already many entrepreneurs, academics, and young people who could share their expertise and experiences.

Pope Francis on the First World Day of the Poor in 2017 described the global scenario of the scandalous growth of poverty in broad sectors of society and urged us not to remain passive and give up.[42] In his address to the participants of an Economy of Communion meeting in Rome, he said,

---

[41] Edmond Eh, "Aristotle, Lubich, and Ratzinger on a New Economic Paradigm," *The Journal of the Macau Ricci Institute*, no. 7 (2021).

[42] Pope Francis, "Message on First World Day of the Poor," November 19, 2017.

The principal ethical dilemma of capitalism is the creation of discarded people, then trying to hide them or make sure they are no longer seen. A serious form of poverty in a civilization is when it is no longer able to see its poor, who are first discarded and then hidden. The economy of communion, if it wants to be faithful to its charism, must not only care for the victims, but build a system where there are ever fewer victims, where possibly there may no longer be any.[43]

For Stefano Zamagni, president of the Pontifical Academy of Social Science, in taking on the many challenges in the economic field today, the mission of EoC is not to offer the possibility of fighting capitalism from a revolutionary perspective or to change the shape of the market economy, but to humanize it. Therefore, EoC's contribution is to emphasize human dignity and participation of employees in the objectives, decision-making, and management of enterprises in a civil economy, and to transform such enterprises from within, starting a process of change in their way of operating.[44]

The encyclical *Fratelli Tutti* uses the parable of the Good Samaritan to describe the issue of human relationships, and comments on the account of creation of the world and of humanity. Cain kills his brother Abel and then hears God ask, "Where is your brother Abel?" Not answering God's question, Cain asks, "Am I my brother's keeper?" (Gen. 4:9). He thus declared he was not Abel's keeper. He committed fratricide because he was not a keeper. Luigino Bruni concludes his reading

---

[43] Pope Francis, "Address to Participants in the Meeting 'Economy of Communion,'" February 4, 2017.

[44] Carlo Cefaloni, "Dialogando con Stefano Zamagni," *Città Nuova*, July 2021, 30–33.

guide to the encyclical with another beautiful account of what biblical brotherhood means.[45] Joseph said to his brothers, "I am Joseph! Is my father still in good health?" But his brothers were not able to answer him, because they were terrified at his presence. Then Joseph said to his brothers, "Come close to me." When they had done so, he said, "I am your brother Joseph, whom you once sold on the road to Egypt" (Gen. 45:3–4). While many are still unaware of the fratricide happening,[46] Pope Francis was making an appeal at the international level, going beyond race, creed, and national boundaries, going beyond the natural fraternity of blood, to that of a fraternity in the spirit.

The Chinese Economic Model with Its Cultural Roots and Future Trajectory

Pope Francis, speaking in *Fratelli Tutti* of the relationship between politics and economics, favored the universal common good and the protection of weaker states. He underlined the role of the state while speaking about political love, saying, "Politics must not be subject to the economy, nor should the economy be subject to the dictates of an efficiency-driven paradigm of technocracy" (*FT* 177).

---

[45] Bruni, *Guida alla lettura dell'Enciclico Fratelli Tutti*, 19–21.

[46] Some thoughtful analysts on human rights emphasize that the most fundamental of rights is the right to life, even in the material sense: for example, the right to food and nutrition. For what does a person do with all the rights, even the noblest ones, if he or she is dying of hunger? If this right was officially recognized and promoted, perhaps rich nations would not waste incredible amounts of money and resources on armaments. Instead, there is an ongoing "fratricide" or "silent genocide of the poor" in the name of a free market. "Silent genocide" is a phrase coined by Professor Abdus Salam in "A Silent Genocide (Rich vs. Poor Nations)," address to Facing the 21st Century: Threats and Promises conference, *UNESCO Courier*, May 1988, 27–28.

Benedict XVI, while still a cardinal, also spoke of the relationship between Church and the economy, and the responsibility for the future of the world economy.[47] The centralized economy is understood to be at the service of the community instead of profit-making, while the market economy is understood to operate on the principles of efficiency instead of the principles of morality. It is believed that, in a centralized economy, market forces can be made to act justly due to state intervention, but a centralized economy entails a form of determinism because it assumes that regulations are always designed to produce what is in the best interest of society at large. Ultimately, the market economy also fails because it entails another form of determinism when market forces are assumed to be intrinsically good and to always produce good outcomes. Therefore, a new economic paradigm that serves as a viable alternative to existing models must take into account both efficiency and ethics. For any economic system to be ethical, it must be guided toward the common good, and this emerging system must strike a balance between the market economy and state intervention.

As mentioned above, China has developed its economic system in recent decades in an experimental way, with resilience, and succeeded. In this process, state intervention has played an important role in the efficient alleviation of poverty. Needless to say, the relationship between the central government and provincial governments is an important topic. Evaluating the performance of local governments that are competing in GDP output has been important for economic efficiency in the past. Nevertheless, it generates other problems, such as corruption and pollution. I have mentioned the shift in the evaluation system to

---

[47] Joseph Ratzinger, "Church and Economy: Responsibility for the Future of the World Economy," *Communio: International Catholic Review* 13 (1986): 199–204.

double down on green GDP and the happiness index. The social teachings of the Church emphasize principles such as subsidiarity, solidarity, and fraternity. For me, China is actually working out an economic system with values consonant to these principles, but perhaps without using the same terms.

At the very beginning of the Chinese economic reform, China was one of the poorest nations in the world, yet it has lifted eight hundred million of its people out of poverty in recent decades.[48] China currently is assisting many African countries and other developing countries to build their infrastructure, bringing in capital, technological know-how, and manpower. According to much international media, this represents another form of colonization. Another way of looking at is that China, with its economic resources, is filling a vacuum in a continent that has been exploited and neglected for centuries. On the geopolitical chessboard, only time will tell of success or failure. One positive effect is that Western developed countries, attempting to counter China, are now paying more attention and offering aid to Africa. Needless to say, it is highly important to use more of the local workforce to generate employment in the host countries. Chinese companies are learning how to collaborate with local governments and are often willing to adjust their policies, including restructuring loans.

In recent times, there has been a lot of talk of competition, tension, conflicts of interest, and strategic rivalry in Chinese-US relations. Ironically, China's endogenous development and success in building its infrastructure perhaps motivated the

---

[48] While 2018 World Bank data indicated that China has lifted 740 million people out of poverty in the past four decades, the United Nations reports the figure of up to 800 million in 2021. See United Nations News, *Economic Development*, March 2021, https://news.un.org/en/story/2021/03/1087472.

Biden administration's infrastructure initiative, Build Back Better (BBB), to boost the US economy. In Trump's second term now, he adopts the Drill Baby Drill approach instead, which represents an opposing vision. BBB emphasizes a sustainable, regulated transition to renewables, while Trump's policies favor immediate fossil-fuel expansion with deregulation. Even within the United States, the debate centers on climate urgency versus short-term economic benefits. For better or for worse, we are all interconnected and interdependent. What will the future bring?

5

Freedom of Religion and the Golden Rule of Reciprocity

The issue of religious freedom affects Sino-Vatican relations. The Roman Catholic Church shares positive values with other cultures that provide common ground for dialogue. Pope Francis emphasized a synodal church projecting outward toward a culture of encounter, working unceasingly for a fraternal dialogue of peace. Chinese President Xi Jinping urges his people to fulfill the Chinese dream, emphasizing the core values of harmony, friendship, civilization, and rejuvenation of the nation. Could this dialogue on values contribute to the spiritual dimension of Chinese civilization? Would normalization of relations between China and the Holy See benefit China and the Catholic Church—and contribute to world peace and harmony? The first part of this chapter tackles these issues, and the second part explores how Catholics practice their faith and face challenges in a rapidly changing China, characterized by urbanization and migration. The chapter also analyzes the mission of the Church in the present situation, formation of the laity and youth, and the testimonies of how Catholic communities are coping with social changes and the new religious policies.

There are two prevailing attitudes regarding the Sino-Vatican relationship and the situation of the Catholic Church in China: one is to engage actively in dialogue, while the other is skeptical about such efforts. Resistance to dialogue can arise from both the Chinese authorities and the Holy See. From the Catholic perspective, those who want to engage actively in dialogue generally take a step-by-step approach.[1] Those who are skeptical about dialogue reason as follows: unless there is complete freedom of religion in China, there can be no genuine dialogue. However, we need to ask, first of all: What is complete freedom of religion, and what does the Chinese Constitution say about religion?

Dialogue between the Holy See and Chinese Authorities

Article 36 of the Chinese Constitution states, "Citizens of the People's Republic of China enjoy freedom of religious belief. No state organ, public organization or individual may compel citizens to believe in, or not to believe in, any religion; nor may they discriminate against citizens who believe in, or do not believe in, any religion. *The state protects normal religious activities.* No one may make use of religion to engage in activities that disrupt public order, impair the health of citizens or interfere with the educational system of the state. Religious bodies and religious affairs are not subject to any foreign domination."[2]

In 2018 we celebrated the seventieth anniversary of the UN Universal Declaration of Human Rights. Article 18 of this declaration states, "Everyone has the right to freedom of thought, conscience and religion; this right includes *freedom* to change his religion or belief, and freedom, either alone or in community

---

[1] See, for example, John Cardinal Tong, "The Future of the Sino-Vatican Dialogue from an Ecclesiological Point of View," *Hong Kong Sunday Examiner*, February 4, 2017.

[2] Constitution of the People's Republic of China, Article 36, December 4, 1982 (emphasis added).

with others and in public or private, *to manifest his religion or belief* in teaching, practice, worship and observance."[3]

If we compare the two articles, we see that both include the freedom to practice and to manifest one's faith and the freedom to change one's religious belief (freedom of conversion). We also see a difference: the Chinese Constitution emphasizes protection and no foreign domination, while the UN declaration emphasizes the freedom to manifest one's religious belief. One focuses inward on protection, and the other focuses outward on manifestation. We may trace this divergence to cultural differences between East and West.

These cultural differences are evident in other universal moral teachings, such as the Golden Rule. This maxim refers to the ethics of reciprocity or reciprocal love, as expressed in a positive or a negative form. Variants of the Golden Rule can be found in many religions and cultures. For Western culture, it is mostly inspired by Jesus's words in the Gospels: "Do to others as you would have them do to you" (Matt. 7:12; Luke 6:31). In China, the rule reflects the wording Confucius gave it: "Do not do to others what you would not want others to do to you." The way of applying or expressing this concept, however, could vary culturally. In the realm of international affairs, for example, China often insists on a policy of not interfering in the internal affairs of others. In contrast, the foreign policy of the United States has often been that of putting pressure on other countries to accept its values and systems. Some Asians want to assert their cultural identity as a response and propose so-called Asian values. Contrary to what many people may think, modernization in Asia does not necessarily mean Westernization.

Another document addresses the meaning of religious freedom: *Christian Witness in a Multi-Religious World:*

---

[3] UN General Assembly, The Universal Declaration of Human Rights, Paris, December 10, 1948 (emphasis mine).

Recommendations for Conduct. This text was signed in 2011 by three major Christian bodies: the Pontifical Council for Interreligious Dialogue (PCID), the World Council of Churches (WCC), and the World Evangelical Alliance (WEA). Despite the nuance of approaches between the Catholic and other Christian churches regarding evangelization, in this 2011 document they were able to come up with an integral approach balancing proclamation and dialogue. The study and consultation were unprecedented, and the subsequent signing of the document was historic, involving interfaith and intercultural—as well as ecumenical—collaboration. Along with principles of service and love of neighbors as witness in multireligious contexts, there is the principle that addresses freedom of religion and belief: "Religious freedom including the right to publicly profess, practice, *propagate* and change one's religion flows from the very dignity of the human person which is grounded in the creation of all human beings in the image and likeness of God (cf. Gen. 1:26). Thus, all human beings have *equal rights and responsibilities.* Where any religion is instrumentalized for political ends, or where religious persecution occurs, Christians are called to engage in a prophetic witness denouncing such actions."[4]

In addition to the freedom to practice and change one's religion, the principle also includes a third element mentioned in the "Christian Witness" document, namely, the freedom to "propagate" one's faith. This freedom is a basic human right but is balanced by certain responsibilities. Another important point is that "religion should not be instrumentalized for political ends," a concern China has also voiced in China-Vatican relations.

---

[4] Pontifical Council for Interreligious Dialogue, World Council of Churches, and World Evangelical Alliance, *Christian Witness in a Multireligious World: Recommendations for Conduct*, Bangkok, January 2011 (emphasis mine).

It is interesting to note that the PCID of the Catholic Church signed this document, together with the WCC Program on Interreligious Dialogue and Cooperation.[5] While some Christian groups—including, for example, Pentecostals and evangelicals—stress that they have a mission to propagate their faith, the Catholic Church emphasizes that this mission best occurs in interreligious dialogue, that is, when all parties are open, and each person or each group has the right to manifest and to propagate its faith and culture, but in a respectful manner.

By clarifying these additional terms crucial for religious dialogue, the 2011 joint document not only represents a step forward for the relationship between the Catholic Church and other Christian churches but also provides relevant ground for China-Vatican rapprochement. As I mentioned earlier, regarding issues of religious freedom, the Chinese Constitution stresses the protection of its citizens from foreign influence rather than manifestation and propagation of faith. Very few people capture this subtle difference. While other churches simply stress propagation of their faith, the Catholic Church stresses respectful proclamation in the spirit of dialogue. In my view, this position of the Catholic Church is more in accord with the Chinese situation.

Inculturation or Sinicization

With regard to the two attitudes mentioned earlier—engaging actively in dialogue or skeptical retreat from dialogue—I opt for the former, for the simple reason that dialogue is a useful tool to bridge any gap or resolve any conflict. I do not personally think that China is doing enough to protect religious freedom. It is

---

[5] Indunil J. Kodithuwakku K., "Christian Witness in a Multi-religious World: Recommendations for Conduct; Thinking Back and Looking Ahead," *International Bulletin of Missionary Research* 37 (2013): 109–113.

engaged in an ongoing process of opening up more and more. Why not facilitate this process through constructive dialogue? In order to define what complete freedom of religion is, we also must listen to the Chinese view and at the same time be open and committed to respectful dialogue. That is, true dialogue needs sincere participation from both sides.

Dialogue requires patience. Chinese leadership may have other priorities. China is governed by consensus building of the collective leadership, with mechanisms of checks and balances.

The Chinese concept of sinicization (i.e., integrating something to be in conformity with Chinese culture or expressing it with Chinese characteristics) is not contradictory to the Catholic concept of inculturation (i.e., a continuous process of the Church to proclaim the gospel so that it enters into the cultures of the peoples without compromising the integrity of the Christian faith). Even in evangelization, there is a mutual influence between the evangelizing and the evangelized cultures ("interculturation"[6]). The emphasis should be that the Catholic Church sees inculturation from a spiritual and religious perspective, while the Chinese authorities see sinicization of religions from the perspective of administration and politics. Keeping in mind the different cultural perspectives and the separate spheres of competence, I believe that controversies and conflicts of interest can be resolved. I suggest that these two concepts, inculturation and sinicization, if tackled well and effectively, are complementary, inasmuch as Christianity can spread in China without the centuries-old label of being a foreign religion, and on the side of China, its rise as a responsible

---

[6] Chiara Lubich first used the term "interculturation" in "Conversation on Inculturation," Nairobi, 1992. See Kin Sheung Chiaretto Yan, *Evangelization in China: Challenges and Prospects* (Maryknoll, NY: Orbis Books, 2014), 134–135.

world power would be welcomed by others while maintaining "socialism with Chinese characteristics in a new era."[7]

Respectful dialogue means expressing one's ideas freely and at the same time respecting the views of the other with openness. A related idea in Confucianism is the notion of being "harmonious while diversified," that is, diversity (distinction) in unity. This concept recognizes that, although people have differences in opinions, interests, preferences, and profiles, they should first maintain peace. People should live in harmony with each other, even as they retain their diversity.

Chinese President Xi Jinping outlined new policies concerning religions in China today. On May 20, 2016, at the Central United Front Work Conference, he stressed that religious activities should (1) actively guide the respective religions to adapt to socialist society, (2) adhere to the principle of sinicization and promote the rule of law in religious activities, and (3) guide religions to promote economic development, social harmony, cultural prosperity, national unity, and the reunification of the motherland.[8]

What consequences will these policies bring about? This question is of particular interest to the Catholic Church in China, especially for the inculturation of the Christian faith in the Chinese context. China has gone through tremendous changes since its open-door policy in 1979. The leader of this

---

[7] The weeklong Nineteenth National Congress of the Communist Party of China (CPC) concluded on October 24, 2017, during which the CPC Constitution was amended to include "Xi Jinping Thought on Socialism with Chinese Characteristics for a New Era" as a new component of the party's guide for action. See *Xinhua News*, October 24, 2017.

[8] President Xi Jinping addressed a conference on religions held in Beijing, April 22–23, 2016. Xi said that religious affairs carry "special importance" in the work of the CPC and the central government, and he promised to fully implement the party's policy on religious freedom and help religions adapt to the socialist society. See *Global Times*, April 25, 2016.

change, Deng Xiaoping, coined the phrase "building socialism with Chinese characteristics." By putting this proposal into practice, enormous potential has been unleashed, and China has experienced unparalleled development.

An article on the editorial page of the *Global Times,* a major newspaper of the Chinese government, mentioned that there is a simple way to describe China's historical development.[9] While the founding of the People's Republic relied on Marxism, China's economic success depended on implementing reforms that opened the country to the global economy. In this implementation, China accepted some modern Western ideologies for the sake of the nation, its people, and the revival of Chinese culture. However, new ideas must be verified through praxis. China is now defining the core values of the Chinese dream that the article suggests must be maintained while accepting modern Western influence. The West and its positive values, in my view, are deeply rooted in Christianity. As such, the future of China's integration of Western and Chinese culture will entail the integration of Christianity.

As mentioned earlier, Matteo Ricci pioneered a successful dialogue based on his vision of inculturating the Christian faith in China, just as the church fathers did centuries before in the encounter between the gospel of Jesus Christ and Greco-Roman culture.[10] Today's dialogue is not limited to Confucianism as with Ricci, but should also take into account Daoism, Chinese Buddhism, and recent developments in Chinese culture, including socialism with Chinese characteristics.

---

[9] Chen Ming, "The Return of Confucianism in Modern Practice Edification," *Global Times*, editorial, Chinese edition, March 21, 2016.

[10] John Paul II, "Message to the Participants in the International Conference Commemorating the Fourth Centenary of the Arrival in Beijing of Father Matteo Ricci," October 24, 2001, 3.

A Culture of Encounter between Christianity and China

I mentioned in chapter 1 that Chinese culture emphasizes harmony and relationships with a dialectical way of thinking. It has a disposition, in this sense, to approach the mystery of the Trinity, which is so essential to Christianity. An in-depth analysis of Daoist dialectics of harmony and Christian Trinitarian theology could contribute to the inculturation of the Christian faith in the Chinese context in ways that could contribute to the Church and to the positive development of Chinese culture in today's world. In chapter 3, I made a comparison between the Chinese and the Christian concept of fraternity. These are underlying themes for dialogue. On the World Day of Peace 2014, Pope Francis gave an important message titled "Fraternity, the Foundation and Pathway to Peace"[11] and instituted a new form of dialogue of fraternity for peace. Other values of the Chinese dream are "prosperity" and "civilization," which correspond to the themes of "a healthy and caring economy for happiness" and an "integral ecology and full human development," as elaborated in Pope Francis's apostolic exhortation *Evangelii Gaudium* and his encyclical *Laudato Si'*. Piero Coda summarizes the vision of Pope Francis for the emerging Church in four words: mercy, poverty, synodality, and encounter.[12]

Mercy. In Latin, mercy is signified by "misericordia." This is two words combined, the Latin *miseriae*, meaning misery, and *cordis*, heart. Pope Francis declared 2016 to be the Jubilee Year of Mercy. He encourages Catholics to have an open heart toward forgiving others, as God forgives each one of us.

---

[11] Pope Francis, "Message for the Celebration of the World Day of Peace: Fraternity, the Foundation and Pathway to Peace," January 1, 2014.

[12] Radio Vatican, "Giubileo dei nunzi, Becciu: Aperti al dialogo, forti nell'identità," interview with Angelo Becciu, Vatican's deputy secretary of state, ANSA News Agency, September 15, 2016.

Poverty. It brings about humility and goes toward the poor and the marginalized. The Church should not rely on aspects of wealth, human power, and human instruments, but must be founded on the power of God.

Synodality. It comes from the Greek word *synodus*, which means walking together and looking in the same direction. This characteristic is a way of being in the Church, as Pope Francis often repeated to us; it is seeing things and living from the standpoint of communion. "Broadly, it refers to the active participation of all the faithful in the life and mission of the Church."[13]

Encounter. We live in a culturally diverse world with many challenges, but there are also many opportunities. Indeed, Christians are constantly challenged by the presence of people of other religions and cultures. The Christian identity lies in opening up to others, creating a relationship with those who are different. Encounter means opening ourselves up to dialogue with others who are different from us.

I would like to conclude this part on religious freedom—with regard to the situation of the Catholic Church in China, and the ongoing dialogue between China and the Holy See—suggesting adherence to some basic attitudes. First, both sides want to continue the dialogue. Second, the Holy See wishes to maintain the unity of the Church and emphasizes reconciliation of the official and the underground communities of Chinese Catholics; likewise, the Chinese authorities would not like the abnormal situation of the Catholic Church to continue to develop in China. Third, the Holy See has concern for the feelings and sentiments of Catholics, whether they belong to the official or the

---

[13] Joint International Commission for Theological Dialogue between the Roman Catholic Church and the Orthodox Church, "Synodality and Primacy during the First Millennium: Towards a Common Understanding in Service to the Unity of the Church," Chiete, September 21, 2016, 3.

underground community. The Chinese authorities want Catholic believers to practice their faith within the boundary of the laws of the state. In the final analysis, the Holy See and the Chinese authorities have two different perspectives: one is religious and spiritual, the other, political and administrative. Both sides have different starting points, but the concrete result could coincide and benefit both sides.

Lest the needed dialogue be threatened, ideological opposition is to be avoided between the official and the underground communities, between the Catholic Church in China and the universal Roman Catholic Church, and between the Catholic Church and the Chinese authorities or the Communist Party. Though at times the other side may seem tough or resolute, still the dialogue must continue. The normalization of relations between the Holy See and the People's Republic of China would certainly be helpful for the healthy development of the Catholic Church in China. Normalization would be beneficial for mutual enrichment, and have positive repercussions for the path of humanity toward a better future.

With regard to the Taiwan issue, there is a common misconception that the Holy See is deciding between Taiwan or Mainland China on the political front. The Holy See for decades has been seeking to normalize relations with the People's Republic of China and to resume the post of apostolic nunciature in Beijing vacant since 1951. The ultimate goal of the Church is proclaiming the faith and taking care of its flock. When the PRC took the place of the Republic of China (ROC) with its government in Taiwan as the sole representative of China in the United Nations in 1971, the head of the mission from the Holy See in Taiwan was downgraded to chargé d'affaires from the rank of nuncio, which was equivalent to that of ambassador. Therefore, the diplomatic ranking of the Holy See mission in Taiwan will have no change, as far as the Church is concerned, no matter what changes take place in the relations between the Holy See and Mainland China. It is important not to be held hostage by politicizing the Taiwan issue.

As Christians, our dream is to fulfill the wish of Jesus and be united in our diversity. To achieve this goal, dialogue is necessary. Dialogue is not a means to an end but is a way of being in the world because it is the life of God, the Trinity. Trinity is relationship; it is infinite dialogue and total reciprocity. Not insignificantly, Jesus calls reciprocal love "his new commandment."

From the perception of the West, there is no religious freedom in China; yet it is guaranteed in the Chinese Constitution. Why is there such a perception when in reality there is a revival of Buddhism and other traditional religions? In the past, there were more Catholics than Protestants, but the Protestants (all churches put together) have since long overtaken the Catholics by a huge margin.[14]

Since the nineteenth century, Christianity, Catholic and Protestant alike, has been associated with Western imperialism in the minds of the Chinese people. The Chinese government, because of this perception, is cautious that religion—particularly Catholicism, which is well organized at the international level—may become a political tool for foreign interference. (Think of

---

[14] According to figures released by the State Council Information Office, Protestant Christians number five times more than Catholics, with a total of thirty-two million Protestants and six million Catholics among the two hundred million believers in China. The State Council Information Office of the People's Republic of China, *China's Policies and Practices on Protecting Freedom of Religious Belief*, April 2018. Pew Research Center statistics indicates that Protestants number six times the total of Catholics, with fifty-eight million Protestants and nine million Catholics in China. Forum on Religion & Public Life Global Christianity, "Christians in China," Pew Research Center, December 2011. Although the Pew Research Center reports a higher total number of Christians in general than the State Council Information Office of China, both statistics show that Protestants outnumber Catholics by a margin of five to six times.

Tibet with Western support for the Dalai Lama, or Xinjiang, wrong as it may be, which is associated with terrorism and separatism.) This is something that neither the government nor ordinary citizens in their common psyche will tolerate. Think of the perceptions expressed in these sayings: "a Christian more, a Chinese less" and now the "patriotic association." Saint John Paul II appealed through Radio Veritas to the Chinese Catholics that there is "no opposition or incompatibility in being at the same time truly Christian and authentically Chinese."[15]

Certainly, to ensure stability, the government is undoubtedly authoritarian, a price the people seem ready to pay. Interestingly, Singapore's political structure could be a point of reference in this regard. This small Southeast Asian city-state with its "authoritarian modernism" became a major reference point for China. Although more than 75 percent of the population of Singapore are ethnic Chinese, it is a multiracial and multireligious society. Therefore, racial and religious harmony are vital to Singapore's social cohesion.[16] In China, likewise, besides the Han Chinese majority, fifty-five other ethnic minority groups are present. Further discussion and comparison could be interesting but is beyond the scope of the present research.

Interculturality, a Two-Way Process, Instead of Unidirectional Inculturation or Sinicization

Cardinal Joseph Ratzinger, who later became Pope Benedict XVI, when speaking to Asian bishops in Hong Kong about the mission of the Church, said, "We should no longer speak of inculturation

---

[15] Pope John Paul II, "Address to the Chinese Catholic Community in Asia," Manila, February 18, 1981, 3–4.

[16] See the Ministry of Home Affairs of Singapore, Maintenance of Religious Harmony Act, for Maintaining Racial and Religious Harmony, November 9, 1990.

but of the meeting of cultures or 'inter-culturality.'" He coined this new term to express more precisely "the meeting of cultures" that takes place when the culture of Christian faith encounters other cultures. "Only if all cultures are potentially universal and open to each other can inter-culturality lead to flourishing new forms."[17] He wanted to promote the encounter of cultures as reciprocal enrichment.

Pope John Paul II spoke openly of the desire for dialogue between China and the whole Catholic Church, which would benefit the whole human family. In an international conference held at the Pontifical Gregorian University commemorating the four hundredth anniversary of Matteo Ricci's arrival in Beijing, John Paul II said, "I hope and pray that the path opened by Father Matteo Ricci between East and West, between Christianity and Chinese culture, will give rise to new instances of dialogue and reciprocal human and spiritual enrichment."[18]

In contrast to the culture of indifference, Pope Francis in recent years advocated a "culture of encounter." He dreams of a Church that is going out for its mission rather than self-preservation.[19] People live in a culturally diverse world with many challenges, but there are also many opportunities. For Pope Francis, Christians are constantly challenged by the presence of people of other religions and cultures. The Christian identity lies in opening up to others, creating a relationship with those who are different.

While recent popes have spoken about interculturality and encounters, I observe that President Xi Jinping also speaks of

---

[17] Joseph Ratzinger, "Christ, Faith and the Challenge of Cultures," meeting with the Doctrinal Commissions in Asia, Hong Kong, March 3, 1993.

[18] John Paul II, Message to Participants of the International Conference Commemorating the Fourth Centenary of the Arrival in Beijing of Fr. Matteo Ricci, October 24, 2001, 7.

[19] Pope Francis, Apostolic Exhortation *Evangelii Gaudium,* November 24, 2013, 27.

the encounter of civilizations to promote an inclusive world civilization.[20] He introduced the Global Civilization Initiative (GCI) for the first time in 2023 at a high-level meeting in dialogue with world political parties. It was ten years after China had launched the initiative of building a community with a shared future for humanity and the Belt and Road Initiative (BRI). Therefore, China is not only keen on promoting infrastructure or economic projects; it now wants to promote exchanges and mutual learning between cultures for the progress of human civilization, while contributing Chinese wisdom and experience.

In 2024 I participated in two academic conferences in China relating to dialogue between civilizations. They were organized by the Institute of Silk Road Studies at the North West University at Xi'an with the support of the government. The first was the Xi'an *Jingjiao* (the luminous religion) Forum, about the famous stele of Xi'an recording the history of the first arrival of Christianity in China via the Silk Road from the Eastern Syriac Church in 635 CE. It was an interdisciplinary conference held from July 5 to 7, with the participation of seven scholars from Italy and twenty-seven other experts in the field from all over China.[21] The other conference was the Global Civilization Dialogue lecture series held in the same institute at Xi'an on October 24. Professors Peter Leander Hofrichter and Dietmar W. Winkler from the University of Salzburg, Austria, gave the first and second lectures: "From Xi'an to Salzburg: Origin, Development and Significance of the Salzburg Conferences on *Jingjiao*," and "The Study of the Church of the East in Central Asia and China as a Challenge for Interdisciplinary Research," respectively. I was among the

---

[20] Xi Jinping, "Join Hands on the Path towards Modernization," Keynote Address at the CPC in Dialogue with World Political Parties High-Level Meeting, State Council Information Office, Beijing, March 15, 2023.

[21] Stefania Falasca, "La croce sulla stele di Xi'an testimone della fede in Cina," *Avvenire*, August 30, 2024, 20.

speakers at both conferences. There were open exchanges with an interdisciplinary approach on such a significant topic as the first arrival of Christian civilization in China, and exploration of possible collaborations between institutions from Europe and China in the future.

Even more significantly, the above initiatives were in response to the resolution proposed by China to establish an International Day for Dialogue among Civilizations. The resolution was unanimously adopted at the seventy-eighth UN General Assembly, advocating respect for the diversity of civilizations. It emphasizes the important role of dialogue among civilizations in maintaining world peace and enhancing human well-being. Beginning in 2025, June 10 is to be designated as the International Day for Dialogue among Civilizations.

Moral Courage beyond Trauma

There have been many difficulties for Catholics living their faith in China in recent decades due to a complex social context and for historical reasons. I would like to narrate from a spiritual perspective some concrete experiences of the faith of Catholics in China.

How Catholics Navigate Changes in China

The Church is missionary by nature. The Second Vatican Council shifted the attention from the Church itself to the interlocutor at whom mission aims.[22] Therefore, let's take a look at the context of China, characterized by huge social mobility and an urban-rural dichotomy in last few decades.

---

[22] See Second Vatican Council, *Gaudium et Spes, Pastoral Constitution on the Church in the Modern World*, 1965, 5.

China has experienced the biggest human migration and urbanization in human history; 50 percent of its population moved from poor rural areas to cities in the last forty years. Social changes have been enormous—and also challenging. Although Catholics comprise less than 1 percent of the Chinese population,[23] the Church in China has had to cope with these changes.

When China inaugurated the reform and opening-up policy in the 1980s, the Christian faith was mainly preserved and spread in rural areas. In the 1990s, the trend of migrant workers entering cities emerged. Different groups have had distinct experiences over the last two decades; I speak here about the importance of formation of the laity and youth. In this research, I concentrate on three groups: students and youth, migrant families, and professionals and entrepreneur Christians.

Important accompaniment is needed according to different life stages and age groups. The laity and the youth have played an active role in evangelization and in the urban-rural mobility:

Teens, youth, and students. Many teens and youth in rural areas have gone through the experience of the so-called left-behind children.[24] They have, for example, faced such problems as lack of communication with parents. Several dioceses in the northern province of Hebei, where about one-fifth of the Catholic population is concentrated, have started an initiative called the one-hundred-day formation program for youth—boys and girls separately. The program concentrates on human promotion, values, and communication

---

[23] The urban population has grown from about 18.6 percent in 1979 to 57.9 percent in 2017. See "China: Urban Population as a Share of Total Population," *World Data Atlas*, accessed April 17, 2018.

[24] These are children left behind with their grandparents or relatives in the countryside while their parents work in the cities. It is a phenomenon due to China's economic and social conditions, especially from the 1980s to the 2000s. They are also called "home-staying children."

skills, and is offered to youth who are free from commitment, work, and studies for a while. It is a good opportunity to take a break from the usual highly competitive environment and to discern a direction in life.

As for university or college students, it is an important time for academic pursuits; at the same time, independent thinking and seeking a meaning for life are important. The youth go to cities for their studies. In some provinces where traditional Catholics are concentrated—such as Hebei, Sichuan, Shanxi, and Shaanxi—youth return during holidays to their hometowns and participate in Church activities, such as group sharing and exchanges, which they continue during the school year. They meet at Sunday Mass in the host city where they study. Little by little, faith and friendship groups are born spontaneously on their own initiatives, helped by their diocese of origin, or by a priest dedicated to youth ministry in the host parish.

There is also a group called YCS (Young Catholic Students) that cares for and pays particular attention to the needs of high school students. According to its guiding principle, youth should animate themselves, although they have priests as spiritual directors. In the light of the Gospel, the teenagers accompany one another in the process of a see-judge-act review of life, and benefit from this group experience. As they grow spiritually and in age, some feel the call to dedicate themselves to helping the younger ones. Therefore, senior high school students will help junior student groups, and some will remain to energize the high school students even after entering college. The annual nationwide *Gaokao* (college entrance exam) is an important event in the life of a student, often under tremendous pressure. A college student of the group will be assigned to, paired with, and praying for the one taking the exam. It is very significant and fruitful that young people are accompanying and giving support to one another.

Migrant families and professionals. For adults, many dioceses have formation centers. Formation programs and activities are regularly held for specific groups, such as pastoral workers, married couples, or professionals such as teachers. Programs help them witness to the gospel in their specific fields and environments. As for migrants in the cities, Bishop Jin Luxian in his 2011 Chinese New Year pastoral letter praised the experience of the faithful from Wenzhou residing in Shanghai as fervent and active Catholics. Shanghai Diocese assigned a priest as their spiritual director. Jin encouraged parishes to dedicate pastoral care aimed at those coming from the countryside and other provinces. He said, "Let them experience that the Church is really a family and we are brothers and sisters."[25] Some bigger dioceses—Xianxian, Handan, and Wenzhou—also sent pastors to visit their faithful.

Entrepreneur Christians. The professionals and well-educated faithful are helpful in communicating with the government and society at large.[26] Some laity form regular Bible study groups. Still others, businesspeople, try to offer Christian testimony in the business environment. There is an enterprise at Ninjin, Hebei, that employs several thousand workers. An entrepreneur Christian, Mr. Geng and his whole family of fervent Catholics instill Christian spirit in the corporate culture and management. The employees are well treated, with paid holidays. They can join wholesome activities organized by the company, working in a family atmosphere, and feeling happy. As a consequence, some are attracted to the Christian faith. When I visited his factory, Mr. Geng shared this experience

---

[25] Aloysius Jin, "Advancing with the Times," Chinese New Year 2011 pastoral letter, February 2, 2011.

[26] Chinese scholars have started to recognize "entrepreneur Christians" [*laoban jidutu*] emerging in economically developed coastal areas. See Cunfu Chen and Tianhai Huang, "The Emergence of a New Type of Christians in China Today," *Review of Religious Research*, December 2001, 83–200.

with me: "Workers work in shifts. Christians were free to attend Sunday Mass. At a certain point, we decided to let everybody free from work on Sunday. In front of workers present, we asked, did our production go down?" They exclaimed loudly: No!

Testimonies of Facing Challenges with Moral Courage

China instituted a new religious policy on March 1, 2022. All religions are now under the supervision of the central government while general guidelines are implemented locally. According to the government, this policy is a response to the need: to avoid religious extremism on the one hand and guarantee social stability on the other. Moreover, the government does not want religions, because of their international affiliation, to be a pretext for foreign intervention, covert or overt. All religions are therefore conditioned by the prevailing political climate. This is more evident for Catholicism because of the distinction between the so-called official (patriotic) and the unofficial (underground) Church, which makes it difficult for the Church to play a prophetic role in society as it should. This presents a significant challenge: How can the Church play a more active role in society? For examples, I offer some concrete experiences of how Catholics in China responded to these challenges in two areas: the new religious policies and restrictions and COVID-19. At times the experiences were traumatic.

City-countryside exchanges. Social changes and mobility present challenges particularly to youth but also create opportunities for them. A positive aspect of the urban-rural mobility is the exchange and reconciliation brought about in Catholic communities, especially among young people who are not burdened by the baggage of divisions of the past. They do not care about the distinction between the official and the underground Church. They go to the church that is nearest or most convenient. Their exchanges and testimony help bring about reconciliation among Catholic communities. Reconciliation is so important for the development of the Catholic Church in China, for only unity and love can offer testimony to other people. Groups of laity spontaneously spring up in the local church in search of a relevant modern-day spirituality. Ecclesial communities with mature experience and spirituality can contribute in collaboration with local clergy in accompanying the youth.

There is the challenge of living with and gaining "space" under the new religious regulations and restrictions. The Chinese government officially recognizes five religions: Buddhism, Daoism, Islam, Catholicism, and Protestantism. Despite this official recognition, all are obliged to observe government regulations. Two new regulations that have a significant impact are prohibition of the use of the internet for religious propagation and a limit on religious education for minors. As a consequence, some minor seminaries were closed. However, Bishop Yang of the National Seminary in Beijing once shared with me how he spoke out, in an official meeting with religious authorities, about minor seminaries being the cradle of priestly vocation. As a fruit of friendly dialogue, an exception to the restriction was made; three minor seminaries are still open in China. Genuine priestly vocations are nurtured and fostered, not only in a seminary, but also in a caring Christian community in the family and in parishes.

As mentioned earlier about Catholic social services, since the beginning of the COVID outbreak, it has been touching to see testimonies of how some Catholic nuns volunteer their mobile clinic ambulances for emergency services. The bishop from Qiqihaer said that some clergy and Catholic faithful volunteered along with others, offering their services in their districts to the needy without attention to belief.

Even the crisis of the pandemic could be a period of good harvest: Fr. Ren from Shanxi Province considered the pandemic a blessing in disguise. He said, "For a few months children didn't have school and had to stay home in the villages in the countryside. I built some facilities for them to play in, and sometimes I had a chance to give them catechetical lessons."

Outdoor activities like camping for children and teens. The Focolare community in Shanghai organized outdoor activities for the children and teens. They visited wetlands to see birds and appreciate nature. These nature visits are a good opportunity to speak to them about ecology, Francis of Assisi, and the pope's encyclical *Laudato Si'*. At some points, Focolare members also initiated Zoom evening prayer meetings with the children and their parents.

Power of prayer, Eucharistic adoration, and reflection. Even for adults, these are occasions for reflection and an opportunity to spend time with family and with nature. Some priests and sisters also promote adoration of the Blessed Sacrament in their diocese. It helps them find inner peace and turn the tide of overemphasis on worldly pursuits, activism, and always being in a hurry.

Internet use for religious services online. A group of young volunteers in Beijing in 2013 developed a digital app called *Tianzhujiao Xiaozhushou* (Catholic assistant), using the public internet social platform Taobao (Alibaba), to provide faith formation and news of the Church in China and from Rome, as well as live transmissions from the Holy Father. It was a good service to the Church and was very successful. However, the platform was temporarily interrupted in 2022 due to stricter Internet Religious Information Service Regulations that had taken effect. It was, however, a pleasant surprise when, after two weeks, the platform migrated and was resurrected under a new name: *Wanyouzhenyuan*. It is associated with the Beijing Catholic

North Cathedral, therefore legally operating under Beijing's state-approved Catholic Church. Coincidentally, when the Northern Cathedral was built, Emperor Kangxi (1703) personally had handwritten on a plaque on the church the inscription *Wanyouzhenyuan*, which means, "the origin of everything," referring to God.

At times, it is not easy to navigate within China's complex religious framework, balancing state oversight and faith practices. What is particularly significant is that this initiative was the fruit of the moral courage of youth group volunteers who continue today to provide their wonderful services throughout China.

Ultimate Analysis and Positive Notes

There is continuity in the efforts of recent popes to foster rapprochement between the Holy See and China. Saint John Paul II initiated a spirit of Vatican II openness, a search for new language, new ardor, and new models for a new evangelization in mission lands like China, where Catholics are a small minority. Pope Benedict XVI's 2007 letter to the Catholic Church in China formed a solid theological base for dialogue with China and encouraged reconciliation within the Catholic Church in China. Under the papacy of Pope Francis, with a humble spirit of reaching out to China, promising signs of normalization of relations emerged, for the good and the development of the Church in China.

Just to cite a few illustrious facts: First, by signing the Provisional Agreement on the Appointment of Bishops on September 22, 2018, Chinese authorities recognized the role and involvement of the pope in appointing bishops in China. Considering the Holy See as an authority from outside, this concession from Chinese authorities is quite exceptional. Therefore, the agreement is indeed historic. Second, as we discussed earlier, from April 29 to October 9, 2019, the Vatican participated in the International Horticultural Exhibition (Beijing Expo) with the Vatican Pavilion highlighting the theme of the Encyclical Letter *Laudato Si'* of Pope Francis "on care for our common home." It is the first time the Holy See participated successfully, exhibiting for six months, in a high-level international event held in China under the official invitation of the Chinese government. Third, in addition to the Holy See Pavilion, the Vatican Museums held an exhibition titled *Beauty Unites Us* at the Palace Museum in the Forbidden City for a month and a half from May to July 2019, exhibiting a collection of seventy-eight Catholic and Chinese artifacts as signs of friendship and cultural exchange. The Expo and the exhibitions, which received millions of visitors, are very significant because the Chinese public had direct contact with the rich patrimony and contributions of the universal Catholic Church to humanity in history, art, culture, and values. On these occasions, the public could receive the Catholic Church in a positive way, which helps dispel prejudices of the past; create acceptance, trust, and good emotions with the public; and present a favorable image of the Catholic Church.

From my observation, under the Catholic social teaching principle of subsidiarity, the normalizing and improving relations between China and the Holy See, at a higher level, are helping local Catholic communities deal with local authorities in settling issues and difficulties. In this way, Catholics can more readily give testimony and be a leaven in society as good Christians and good citizens in the eyes of the general public.

With the coronavirus outbreak in Wuhan in January 2020, little was known at the beginning. Many people were stunned by the government's drastic measures. Wuhan was locked down on January 23, together with other nearby areas of Hebei Province, and travel restrictions were implemented. It was just two days before the Lunar New Year, when the home visit travel season had just started. It is a long-held tradition for most Chinese people to reunite with their families during the Chinese New Year. With the advent of the efficient high-speed railway systems in China, a total of three billion passenger trips were expected during this Spring Festival season of the New Year. The movement of people during the Chinese New Year holiday season has been called the largest annual human migration in the world.

During the Lunar New Year of 2020, I was particularly touched by the Holy Father when he publicly sent his Lunar New Year greetings and blessings twice in a scroll to people in Asia. At the end of a general audience, he said, "In the Far East and in various other parts of the world, many millions of men and women will celebrate the Lunar New Year. I send them my cordial greetings, wishing them in particular to be places of education in the virtues of welcome, wisdom, respect for each person and harmony with creation. I invite all to pray also for peace, dialogue and solidarity among nations: gifts which are so necessary in the world today."[27] It is precisely this emphasis on the virtues that helped people endure the pandemic.

The prolonged effect of the pandemic "brought to light not only our false securities, but also the inability of the world's countries to work together,"[28] as the Holy Father pointed out. Nevertheless, the pandemic prompted us to rethink our values. I also observed that at the beginning of the COVID outbreak in China, as far as I could tell within Catholic circles, we received much help and support from abroad. When the situation in China was more or less brought under control two months

---

[27] Pope Francis, "Special Greetings," general audience, January 22, 2020.

[28] Pope Francis, "Message of His Holiness on the Occasion of the Plenary Session of the Pontifical Academy of Sciences," October 7, 2020.

later, it had become a pandemic and the situation abroad grew worse. Motivated by a non-Christian friend who wanted to donate ten thousand sanitary masks to Italy, I personally became involved with Jinde Charities and Yahvé Caritas in sending tens of thousands of sanitary masks and protective gear to Italy and other countries. I have witnessed that the power of love is even more contagious and goes beyond the distinction of creeds. It has been very encouraging. Also, as a professor of religious studies, I am aware, as the Muslims would say, that the original meaning of *jihad* is first and foremost the struggle within oneself against infidelity to God, rather than committing an external act of violence in the face of adversities and challenges. As Christians we too are called to exhibit moral courage, continue to live our faith, and navigate changes in society with wisdom.

In spite of the changing social environment and the stricter religious regulations in China, I find resilience in how some Chinese Catholics face challenges with creativity. For example, parents get involved in catechism classes in venues close to the church. Even though, as in other countries, there is a general decline in vocations to the priesthood, the seminary of Chendu has managed to begin again to cater to the needs of the southwestern region of China. Even some minor seminaries manage to continue under exceptional circumstances.

Mary, Mother of Hope and Tenderness

It was a happy coincidence that on May 24, 2020—the feast day of Our Lady of Sheshan, so dear to Chinese Catholics—Pope Francis also launched a year to reflect on *Laudato Si'*. He voiced his closeness to the Chinese faithful and their country. Pope Francis emphasized that the Chinese faithful are an "integral part" of the universal Church. He assured us of his love and the strong bond with the universal Church. Although there are difficulties, he encouraged us "to be strong in faith and steadfast in fraternal union, joyful witnesses, promoters of charity and hope, and good citizens." With a special Apostolic Blessing, he prayed for "a new outpouring of the Holy Spirit," with the light and beauty of the gospel "shining from within."[29]

Apart from the culture of care, Pope Francis spoke so often of the tenderness of God. He is the creator of heaven and earth. We pray to God through Christ, under the loving gaze of Mary, Help of Christians and Patroness of China, that the Holy Spirit will guide the Church in China to be a living witness of the gospel and to be promoters of charity, fraternal hope, and good citizenship.

With the hope of light and resurrection, China has an important role to play in this epochal change in the world today. The country has gone through a period of atheist materialism, concentrating on material well-being and economic development to overcome material poverty. God has a loving plan for all peoples. Chinese Catholics are serious about their life of faith and make a radical choice to live it. I am convinced that the time will come for more Chinese to be open to spiritual transformations. Jesus also went through his dark night, forsaken by the Father on the cross. The Resurrection came only after. After this period of trial and deeper discernment, the Chinese Catholic Church will be more prepared to engage in dialogue with atheism. Atheism, after all, is a cry of humanity—like the cry of Jesus forsaken on the cross.

---

[29] Pope Francis, *Regina Caeli*, May 24, 2020.

Conclusion

Everyone has a dream. There are also common dreams of a people. For example, the dream of the Chinese people is to satisfy their need for a better life. The point of departure for the Chinese dream, both for the people and for their leaders, comes from a human or sociopolitical point of view. As for me, the Chinese dream needs a deeper spiritual dimension! A main theme of this book is the belief, no matter where we depart from, that once we are on board, we will all meet at some point. As a conclusion, I offer some points to ponder, and suggest three images that may serve as inspiration.

Some Articulating Points of This Book

Leitmotiv: Culture of Encounter

I have written this book in the spirit of the culture of encounter, intending to be faithful to the teachings of the Catholic Church on inculturation. I go back to the primary source, revelation, recognizing that the gospel message is for all cultures, and informed by the Trinitarian logic as a guide to this Christianity-China dialogue. The Trinitarian vision at the heart of Church doctrine, and the spirituality of the charism of unity of Chiara Lubich, is the leitmotif throughout the different areas of this research.

Conclusion

An Opportunity Not to Be Missed

Pope Francis was committed to the culture of dialogue and encounter with China. He loved the Chinese people and had always looked upon China as a land of great opportunities, with its profound culture and wisdom. In his message to Catholics in China and the Universal Church on September 6, 2018, he indicated that the signing of the Provisional Agreement between the Holy See and the Chinese authorities on nomination of bishops in China was meant for evangelization and pastoral purposes. The pope called for the Catholic community to unify and overcome the divisions of the past that have caused much suffering. He encouraged "walking together" to build a common future of harmony. The agreement set in place an element of cooperation between the state authorities and the Apostolic See to provide bishops for Catholics in China, for the first time since 1949. The Holy Father also urged the Universal Church to accompany Catholics in China with fraternal friendship, as a way to integrate together into the Universal Church, which will be enriched by authentic Chinese spiritual and cultural treasures. Moreover, Francis invited the Chinese leaders to continue, with trust and farsightedness, the dialogue for greater friendship and for avoiding misunderstandings in order to build a future of peace and fraternity among peoples.[1]

Inculturation = Interculturality

Interculturality refers to the existence and equitable interaction of diverse cultures and the possibility of generating shared cultural expressions through dialogue and mutual respect.[2]

---

[1] Pope Francis, "Message to the Catholics of China and the Universal Church," September 2018.

[2] UNESCO, Convention on the Protection and Promotion of the Diversity of Cultural Expressions, Paris, October 20, 2005, Article 4.8.

Cardinal Joseph Ratzinger, when head of the Vatican Congregation for the Doctrine of the Faith, urged the bishops of Asia to regard the mission of the Church in Asia more in terms of "interculturality" instead of "inculturation." He coined this new term and urged its use to express more precisely "the meeting of cultures" that takes place when the culture of Christian faith encounters other cultures. "Inculturation" should no longer be used,[3] because this word "presumes that a faith stripped of culture is transplanted into a religiously indifferent culture whereby two subjects, formally unknown to each other, meet and fuse." He wanted to promote the encounter of cultures as reciprocal enrichment.

Two interrelated issues in the life of the Church are evangelization of cultures and cultural understanding of the gospel. In this context, Pope John Paul II said in 1982, "The synthesis between culture and faith is not only a requirement of culture, but also of faith.... Faith that does not become culture is not fully accepted, nor entirely reflected upon, or faithfully experienced."[4]

Saint John Paul II was convinced that Christianity would further uplift Chinese culture in its spiritual dimension, and vice versa: that Chinese culture, with its human experiences, would greatly enrich the Church.[5] As theologian Piero Rossano also said, "The Christian economy will not be known and developed in all its values until it has been conceived, interpreted, and lived through the religious categories of all peoples."[6] John Paul

---

[3] The cardinal said this to twenty-five Asian bishops with whom he met in Hong Kong, March 2–6, 1993.

[4] Pope John Paul II, "Speech to the Participants of the National Congress Movimento Ecclesiale di Impegno Culturale," January 16, 1982.

[5] John Paul II, "Message to Participants of the International Conference Commemorating the Fourth Centenary of the Arrival in Beijing of Fr. Matteo Ricci," October 24, 2001, 7.

[6] Giulio Osto, *La testimonianza del dialogo Piero Rossano tra Bibbia, religioni e cultura* (Roma: Glossa, 2019), 3.

Conclusion

II hoped that once the difficulties and misunderstandings have been overcome, the dialogue will bring about a new encounter of reciprocal human and spiritual enrichment. Pope Benedict XVI's Letter to the Church in China invited the Chinese authorities to overcome misunderstandings of the past and to establish concrete forms of communication, cooperation, and open dialogue.

Vatican-China: An Icebreaker

While the desire of recent pontiffs to bring about rapprochement with China has been continuous and consistent, the acceptance from Beijing that the bishop of Rome has the final say in the appointment of bishops in China is truly unprecedented in recent Chinese history. Although some critics of the agreement worry that the Holy See is making too much of a concession to China, according to some Chinese scholars, the agreement is truly historic and constitutes an even bigger concession on the part of the top leader in China.

ABCs (Foundations) of Chinese Culture

Confucianism—which emphasizes benevolence, righteousness, and fraternal love—is at the root of Chinese culture. To cite some of the most representative ancient Chinese philosophers, Confucius spoke of the need "to be *ren*," that is, to foster a benevolent relationship among human beings. Mencius spoke of "choosing righteousness over one's own life." Mozi spoke of "universal love," a principle forgotten for some time but one that is making a return because of its contemporary relevance. Traditional culture in China is characterized by Confucian teaching, while Daoism plays a complementary role in Chinese cultural history. While Confucianism emphasizes making a change, Daoism stresses *wuwei*, letting nature take its own course. Laozi spoke of "being" and "non-being" generating one another, reciprocally transforming one another in a dialectic of harmony. These are just a few examples of elements in Chinese culture that illustrate a basis for dialogue and a contribution to world culture. My main objective is to discover more, and to open further reflections on the compatibility of Chinese culture with Christianity.

Trailblazers to Bridges

By following in the footsteps of Matteo Ricci, respectful dialogue between East and West, between Christianity and Chinese culture, is possible—and will bring about reciprocal enrichment that will benefit the whole human family.

In this book's five chapters, I have demonstrated that there are many values in common between Christianity and Chinese culture, though at times they are articulated in different ways—especially values such as harmony and unity, ecological civilization and integral ecology, fraternity and social friendship, poverty reduction and common prosperity, and freedom of religious practice and reciprocity. As I mentioned at the beginning of this book, I did not intend to go into extensive analysis of each of the Chinese concepts selected for comparison because of the huge number of studies that have analyzed these concepts' evolving meanings. For the broad framework of intercultural and interreligious study adopted in this research, I remain committed to borrowing the results from professional scholars in Chinese history and philosophy.

Finally, in order to help readers view the book's key findings, I present here a summary of highlights from each chapter. These overall points are in no way exhaustive but can serve as a bridge to dialogue. The topics are worthy of extended reflection. It is a modest attempt to arouse resonance in other scholars to ponder these topics in a continuous process of further discussion and elaboration.

Summary of Each Chapter

Chapter 1: Dialectic of Harmony in Dialogue with Trinitarian Relationship

I distinguish between the dialectics of thesis-antithesis-synthesis of Hegel, the dialectics of love of Lubich, and the dialectics of harmony of Laozi.[7] Hegel's dialectics illustrated in the bud-blossom-fruit example, with each former disappearing and being refuted by the latter, are criticized. Marxism even justifies violence as part of the revolution in this dialectical process. While in Lubich's dialectics of love, Jesus is forsaken on the cross; instead of denying the Father, he lives a total self-denial in his *kenosis*, entrusting himself completely to the will of the Father. In Laozi, there is a dialectics of harmony, with *dao-de, yin-yang* harmonizing, and being-nothingness mutually generating.

I conclude that the Chinese mindset of dialectics of harmony offers a starting point for understanding Trinitarian relationships, preferable in some ways to the approach of Scholastic philosophy. Instead of just comparing the *Logos* with the *Dao* in the effort of inculturation, there needs to be a rethinking of the relationship between *Dao-De*-harmony, and the love between Father and the Son in the Trinity. Again, this dialogue and relational dialectics of harmony and reconciliation offer the through line for the book's five chapters.

---

[7] Kin Sheung Chiaretto Yan, "Prolegomenon to Interreligious Dialogue in China: Daoism, the Trinitarian Relationship, and Christian Inculturation," *Claritas: Journal of Dialogue and Culture* 6 (2017): 43–44, 55.

Chapter 2: Ecological Civilization in Dialogue with Integral Ecology

Daoism reminds us of our relationships in creation. Daoists were the first ecologists because of their concept of being in harmony with nature, blending in with the environment, and doing no harm to nature.

However, China has in recent decades developed from a backward economy by means of heavy industrialization. The world knows well that this entailed acute pollution; but few are aware that air quality across China has improved in recent years due to countless small- and large-scale green initiatives. China has the duty to share its experience with developing countries to strike a balance between economic development and environmental protection.

I had the privilege to serve as the coordinator of the Holy See Pavilion at the Beijing Expo 2019 on Horticulture; the theme of *Laudato Si'* was well-presented with a painting of Adam and Eve in the Garden of Eden and other artistic elements. As Pope Francis wrote in the encyclical, empirical data have shown humankind's negative effects on the environment. He stressed the need for an integral approach and concerted effort to combat this ecological crisis. In the Genesis account, humans are created in God's image, but a distorted interpretation gives humans absolute domination over nature and other creatures (Gen. 1:28).[8] Rather than as the text might indicate, they are to be caretakers (Gen. 2:15) to glorify God with other creatures. Humans have disobeyed God. They have ruined not only the harmonious relationship between humans and God, but also between humans and nature, as well as human-to-human

---

[8] Francis, *Laudato Si'*, Encyclical Letter on Care for Our Common Home, May 24, 2015, 66.

relationships. Instead of a distorted anthropocentric position, the social doctrine of the Church orients us toward an "anthropocentrism of Christ."[9] Jesus, the New Adam, through the cross, restores these relationships.

Although Xi made no suggestion or mention of God and creation in his inaugural speech at the Expo, I found certain consonance in that speech with the spirit of *Laudato Si'*. President Xi emphasized human wisdom, scientific policies and research to create a harmonious ecosystem, and following laws of nature, the earth, "our common homeland." Nature punishes and rewards. The rise or fall of a society is dependent on its relationship with nature. Industrialization generated material wealth but damaged nature. All humans live in community with a shared future and need to collaborate to tackle environmental issues, to have a balanced ecosystem, to accelerate an "ecological civilization," to raise people's awareness, and to work together with other countries to achieve the UN's Sustainable Development Goals (SDGs). Xi also spoke of responsibility toward future generations.[10]

Chapter 3: Universal Brotherhood, Fraternity for Peace, and Social Friendship

In Chinese culture, the concept of fraternity and love is expressed in the following terms: *ren'ai, jian'ai*, and *bo'ai*. *Ren'ai* has a rich connotation of benevolence, forgiveness, humanity, and

---

[9] See Sergio Rondinara, "Custodire ciò che è salvato," in *Per un umanesimo degno dell'amore: Il Compendio della Dottrina Sociale della Chiesa*, ed. Paolo Carlotti and Mario Toso (Roma: Editrice LAS, 2005), 437. See also Pontifical Council for Justice and Peace, *Compendium of the Social Doctrine of the Church*, 463.

[10] See "Xi Jinping's Keynote Speech at the Opening Ceremony of the International Horticultural Exhibition 2019 (Edited Excerpt)," *Beijing Review*, September 3, 2019.

human-heartedness. *Jian'ai*, all-embracing love, was introduced by Mozi immediately after the time of Confucius, but it was deemed too abstract and has become a forgotten principle. *Bo'ai* was influenced by the concept of *agape* in Christianity, introduced by Dr. Sun Yatsen, the founding father of modern China. With the inroads of Christianity and the influence of Western ideas such as the motto of the French Revolution, the term taken from Chinese classics is made popular to express the idea of universal love and fraternity.

The relationship of fraternity is also expressed in an idiomatic expression: "a relationship as close as one's hands and feet." In recent years, President Xi has stressed that distinguished Chinese traditional culture fosters socialist core values—including *youshan* (friendliness and fraternity)—that are alive in people's hearts. This friendship applies not only at the personal or social level but also to relationships between nations.

In the history of Christianity, brotherhood is intrinsic to a strong spiritual meaning of fraternity in Christ, and thus manifests itself in the sharing of goods in a community and helping the poor. It contributed to the abolition of slavery in Christian society. As the motto of the French Revolution was "Liberty, Equality, and Fraternity," the notion of fraternity has become a political category. In much of the twentieth century, the principles of freedom in liberalism or equality in socialism were emphasized in one political system or another, but the triptych motto was not taken altogether as a whole; fraternity has become a forgotten principle.

Pope Francis signed the joint declaration "Human Fraternity for World Peace and Living Together," with Sheikh Ahmed Al-Tayeb representing the Muslim world, at Abu Dhabi in February 2019. The Holy Father has a gradual approach. The point of departure is the recognition that all persons in the world are to live as brothers and sisters in the one human family. Faith in God is the starting point of this fraternity, but the benevolent gaze of God includes every person in the human family. This fraternity is destined to extend to people of all religions and cultures.[11]

Consonant with the Confucian tradition, the concept of fraternity starts within the family with the emphasis on benevolence (*ren*). Such love should then be extended until it includes distant members of society as well. "Honor the elderly and care for the young in other families as we do to those in our own" (*Mencius* 1A7). This extension is also well expressed in another verse of the *Analects*: "Now the man of perfect virtue, wishing to build up himself as such, seeks to build up others as well; wishing to enhance himself, seeks also to enhance others" (*Analects* 7.2).

Chapter 4: Poverty Alleviation and a New Economic Model

China's success in poverty alleviation is the result of long-term planning and continuous effort, typical of the Confucian spirit of making a change. State policies and guidance have been important for delivering results in poverty alleviation: the Targeted Poverty Alleviation strategy, the Chinese experience of prosperous coastal provinces paired to help poor provinces in western China, and putting into practice an age-old saying, "Give a man a fish and he will eat for a day. Teach him how to fish and you feed him for a lifetime."

---

[11] Pope Francis affirms that man is made for love, so he must go beyond the self toward others to find fuller existence. Love is capable of transcending borders of regions or countries. He says, "The ever-increasing number of interconnections and communications in today's world makes us powerfully aware of the unity and common destiny of the nations." Francis, *Fratelli Tutti*, Encyclical Letter on Fraternity and Social Friendship, October 3, 2020, 96.

Endogenous development refers to a model of development from within a culture.[12] It also means harnessing cultural values, particularly Asian and Confucian values, of being industrious, frugal, and high-saving; emphasizing education and political stability; and pursuing continuous reform, government competency, and improvement of people's livelihood. China has worked out a development path in many aspects that is consonant with its own culture and adequate for its stage of development.

China's experience can be a reference on one hand for developing countries—but on the other hand, because of the nation's sheer size and unique characteristics, others may not easily emulate the example. Each country needs to find a model suitable for its conditions and its present stage of development. China has taken the path with what it calls "Chinese characteristics." Success depends internally on administering the country well, and externally in adapting to the international environment.

Can the China experience provide a new paradigm for the world economy? The new economic reform of China is in some ways in line with Pope Francis's thoughts. As mentioned before, the Holy Father sees the crisis of the pandemic as an opportunity for radical changes in the economic system, and he emphasizes the culture of care. By caring, even the pandemic becomes a lesson for people at times of adversity to spend more time with family. New policies in China are, after all, aimed at reducing the social ills of materialism and the stress of too much competition for Chinese kids, youth, and parents.

For the education of future generations toward a more sober lifestyle, exemplary testimonies from both East and West are available. While Pope Francis mentioned in his encyclical St.

---

[12] Yan Kin Sheung Chiaretto, "The China Experience as Contribution for a New Economic Paradigm," *The Journal of the Macau Ricci Institute* (Macau), no. 7 (May 2020): 91–95.

Francis of Assisi (1181–1226) and St. Charles de Foucauld (1858–1916), I cite inspiring figures such as Zhang Zai (1020–1077), whose writings highlight the unity of heaven, earth, and all beings. Another figure is Tao Yuanming (365–427), who abandoned his career in the capital and returned to his small town to live a sober life and left his poems for future generations, who still read them today.

Chapter 5: Freedom of Religion and the Golden Rule of Reciprocity

If we compare the Universal Declaration of Human Rights and the Constitution of the People's Republic of China on freedom of religion, we see that both include the freedom to practice and to manifest one's faith and the freedom to change one's religious belief (freedom of conversion).

However, while the UN Declaration emphasizes the freedom to manifest one's religious belief due to inherent human dignity and rights,[13] China emphasizes protection of the religions so that none is allowed to foster fanaticism or extremism and to ensure that no foreign interference may use "religious freedom" as a pretext for destabilizing the course of development for the country.[14] One focuses on outward manifestation while the other focuses on protection. This subtle divergence is also reflected in the cultural differences between East and West. Both Jesus and Confucius spoke of the Golden Rule on reciprocity. Confucius used the passive form: "Do not do to others what you would not

---

[13] See United Nations General Assembly, Universal Declaration of Human Rights, Paris, December 10, 1948), preface, articles 18 and 26.

[14] See National People's Congress of the People's Republic of China, Constitution of the People's Republic of China, Amendment at the First Session of the Thirteenth National People's Congress, Beijing, March 11, 2018, articles 33–38.

want others to do to you." From the point of view of ethics, it is more practical to establish as a rule at least not to harm others while it is more demanding to establish reciprocal love as a rule.

Another very significant document on religious freedom, signed in 2011 by the Pontifical Council for Interreligious Dialogue, the World Council of Churches, and the World Evangelical Alliance, is titled *Christian Witness in a Multi-Religious World: Recommendations for Conduct*. In this text, the right of freedom to promulgate one's faith is also balanced by responsibilities. These responsibilities include not only the witness of service and love to neighbors in multireligious contexts, but also that religion should not be instrumentalized for political ends.[15] Therefore, it is a legitimate concern not to interfere in other countries' internal affairs under the pretext of religion. Interestingly, while China raises this concern with the United States for interfering in other countries' internal affairs under the pretext of religion, this obstacle has not been mentioned in recent years in the process of normalizing Holy See–China relations under the papacy of Pope Francis.

While some Christian groups stress the mission to propagate their faith, the Catholic Church emphasizes that this mission best occurs in interreligious dialogue—when all parties are open and each person or group has the right to manifest and to propagate its faith and culture in a respectful manner.

For the specific nature of the Church's mission in the world, the Holy Father has repeated on numerous occasions that evangelization is not "proselytism," and that the Church grows "by attraction" and "by witnesses."

---

[15] See Pontifical Council for Interreligious Dialogue, World Council of Churches, and World Evangelical Alliance, *Christian Witness in a Multi-religious World: Recommendations for Conduct*, Bangkok, January 2011, 5.

The Church is missionary by nature. Vatican II has shifted the Church's attention from the object of faith to the greater discovery of the interlocutor to whom mission is aimed. Improved Holy See–China relations offer hope and emphasis on the testimony of Catholics as good citizens, thereby changing relationships with the government and the general public. Christians are called to be instruments of peace in times of "lights and shadows" in the course of human history. Catholics in China, small in number but aware of their historical responsibility, may change the landscape of the Catholic Church in due time.

Thoughts and Afterthoughts

I quote extensively Pope Francis and his Magisterium; on the other hand, I quote Chinese classics and Xi Jinping. Do they match? Sometimes they are incompatible; nevertheless, there are points of convergence, at least on the theoretical level. Why not take advantage of them? China is contributing important Chinese values, on equal footing in the dialogue, with the West. The Catholic Church as a mediator without political or economic interest can facilitate this process to improve relations between China and the West, and specifically to ease US-China tensions.

Bergoglio and Xi were elected at almost the same time in March 2013—one as pope, the other as president of China—at a time when China–Holy See relations were strained. During the pontificate of Pope Francis, relations improved greatly. Both sides resumed talks in 2014. That year and thereafter, Pope Francis became the first pope authorized to fly over Chinese airspace in his apostolic journeys in Asia. On September 22, 2018, the Holy See and China signed a Provisional Agreement on the Appointment of Bishops. Although the contents of the agreement have not been fully revealed, the Chinese government's recognition of the pope's role, an authority outside China, in appointing bishops in China was quite exceptional. New bishops have been ordained according to the agreement, and the civil authorities have recognized some underground bishops in the process. The agreement was renewed on October 22, 2024, for the third time,[16] this time for four years instead of two, signaling more stable relations on both sides.

There are still unsettled issues regarding the boundaries of dioceses, registration of underground bishops and clergy, the criteria for normal practice of faith within the Chinese legal framework, and the rectification of canonical irregularities. These issues take time and patience to resolve, but they are more limited to the religious sphere.

To my mind, from a wider perspective worldwide, the dialogue and consultations between the Holy See and China should not be limited only to the religious sphere, but extended to other fronts with the assistance of specific teams of experts. Though Pope Francis extended sincere gestures to China, the Chinese response was not always so apparent. Further trust on the part of China toward the Catholic Church will be required for progress.

On the sidelines of the International Conference for the one hundredth anniversary of *Concilium Sinense*, Cardinal Secretary of State Pietro Parolin hinted at the desire to establish a certain "stable presence in China."[17] In case the appointment of an apostolic nunciature is not immediately possible, the dialogue regarding religious matters can continue with delegations from

---

[16] Analysis before renewal of the agreement appears in Chiaretto Yan, "Holy See–China Provisional Agreement: Balance Sheet Five and a Half Years After," *China Source*, October 14, 2024, https://chinasource.org/resource-library/articles/holy-see-china-provisional-agreement/.

[17] Salvatore Cernuzio, "Cardinal Parolin on China: Obedience to the Pope Enlivens Love for Country," *Vatican News*, May 21, 2024.

both sides. A stable presence may take a wider scope beyond purely religious matters. There have already been initiatives, such as the exhibition of the Holy See Pavilion at the Beijing Expo 2019, and exchanges between the Vatican Museum and the Palace Museum at the Forbidden City, as well as libraries from both sides. The Holy See should establish an office or a platform in China—even with the help of a third party, perhaps a nonreligious entity—to collaborate in projects of common interest, such as cultural exchanges, dialogue among civilizations, poverty alleviation, ecology, and world peace.

After the 2019–2020 social unrest in Hong Kong, and Beijing's passing of the National Security Law, some Hong Kong families are emigrating. There is also a great tension in the relationship between the two sides of the Strait of Taiwan. Saint John Paul II spoke of the diaspora of overseas Chinese, who share the same cultural roots, and encouraged Catholic Chinese to live, suffer, pray, and be open to the plan of God and to discover the victorious love of Christ in history. He also stressed that Catholics in Taiwan, Hong Kong, and Macau should be a "bridge church," for they belong to the one Chinese people as a great unified reality. It is a "wonderful task."[18] It is also a challenge that, if successful, could prove to be a game-changer. It is important to stress fraternity of blood, but more so, fraternity in the spirit, which is so much in need today for world peace.

With the tension between the United States and China ongoing and increasing—with accusations, true or twisted, on the side of the United States and its allies—a critical issue is the US position on Taiwan's independence. Just one miscalculation could

---

[18] John Paul II, "To the Taiwan Bishops and the Chinese Diaspora," February 28, 1984, in *Papal Documents Related to China 1937–2005*, ed. E. Wurth and B. A. Maheu (Hong Kong: Holy Spirit Study Centre, 2006), 262–266.

lead to hot war. In the present cold war, the United States is seen as containing China with its economic and military alliances. War must be avoided at all costs as there will be no winners.

While the United States emphasizes individual freedom, China emphasizes the collective interests of the state. On one side, there is the risk of individualism that makes people indifferent to others' needs, forgetting about the common good and even giving rise to xenophobia. On the other side, there is a risk that the spirit of the state is overemphasized at the expense of respect for the dignity of an individual person. China needs to have an open dialogue with the West, assuming that both sides are open to it. China can draw from the original inspiration of the culture of harmony in Chinese tradition to promote its soft power to defuse tensions and promote mutual acceptance.

Many Chinese are going abroad for visits and studies. More exchanges among young people and students will contribute to mutual understanding. In the education system in China, there is much stress from competition. An overemphasis on science needs to be balanced by the arts and letters. Study of technology and business should be complemented with the humanities. In the present book, I have quoted extensively from Chinese classics and the poetry of Zhang Zai and Tao Yuanming, as well as biblical narratives that contain poetry and wise sayings. They are consistent with one another. Modern poetry should also be encouraged, as reflection leads to interiority and dialogue about transcendental reality. It is consistent with Chinese culture's emphasis on forming a well-rounded person. Pope Francis told young people to be like water. "When water flows, it's good," he said, "but when water stops, it ends badly."[19] He encouraged young people to look forward with courage and joy. During the

---

[19] Kielce Gussie, "Pope to Young People of the Synod: 'Keep Moving Forward,'" *Vatican News*, October 23, 2024.

2023 World Youth Day, Francis also stressed the importance of friendship and healthy relationships with others. He told the youth to face their crises together and go forth.

Pope Francis inspired many young people. They will build a world of friendship and hope. Much can be said about the legacy of Pope Francis. He was the pope of the people, of those who are even far from God. During his twelve-year pontificate, he made several apostolic journeys to Asia and flew over China on several occasions. The pope truly believed that China was a great country capable of dialogue that transcended different institutional systems. He loved China and praised China's "great culture" and "infinite wisdom." For me, Pope Francis was a game-changer. Whether in his life or death, he changed China–Holy See relations forever. This improvement will have an impact on China's relations with the West. As Pope Francis used to say, "God always surprises us." I hope that the United States and China will prioritize collaboration over competition—and as such act as a catalyst for a more stable, equitable, and cooperative international order.

Based on my firsthand experiences, sincerity can touch people's hearts. I believe that we really can engage in constructive dialogue if we are open to each other, without holding a biased or absolute attitude. There is a Trinitarian vision at the heart of the charism of unity. Jesus prayed to the Father that "may they all be one as you and I are one," and he showed us the way in the emptying of himself on the cross of how to reconcile humankind with God and among ourselves. This Trinitarian dynamism of the Christian revelation is open to dialogue with all cultures. There is something that corresponds to the profound needs not only in Western culture, but in all cultures and, particularly for me, as a Chinese, in my own.

A Postscript

I would like to close with three inspiring images:

Our Lady of the Knots in Munich

In observing recent developments of the Catholic Church in China, certain knots need to be untied. Among the five established religions officially recognized in China, Buddhism and Protestantism have grown rapidly amid a nationwide religious revival in recent decades. Catholicism is the only one not growing in numbers. Why? Maybe it has fallen victim to politicization, with controversies easily played up by the media. Maybe there should be more emphasis on reconciliation and mutual love among Catholics. Saint Pope John Paul II appealed to Catholics in China through Radio Veritas during his first visit to the Philippines, stating that there is "no opposition or incompatibility in being at the same time truly Christian and authentically Chinese."[20] This appeal has been repeated by his successors. Pope Francis emphasized the culture of encounter. Rather than self-preservation of the Church, he encouraged the Church to go out, offering testimony and dialogue. I remember paying a visit to a church in Augsburg, Germany, a few years ago. There I saw the painting of Mary, Untier of Knots. I was told that Pope Francis saw that image while in Germany as a student and promoted her veneration in Latin America. Since then, I often pray that through the intercession of Mary, the witness of Pope Francis, and our own as authentic Catholics, the knots surrounding the Church in China will gradually be untied.

---

[20] Pope John Paul II, "Address to the Chinese Catholic Community in Asia," Manila, February 18, 1981, 3–4.

The Lighthouse at the Bund of Shanghai

I remember one casual evening in 1995, strolling and viewing from the Pudong the new area on the other side of the river. All lights on the Bund were turned off at 10 pm. I saw in the dim light a cross on top of the lighthouse. It made a strong impression on me. I was surprised to see a cross in the dim light, in a socialist country, officially atheist. The following morning, I found out that on top of the lighthouse, what I thought was a cross was just a wind-measuring instrument in the shape of a cross. I was also struck by the Monument to the People's Heroes on the other end of the Bund, for it was dedicated not only to Communist revolutionaries but to all persons who have contributed to the renewal of the Chinese nation in the last two hundred years. China was called the "sick man of Asia" at the turn of the nineteenth century. China has lifted eight hundred million people out of poverty in recent decades. Nowadays, you will find more and more Chinese students and tourists everywhere in the world. Whether China can achieve its long-term goals is open to debate, but it surely has entered a new era and is committed to moving toward "building a community of shared future for mankind." The instrument on top of the lighthouse may not have been originally designed as a cross, but for me there is always a design in the loving plan of God, whether in a person's life, in a country, or in the whole of humanity.

The Unfinished Bird in Beijing

There was a subtle message in the design of the Holy See Pavilion in the Beijing Expo 2019. The environmental crisis humanity faces is seen in the light of the consequence of the fall of man. Distancing himself from the original design God had for creation and for humanity, man ruins harmony in nature and relationships, but Jesus, the New Adam, with his death and resurrection, restores what was broken. God speaks to the hearts of men and women in many ways, as the wind-measuring instrument on top of a lighthouse in the dark resembling a cross spoke to me so strikingly many years ago. In the painting *Adam and Eve in the Garden of Eden*, displayed during the Beijing Expo, among the many animals and birds depicted, there was a sketch of a small bird forgotten by the painter Peter Wenzel. During the exhibition, we organized activities to let children participate in painting the "forgotten bird" on postcards and on canvases. It was not only something educational for the children who participated in such a program; it was also very significant for parents, teachers, and volunteers of the Expo who joined in the activities. I am convinced that whatever we do—whether painting the forgotten bird, taking actions in lifestyle conversion for an integral ecology, praying for wisdom in dealing with climate change, or constructing peace in our daily relationships—is a contribution, adding colors and strokes to the "unfinished work"—the unfinished work of building bridges and fostering dialogue.

Bibliography

Papal Documents and Official Church Documents
[All papal and Church documents are available online at Vatican.va]

Catechism of the Catholic Church. 1993.

Holy See Press Office. "Document on Human Fraternity for World Peace and Living Together," signed by His Holiness Pope Francis and the Grand Imam of Al-Azhar Ahmed Al-Tayeb. Abu Dhabi, February 4, 2019.

International Theological Commission. *Communion and Stewardship: Human Persons Created in the Image of God.* 2002.

Joint International Commission for Theological Dialogue between the Roman Catholic Church and the Orthodox Church. "Synodality and Primacy during the First Millennium: Towards a Common Understanding in Service to the Unity of the Church." September 21, 2016.

Pontifical Council for Interreligious Dialogue (PCID), World Council of Churches (WCC), and World Evangelical Alliance (WEA). *Christian Witness in a Multi-religious World: Recommendations for Conduct.* Bangkok, January 2011.

Pontifical Council for Justice and Peace. *Compendium of the Social Doctrine of the Church.* 2004.

Pope Benedict XVI. *Caritas in Veritate.* June 29, 2009.

Pope Francis. "Address to Participants in the Meeting 'Economy of Communion.'" Sponsored by the Focolare Movement. February 4, 2017.

———. "Address at the Pastoral Visit to Loppiano, the International Center of the Focolare Movement." May 10, 2018.

———. "Apostolic Blessing '*Urbi et Orbi*' and First Greeting of the Holy Father Pope Francis." March 13, 2013.

———. "Catechism on Prayer." General Audience at the Library of the Apostolic Palace. May 20, 2020.

———. *Evangelii Gaudium, Apostolic Exhortation on the Proclamation of the Gospel in Today's World*. November 24, 2013.

———. *Fratelli Tutti*. Encyclical Letter on Fraternity and Social Friendship. April 3, 2020.

———. General Audience on the Occasion of the Fiftieth Earth Day. April 22, 2020.

———. Interreligious General Audience on the Occasion of the Fiftieth Anniversary of the Promulgation of the Conciliar Declaration *Nostra Aetate*. October 28, 2015.

———. Interreligious Meeting Address of His Holiness. Apostolic Journey of His Holiness Pope Francis to the United Arab Emirates, Founder's Memorial, Abu Dhabi, February 4, 2019.

———. *Laudato Si'*. Encyclical Letter on Care for Our Common Home. May 24, 2015.

———. "Letter to a Non-believer: Pope Francis Responds to Dr. Eugenio Scalfari, Journalist from the Italian Newspaper *La Repubblica*." September 4, 2013.

———. "Message to the Catholics of China and the Universal Church." September 26, 2018.

———. "Message for the Celebration of the World Day of Peace: Fraternity, the Foundation and Pathway to Peace." January 1, 2014.

———. "Message on First World Day of the Poor." November 19, 2017.

———. "Message of His Holiness on the Occasion of the Plenary Session of the Pontifical Academy of Sciences." October 7, 2020.

———. "Message on World Day of the Poor." November 18, 2018.

———. *Regina Caeli*. May 24, 2020.

———. "Special Greetings," general audience. January 22, 2020.

———. *Veritatis Gaudium, Apostolic Constitution on Ecclesiastical Universities and Faculties*. January 29, 2018.

Pope John Paul II. "Address to the Chinese Catholic Community in Asia." Manila, February 18, 1981.

———. *Centesimus Annus*. Encyclical letter. 1991.

———. *Fides et Ratio*. Encyclical on the Relationship between Faith and Reason. 1998.

———. "Message to the Participants in the International Conference Commemorating the Fourth Centenary of the Arrival in Beijing of Father Matteo Ricci." October 24, 2001.

———. "Speech to the Participants of the National Congress of the Movimento Ecclesiale di Impegno Culturale." January 16, 1982.

Second Vatican Council. *Ad Gentes, Decree on the Mission Activity of the Church*. 1965.

———. *Dei Verbum, Dogmatic Constitution on Divine Revelation*. 1965.

———. *Gaudium et Spes, Pastoral Constitution on the Church in the Modern World*. 1965.

———. *Lumen Gentium, Dogmatic Constitution on the Church*. 1964.

Chinese Classics and Their Translations

Chan Wing-tsit, ed. *A Source Book in Chinese Philosophy*. Princeton, NJ: Princeton University Press, 1963.

Chen Guying. *The Interpretation and Translation of Laozi Today*. Beijing: Beijing Commercial Press, 2006.

———. *The Translation and Review of Laozi*. Hong Kong: Chunghua Book, 2012.

Ding Yuanzhi. *Guodianzhujian Interpretation and Research on Laozi*. Taipei: Wanjuanlou Publishing, 1999.

Hui Neng. *Teachings of Sakyamuni Master Huineng, the Sixth Patriarch of Zen Buddhism*. Translation from Key Concepts in Chinese Thought and Culture.

Laozi. *Daodejing*. Translation from Key Concepts in Chinese Thought and Culture.

Legge, James, ed. and trans. *The Works of Mencius*. Oxford: Clarendon Press, 1895.

———. *The Analects by Confucius*. Oxford: Clarendon Press, 1893.

Li X. F. *Daodejing*. A New Millennium Translation. Bethesda, MD: Premier Publishing, 2001.

Liu Kezhuang. "The Tenth Poem." *Ten Six-Character-per-Line Poems*. (English translation mine)

Loy Hui-chieh. "Mozi." *Internet Encyclopedia of Philosophy*. https://iep.utm.edu/.

Wang Keping, Yuan Jixi, Zhao Tingyang, et al. *Key Concepts in Chinese Thought and Culture.* Shanghai: Palgrave Macmillan, 2019.

Zhang Zai. *Enlightenment through Confucian Teachings.* Translation from Key Concepts in Chinese Thought and Culture.

Books, Articles, and Other Sources

Amendments to the Constitution of the People's Republic of China. Adopted at the Second Session of the Tenth National People's Congress and Promulgated for Implementation by the Announcement of the National People's Congress. Beijing. March 14, 2004.

Amery, C. *Das Ende der Vorsehung. Die gnadenlosen Folgen des Christentums.* Reinbek bei Hamburg: Rowohlt, 1972.

Ames, Roger T. "Putting the *Te* Back into Taoism." In *Nature in Asian Traditions of Thought*, edited by J. Baird Callicott and Roger T. Ames. Albany: State University of New York Press, 1989.

Ames, Roger T., and D. Hall. *Anticipating China: Thinking Through the Narratives of Chinese and Western Culture.* Albany: State University of New York Press, 1995.

Baggio, A. M. *Caino e I suoi fratelli, il fondamento relazionale nella politica e nel diritto.* Roma: Città Nuova, 2012.

———. "The Forgotten Principle: Fraternity in Its Public Dimension." *Claritas: Journal of Dialogue and Culture* 2, no. 2 (October 2013).

———. *Il principio dimenticato. La fraternità nella riflessione politologica contemporanea.* Roma: Città Nuova, 2007.

———. *Il principio dimenticato. Percorsi e prospettive della fraternità nella riflessione politologica contemporanea.* Roma: Città Nuova, 2007.

———. "Love of All Loves: Politics and Fraternity in the Charismatic Vision of Chiara Lubich (Sophia University Institute). *Claritas: Journal of Dialogue and Culture* 2, no. 2 (October 2013): 53–65.

Bao Leiping. "Youth Idols in China since 1949 from the Structural Perspective." *Youth Research* 1 (2009): 67–75.

Bauckham, Richard. *Bible and Ecology*, London: DLT, 2010.

Benton, Andrew. "China Releases 2021–2035 Transport Plan." *International Railway Journal*, May 11, 2021.

Berry, R. J., ed. *Environmental Stewardship: Critical Perspectives, Past and Present*. London: T&T Clark, 2006.

Brodie, Thomas L. *The Gospel according to John*. New York: Oxford University Press, 1993.

Bruni, Lugino, and Bernhard Callebaut. "The Economy of Communion as a Charismatic Practice." In H. Opdebeeck (ed.), *Schumacher Reconsidered. Advances in Responsible Economics*. New York: Peter Lang, 2012, 150–172.

Bruni, Luigino. *Guida alla lettura dell'Enciclico Fratelli Tutti* [Guide to Reading Fratelli Tutti]. Milano: Paolini Edizioni, 2020.

Bruni, Lugino, and P. L. Porta. *Economics and Happiness: Framing the Analysis*. Cambridge: Cambridge University Press, 2005.

Caldecott, Stratford. *Catholicism and Other Religions: Introducing Interfaith Dialogue*. London: Catholic Truth Society, 2009.

Callebaut, Bernhard. "Economy of Communion, a Sociological Inquiry on a Contemporary Charismatic Inspiration in Economic and Social Life." *Claritas: Journal of Dialogue & Culture* 1, no. 1 (March 2012).

———. "A Sociological Reading of a New Cultural Scene." *Claritas: Journal of Dialogue & Culture* 4, no. 1 (March 2015).

Cambon, E. *Trinità, modello sociale*. Roma: Città Nuova, 1999.

Campanini, G. *Bene comune: Declino e riscoperta di un concetto*. Bologna: Edizioni Dehoniane, 2014.

———. *Il pensiero politico ed ecclesiologico di Antonio Rosmini*. Bologna: Edizioni Rosminiane, 2014.

Casanova, J. *Public Religions in the Modern World*. Chicago: University of Chicago Press, 1994.

Catholic News Agency. *Full Text: Pope Francis' In-Flight Press Conference from Slovakia*. September 21, 2021.

Cefaloni, Carlo. "Dialogando con Stefano Zamagni." *Città Nuova*. July 2021, 30–33.

Cernuzio, Salvatore. "Cardinal Parolin on China: Obedience to the Pope Enlivens Love for Country," *Vatican News*, May 21, 2024.

Charbonnier, Jean-Pierre. *Christians in China, AD 600–2000*. San Francisco: Ignatius Press, 2007.

Chen Cunfu and Huang Tianhai. "The Emergence of a New Type of Christians in China Today." *Review of Religious Research* (December 2001): 83–200.

Chen Ling and Barry Naughton. "An Institutionalized Policy-Making Mechanism: China's Return to Techno-Industrial Policy." *Research Policy* 45 2016, 2138–2152.

Chen Xie. "The Other Side of the Global Imbalances: The Politics of Economic Reform in China under the 'New Normal,'" PhD diss., University of York, March 2018, 175–176.

Chen Ming. "The Return of Confucianism in Modern Practice Edification." *Global Times* (editorial) (Chinese edition), March 21, 2016.

Cobb, John B., and I. Castuera, eds. *For Our Common Home: Process-Relational Response to Laudato Si'*. Anoka, MN: Process Century Press, 2015.

Cobb, John B., and Andre Vltchek. *China and Ecological Civilization: John B. Cobb, Jr., in Conversation with Andre Vltchek*. Kindle edition, 2019.

Coda, Piero, "Creation in Christ and the New Creation in the Mysticism of Chiara Lubich." *Claritas: Journal of Dialogue and Culture* 5, no. 1 (2016): article 3.

———. *Dalla Trinità. L'avvento di Dio tra storia e profezia*. Roma: Città Nuova, 2011.

———. *Il logos e il nulla. Trinità religioni mistica*. Roma: Città Nuova, 2003.

———. *La trinità, quando il racconto di Dio diventa il racconto dell'uomo*. Rome: Marcianum Press, 2015.

———. *Pensare la Trinità*, Roma: Città Nuova, 2013.

———. "Per una fondazione teologica della categoria politica della fraternità," in Antonio M. Baggio, *Il principio dimenticato: La fraternità nella riflessione politologica contemporanea*. Roma: Città Nuova, 2007, 107–108.

———. *Sul luogo della Trinità. Rileggendo il De Trinitate di Agostino*. Roma: Città Nuova, 2008.

———. "Trinitarian Ontology." Lecture, Sophia University Institute, Figline and Incisa Valdarno, Florence, March 11, 2014.

Coda, P., et al. *Manifesto, Dizionario dinamico di Ontologia Trinitaria.* Roma: Città Nuova, 2021.
Constitution of the Communist Party of China. Revised and Adopted at the Nineteenth National Congress of the Communist Party of China. Beijing, October 24, 2017.
Constitution of the People's Republic of China. December 4, 1982.
Corsetti, Gabriel. "An Analysis of Online Fundraising in China." *China Development Brief,* August 31, 2018.
Costa, G., and P. Foglizzo. "L'ecologia integrale." *Aggiornamenti Sociali,* August–September 2015.
Cotter, Kevin. "The Best 2-Page Summary of *Laudato Si'*." Global Catholic Climate Movement (GCCM). August 11, 2016.
Cousins, Ewert. *Christ of the 21st Century.* New York: Continuum, 1998.
De Bary, W. Theodore, ed. *Sources of Chinese Tradition.* New York: Columbia University Press, 1960.
De Vitry, Jacques. "History of the Orient." In *St. Francis of Assisi, Omnibus of Sources.* Cincinnati: St. Anthony Messenger Press, 2008.
Di Sante, Carmine. *Responsabilità, L'io-per-l'altro.* Roma: Edizioni Lavoro-Esperienze, Fossano, 1996.
Donati, P. *Relational Sociology: A New Paradigm for the Social Sciences.* London: Routledge, 2011.
Dong Zhongshu. "Luxuriant Gems." In *The Spring and Autumn Annals.* Translation from Key Concepts in Chinese Thought and Culture.
Eh, Edmond. "Aristotle, Lubich, and Ratzinger on a New Economic Paradigm." *The Journal of the Macau Ricci Institute,* no. 7 (2021).
Epps, Henry. *Ethics Vol. II: Universal Ethics and Morality.* Scotts Valley, CA: Lulu, 2012.
Faggioli, M. *Sorting Out Catholicism,* Wilmington, DE: Michael Glazier Book, 2014.
Falasca, Stefania. "La croce sulla stele di Xi'an testimone della fede in Cina." *Avvenire.* August 30, 2024, 20.
Federation of Asian Bishops' Conferences. *Theology of Dialogue.* Tagaytay City, Philippines, 1988.

Feng Youlan (Fung Yu-lan). *Collection of Discussions on the Philosophy of Laozi*. Beijing: Zhonghua Book Company, 1959. Chinese edition.

———. *A Short History of Chinese Philosophy*. New York: Macmillan Publishing Company, 1948.

———. "Why China Has No Science." *International Journal of Ethics* 32, no. 3 (1922): 237–263.

Ferrara, Pasquale. *Il mondo di Francisco: Bergoglio e la politica internazionale*. Milan, 2016.

Francis of Assisi. "Canticle of the Creatures." In *Francis of Assisi: Early Documents*. New York: New City Press, 1999.

Fraser, Chris. "Mohism: Book 16, 'Inclusive Care' of Mozi." *Stanford Encyclopedia of Philosophy*, 2015.

Friedman, Maurice S. "Martin Buber: The Life of Dialogue." *The Religion*, June 9, 2020, https://religion-online.org/book-chapter/chapter-12-the-eternal-thou.

Galimberti, U. *Psyche and Techne: Man in the Age of Technology*. Milan: Feltrinelli, 1999.

Gallagher, Jim. *Woman's Work: Story of the Focolare Movement and Its Founder*. New York: New City Press, 1998.

Gao Pengcheng. "The French Revolution Never Mentioned the Motto of Bo'ai." *Qinghai Social Science*, no. 2 (2014).

Gillies, D., and G. Giorello. *La filosofia della scienza nel XX secolo*. Rome: Editore Laterza, 2007.

Goossaert, Vincent. "1898: The Beginning of the End for Chinese Religion?" *Journal of Asian Studies* 65, no. 2 (2006).

Gussie, Kielce. "Pope to Young People of the Synod: 'Keep Moving Forward.'" *Vatican News*. October 23, 2024.

Gutheinz, Luis. *The Mystery of God*. Taipei: Guangqi Press, 1990.

———. *Theological Anthropology*. Taipei: Guangqi Press, 2008.

Hao Changchi. "Is Mozi a Utilitarian Philosopher?" *Frontiers of Philosophy in China* 1, no. 3 (2006).

Heng, Quan. "Navigating China's Economic Development in the New Era: From High-Speed to High-Quality Growth." *China Quarterly of International Strategic Studies* 4, no. 2, 2018, 177–192.

Hegel, Georg Wilhelm Friedrich. *The Phenomenology of Spirit: Volume 1*. Trans. J. B. Baillie. New York: Cosimo Classics, 2005.

Hofman, Bert. "Reflections on Forty Years of China's Reforms." Keynote Speech at Fudan University's Fanhai School of International Finance, Shanghai, January 2018.

Hou Sheng (Zhao Zhengping). "The Philosophy of Universal Love." *Southern Newspaper*, no. 3 (November 1910). In *Selected Works of the Ten Years before the Revolution of 1911*. Volume 3. Hong Kong: Sanlian Bookstore, 1960.

Hu, Philipp K. T. "The Creation of the Universe from Nothingness by Laozi from the Perspective of Nothingness in the Christian Tradition." *Sophia* 13, no. 1, 2021, 75–92.

———. "La volontà del cielo nell'antica sapienza cinese introduzione, traduzione e commento dei capitoli 26–28 di Mozi." *Nuova Umanità*, no. 217 (2015): 65–89.

Hua Hua. "A Survey on College Students' Christian Belief: Taking Some Shanghai Students as Example." *Youth Studies*, vol. 1. Shanghai, 2008.

Huang Songkang. "The Ultimate Realization of the Confucian Ideal Universal Harmony as Seen by China's Revolutionary Thinker Li Dazhao (1889–1927)." *Ultimate Reality and Meaning* 9, no. 3 (1986).

Huntington, Samuel. *The Clash of Civilizations and the Remaking of World Order*. New York: Simon and Schuster, 1996.

Indunil, J. Kodithuwakku K. "Christian Witness in a Multi-religious World: Recommendations for Conduct; Thinking Back and Looking Ahead." *International Bulletin of Missionary Research* 37 (2013).

Information Office of the People's Republic of China. "Seeking Happiness for People: 70 Years of Progress on Human Rights in China." White Paper Issued by the State Council, Beijing, September 2019.

Inglehart, Ronald. "Post-materialism." Encyclopedia Britannica Online. November 16, 2016.

Ivanhoe, Philip J. "The Concept of *De* ('Virtue') in the *Laozi*." In *Religious and Philosophical Aspects of the Laozi*, edited by Mark Csikszentmihalyi and Philip J. Ivanhoe. Albany: State University of New York Press, 1999.

Jaspers, Karl. *Origin and Goal of History*. New Haven, CT: Yale University Press, 1953.

Jin, Aloysius. "Advancing with the Times." Chinese New Year 2011 Pastoral Letter. Shanghai, February 2, 2011.

Jin Keyu. *The New China Playbook: Beyond Socialism and Capitalism*. London: Swift Press, 2023.

Kang Youwei. "The French Revolution." In *Political Theory of Kang Youwei*. Beijing: Zhonghua Book Company, 1981.

Kwok, Edmund. "Epilogue: From Fraternity to Integrality—An Integral Reflection on *Fratelli Tutti*." In *Intercultural and Interreligious Reflection on* Fratelli Tutti. Edited by Edmund Kwok. In Tripod, no. 201. Hong Kong: Holy Spirit Study Centre, 2022, 209–236.

Kwok, Edmund. "Humanism of the Third Generation Confucianism." In *Anthology of Celebrative Essays of Mr. Tu Weiming's 80th Birthday*. Edited by Chen Lai. Beijing: People's Press, 2019, 601–603.

Kwok, Edmund. "Review of *Confucianism and Christianity: Interreligious Dialogue on the Theology of Mission*." Edited by Edmund Kee-Fook Chia. In *Tripod*, no. 200. Hong Kong: Holy Spirit Study Centre, 2022, 209–217.

Lai Panchiu. "God of Life and Ecological Theology: A Chinese Christian Perspective." *Ecumenical Review* 65, no. 1 (March 2013): 67–82.

Leahy, B. *Ecclesial Movements and Communities*. New York: New City Press, 2011.

Leaman, Oliver. *Key Concepts in Eastern Philosophy*. New York: Routledge, 1999.

Lent, Jeremy. "Can China Really Lead the Way to an 'Ecological Civilization'?" ENSIA at the University of Minnesota's Institute on the Environment, Minneapolis, August 29, 2018.

Li Chien-Chiu, Bernard. "Dao-Logos: Lao Zi and Philo." *Euntes Docente* 1 / Anno LXII (2009).

Li Shi. *History of Thoughts in the Qing Dynasty*. Deep Into China Histories series (2019).

Li X. P. "Social Consensus, Core Values and Way of Faith of the Chinese." *North-Western People's University Journal* 6 (2014).

Liu Xinyong. "China Focus: Reform, Opening-Up Create New Wonders in Human History." Xinhua Net, December 17, 2018.

Lubich, Chiara. *The Cry of Jesus Crucified and Forsaken.* Foreword by Cardinal Paul Poupard. New York: New City Press, 2001.
———. *Essential Writings.* New York: New City Press, 2007.
———. "The Experience of the 'Economy of Communion': A Proposal of Economic Action from the Spirituality of Unity." In *The Economy of Communion: Toward a Multi-dimensional Economic Culture*, edited by Luigino Bruni, 15–16. New York: New City Press, 2002.
———. "Lubich's Talk on the Theme about the Eucharist to Members of the Focolare." Rocca di Papa, Italy, October 10, 1976.
———. "The Movement for Unity and a Politics of Communion." Address to the International Conference of the Movement of Unity in Politics. Castel Gandolfo, Rome, June 9, 2000.
———. "A Transforming Power." *Living City.* April 2015.
———. *Unity and Jesus Forsaken.* New York: New City Press, 1985.
Machle, E. J. *Nature and Heaven in the Xunzi: A Study of the Tian Lun.* Albany: State University of New York Press, 1993.
Manjunath, R. *Understanding the Universe: Quarks, Leptons and the Big Bang.* Bangalore, 2020.
Maritain, Jacques. *Existence and the Existent.* Mahwah, NJ: Paulist Press, 2015.
Masters, T., and A. Uelmen. *Focolare: Living a Spirituality of Unity in the United States.* New York: New City Press, 2011.
Meissner, Werner. "China's Search for Cultural and National Identity from the Nineteenth Century to the Present." *China Perspectives*, no. 68, 2006.
Mitchell, Donald W. "Dazzling Darkness, Buddhism and Chiara Lubich's Mystical Writings." *Claritas: Journal of Dialogue and Culture* 6, no. 2. October 2017, 6–13.
Mitchell, Donald W., and James Wiseman. *Transforming Suffering: Reflections on Finding Peace in Troubled Times.* New York: Lantern Books, 2010.
Moeller, Hans-Georg. "Basic Aspects of Daoist Philosophy." *International Communication of Chinese Culture* 2 (2015).
Moriggi, A. "Chinese Women at the Forefront of Environmental Activism: Wang Yongchen, Liao Xiaoyi and Tian Guirong." *DEP (Deportate, Esuli e Profughe) Journal*, no. 35 (2017).

Naughton, Barry. *Growing Out of the Plan: Chinese Economic Reforms 1978–1993.* Cambridge: Cambridge University Press, 1995.

Norton, Brian. *Why Preserve Natural Variety?* Princeton, NJ: Princeton University Press, 1991.

Osto, Giulio. *La testimonianza del dialogo Piero Rossano tra Bibbia, religioni e cultura.* Roma: Glossa, 2019.

Ozouf, Mona. "Liberté, Égalité, Fraternité Stands for Peace, Country, and War." In *Lieux de Mémoire,* Tome III, edited by Pierre Nora, 53–89. Paris: Quarto Gallimard, 1997.

Passmore, John. *Man's Responsibility for Nature: Ecological Problems and Western Tradition.* New York: Scribner's, 1974.

Pelli, Anna. "Verità e dialogo: la dinamica relazionale del conoscere." Sophia University Institute, Florence, 2013–2014.

People's Daily. "Build a New Type of International Relations and a Community with a Shared Future for Mankind." October 29, 2019.

———. "Highlights of Xi's Speech at a Conference Celebrating 40 Years of Reform, Opening-Up." December 18, 2018.

Perry, Marvin. *Western Civilization: A Brief History.* Boston: Wadsworth/Cengage, 2013.

Persico, Nicola. "Fighting Pollution: What China Can Learn from Britain." *Fortune,* March 10, 2015.

Pew Forum on Religion & Public Life. "The Global Religious Landscape." Pew Research Center. December 18, 2012.

Piryns, E. D. "Evangelization, Mission and Missionary Activity in a Dialogical Context." University of Santo Tomas, Manila, 1983.

Pollitt, Hector. "Analysis: Going Carbon Neutral by 2060 'Will Make China Richer.'" *Carbon Brief,* September 24, 2020.

Povilus, Judith M. *United in His Name: Jesus in Our Midst in the Experience and Thought of Chiara Lubich.* New York: New City Press, 1992.

Radio Vatican. "Giubileo dei nunzi, Becciu: Aperti al dialogo, forti nell'identità." Interview with Angelo Becciu, Vatican Deputy Secretary of State. ANSA News Agency. September 15, 2016.

Ratzinger, Joseph. "Christ, Faith and the Challenge of Cultures." Meeting with the Doctrinal Commissions in Asia. Hong Kong, March 3, 1993.

———. "Church and Economy: Responsibility for the Future of the World Economy." *Communio: International Catholic Review* 13 (1986): 199–204.

———. *The Meaning of Christian Brotherhood*. San Francisco: Ignatius Press, 1993.

———. *Principles of Catholic Theology*. San Francisco: Ignatius Press, 1987.

Reis, Bernadette Mary. "A Celebration on Human Fraternity." *Vatican News*, September 21, 2019.

Ren Andao. "A Christian between Tien and Humans." *Fountains Periodical* (Taipei), no. 95, 2018.

Ren Jiyu. "The Dialectic of Simplicity." *Teaching and Research*, no. 2, 1962.

Ricci, Matteo. *Fonti Ricciani*. Edited by P. M. d'Elia. 3 volumes. Roma: Libreria dello Stato, 1942–1949.

———. *The True Meaning of the Lord of Heaven*. Edited by E. J. Malatesta. Taipei: Ricci Institute, 1985.

Rondinara, Sergio. "Custodire ciò che è salvato." In *Per un umanesimo degno dell'amore: Il Compendio della Dottrina Sociale della Chiesa*, edited by Paolo Carlotti and Mario Toso. Roma: Editrice LAS, 2005.

———. "Relazione persona-natura: Il recupero dei significati." *Nuova Umanità*, no. 224 (2016).

Rosse, Gerard. "Il grido del crocifisso, approccio biblico." Sophia University Institute, Florence, 2010.

Rosse, Gerard, and Piero Coda. *Il grido d'abbandono, Scrittura Mistica Teologia*. Sophia University Institute, Florence, 2020.

Schnackenburg, Rudolf. *The Johannine Epistle: A Commentary*. New York: Crossroad, 1992.

Scott, Sarah. "Martin Buber (1878–1965)." *Internet Encyclopedia of Philosophy*, June 9, 2020.

Shen W. X. "Logical Relationship from Socialist Core Value System to China Dream." *Journal of China Executive Leadership Academy*, 2014.

Shrader-Freccette, Kristin. *Environmental Ethics*. Pacific Grove, CA: Boxwood Press, 1981.

Smith, H. *The World's Religions*. San Francisco: HarperCollins, 1991.

Smith, Richard. "China's Drivers and Planetary Ecological Collapse." *Real-World Economics Review*, no. 82 (2017).
South China Morning Post. "Grinding Poverty in China: Is Xi Jinping's Alleviation Campaign Making Any Difference?" March 25, 2018.
Sun Yatsen, "The Revolutionary Strategy of the Chinese Alliance." In *The Complete Works of Sun Yatsen*. Volume 1. Beijing: Zhonghua Book Company, 1981.
———. "Three People's Principles? Nationalism? Sixth Lecture" (March 16, 1924). In *The Complete Works of Sun Yatsen*, Volume 9. Beijing: Zhonghua Book Company, 1986.
Tang, Frank. "China Launches New Go West Development Drive to Counter Post-coronavirus Geopolitical Risks." *South China Morning Post*, June 22, 2020.
Tao Li, "Parents of Ofo's Bike User Sue Company for Negligence after Accident." *South China Morning Post*, October 27, 2017.
Tertullian. *Apology*. Trans. T. H. Bindley. 1890.
Thérèse of Lisieux. *The Story of a Soul*. New York: Doubleday, 2001.
Tocqueville, A. de. *The Old Regime and the French Revolution*. New York: Anchor Books, 1955.
Tong, John. "The Future of the Sino-Vatican Dialogue from an Ecclesiological Point of View." *Hong Kong Sunday Examiner*, February 4, 2017.
UCANews. "First Catholic-Run Non-profit Organization Registered with Chinese Government." August 3, 2006.
United Nations. "Inequality—Bridging the Divide." *UN's 75th Anniversary Report: Shaping Our Future Together*. Geneva, 2020, https://un.org/en/un75/inequality-bridging-divide.
United Nations General Assembly. The Universal Declaration of Human Rights. Paris, December 10, 1948.
Valente, Gianni. "The Pope and Mission: Without Jesus We Can Do Nothing." Extracts from *Senza di lui non possiamo far nulla: Essere missionari oggi nel mondo: Una conversazione con Gianni Valente di Francesco*. Rome: Agenzia Fedes Information Service, November 4, 2019.
Wang Qi. "China Launches Clean Plate Campaign 2.0 as Xi Calls for End to Food Wastage." *Global Times*, August 12, 2020.
Wang X., Dao. "Logos and Social and Historical Changes." *Journal of Lanzhou University*, 1998.

Wang Zhihe and Fan Meijun. "Hope Lies in Change." In *For Our Common Home: Process-Relational Response to Laudato Si'*, edited by J. B. Cobb and I. Castuero. Anoka, MN: Process Century Press, 2015.

———. *Second Enlightenment*. Beijing: University of Peking Press, 2011.

Watson, Burton. *Chinese Lyricism: Shih Poetry from the Second to the Twelfth Century*. New York: Columbia University Press, 1971.

Westermann, Claus. *Genesis*. Trans. David E. Orton. Edinburgh: T&T Clark, 1988.

White, Lynn, Jr. "The Historical Roots of Our Ecologic Crisis." *Science* 155 (1967).

Wintz, Jack. "Franciscans and Muslims: Eight Centuries of Seeking God." Franciscan Media, 2019.

Wong, Joseph H. "*Logos* and *Tao*: Johannine Christology and a Taoist Perspective." *Path: Pontificia Academia Theologica* 2 (2003).

Wurth, E., and B. A. Maheu. *Papal Documents Related to China, 1937–2005*. Hong Kong: Holy Spirit Study Centre, 2006.

Xi Jinping. "Exclusive Q&A with Chinese President Xi Jinping." Reuters. October 18, 2015.

———. *The Governance of China*. Beijing: Foreign Languages Press, 2014.

———. "Highlights of Xi's Speech at Beijing Horticultural Expo Opening Ceremony." China Global Television Network. April 28, 2019.

———. "Xi Jinping: If the People Have Faith, the Nation Has Hope, and the Country Has Strength." Xinhuanet, February 28, 2015.

———. "Join Hands on the Path towards Modernization," Keynote Address at the CPC in Dialogue with World Political Parties High-Level Meeting, State Council Information Office, Beijing, March 15, 2023.

———. "Xi's Keynote Speech at the Opening Ceremony of the International Horticultural Exhibition 2019 (Edited Excerpt)." *Beijing Review*, September 3, 2019.

———. *The 19th National Congress of the Communist Party of China Report*. Beijing, October 18, 2017.

———. "To Promote Common Prosperity on Solid Ground." *Qiushi Journal*. October 15, 2021.

———. "Speech of President Xi Jinping on the 70th Anniversary of the Founding of the People's Republic of China." *Xinhua News*, September 30, 2019.

———. "Working Together to Build a Human Community with a Shared Future." Speech at the United Nations Office in Geneva, January 18, 2017. In *On Building a Human Community with a Shared Future*, 427–440. Beijing: Central Compilation and Translation Press, 2019.

Xu Chenggang. "How China's Economy Actually Works." Transcript from *New Economic Thinking*, April 22, 2021.

Yan, Kin Sheung Chiaretto. "The China Experience as Contribution for a New Economic Paradigm." *Journal of the Macau Ricci Institute* (Macau), no. 7. May 2020, 91–95.

———. *Evangelization in China: Challenges and Prospects.* Maryknoll, NY: Orbis Books, 2014.

———. "Prolegomenon to Interreligious Dialogue in China: Daoism, the Trinitarian Relationship, and Christian Inculturation." *Claritas: Journal of Dialogue and Culture* 6, 2017.

———. *Seasons for Relationships: Youth in China and the Mission of the Church.* Macau: Claretian Publications, 2019.

Yong Lina. "Research on Theological Education in the Church of China." Conference Paper, November 18–19, 2014.

Zhang Qiang et al. "Drivers of Improved PM2.5 Air Quality in China from 2013 to 2017." *Proceedings of National Academy of Science (PNAS)*, December 3, 2019.

Zhao X. "The Critical Discourse Analysis of Xi Jinping's Speech on China Dream." Master's thesis, National University of Singapore, 2014.

Zhuo Xinping. "Responsibility of a Scholar and Future of Religious Studies." *Chinese Culture Research*, no. 1 (2018).

Index

Adam and Eve, 45, 47
  dominion over the earth, as granted, 42, 184
  I-Thou relationship, betraying, 56–57
  temptation, falling into, 33, 43, 56, 59, 92, 95
Adam and Eve in the Garden of Eden (painting), 33, 43, 44, 184, 198
agape (unconditional love), 79, 89, 95, 186
al-Malik al-Kamil, 97–98
Ames, Roger, 26
Andao, Ren, 56
Aquinas, Thomas, xxv, 36
Aristotle, 21, 36
Armstrong, Karen, 21
Augustine of Hippo, Saint, 1, 15
Axial Age, 21, 53

Bacon, Francis, 45–46
Baggio, Antonio, 96, 97, 115, 116
Bao Leiping, 132
Beijing Horticultural Expo, 32–33, 69, 78, 174, 184, 197–98
Benedict XVI, Pope, 141–42, 148, 173, 181

benevolence, 89, 181
  the family, benevolence within, 86, 103, 187
  God, benevolent gaze of, 102, 187
  ren, connotation of benevolence in, 83, 110, 185
Biden, Joe—Biden administration, 77, 150
bike-sharing system, 123, 133
Birthday Tree Planting project, 67
bo'ai (universal love), 83, 90
  agape, influenced by the concept of, 79, 186
  fraternity, expressed as, 80, 81–82, 185
  Sun Yat-sen as championing term, 88, 89, 108
Boff, Leonardo, 143
Bruni, Luigino, 144, 146–47
Buber, Martin, 56–57
Buddhism, 3, 53, 171
  Chinese culture, as part of, 1, 158
  on equality for all sentient beings, 35, 40, 41, 55
  Mahayana Buddhism, 4, 34, 40
  revival of Buddhism in China, 162, 196

Cain and Abel, 62, 92, 146
Caldecott, Stratford, 52
Callebaut, Bernhard, 143, 144
Caritas charity group, 134, 137, 176
Caritas in Veritate encyclical, 142
Catholic Social Services, 134–35
Catholic social teaching, 60, 115, 149, 174
Chai Jing, 50
Chan Wing-tsit, 7–8
charism of unity, 57–58, 178, 195
Chen Guying, 10
Chen Kuying, 28
Chien-Chiu, Bernard Li, 27
city-countryside exchanges, 170–72
Cobb, John, 73–74, 128
Coda, Piero, 15, 19, 92, 95, 159
common good, 106, 116, 128, 145, 148, 194
    Francis as promoting, 112, 114
    in *Fratelli Tutti*, 140, 147
    Sun Yat-sen as advocating for, 88, 108
common prosperity, 120, 126, 182
Concilium Sinense (Shanghai Council), 192
Confucianism, 5, 21, 27, 78, 89, 94, 105, 128
    Analects of Confucius, 84, 187
    change, emphasis on making, 181–82, 187
    Chinese culture, at the root of, 1, 181
    Classic of Filial Piety, 88
    as complementary to Daoism and Buddhism, 3–4, 29, 34
    Confucian state exams, 131
    Confucian values, 188
    Golden Rule of Confucius, 89, 153, 189
    on harmony while diversified, 104, 157
    on heaven and man united as one, 35, 37, 38, 55
    Mohism as an alternative philosophy, 54, 80, 86
    principle of gradation, tradition based on, 107
    reciprocity and altruism, upholding, 106
    relationship between humans and nature in, 37–39, 41
    on *ren'ai* as human-heartedness, 82–84, 90, 108, 110, 185–86
    Ricci as inaugurating dialogue with Christianity, 2, 158
    tianxia, emphasizing concept of, 103, 111
Costa, Giacomo, 63
Cousins, Ewert, 21
culture of harmony, xxviii–xxxi, xxxii, 194

Daoism, 41, 71, 89, 158, 171, 182, 183
    in Chinese cultural tradition, 1, 55, 181

as complementary to Confucianism and Buddhism, 3–4, 34
dao fa ziran as "*Dao* follows self-so," 35–36
Daodejing, 5, 6, 7, 9, 10–11, 24, 25, 26, 37, 53, 54, 104
Daoists as the first ecologists, 59, 184
de as a Daoist virtue, 4, 24, 26–29
harmony, Daoist notion of, 61, 103, 159
Logos, translated as, 22, 26, 28–29
yin and *yang* elements in, 12, 24
Deng Xiaoping, 121, 126, 129, 158
Descartes, René, 46, 48
Di Sante, Carmine, 6
dialectic of harmony
being and nonbeing in, 182
Laozi on mutual generation in, 183
social life, as a guide for, 8, 104
Trinitarian theology, applying to, 1, 24–25, 29, 183
yin-yang, as a method of, 7, 9
dialectic of simplicity, 7–9
dialogue, 68, 95, 108, 141, 157, 164, 171, 175
daily commitment to dialogue, 100, 105, 109
dialogue of action, 75–76
of ecological civilization with integral ecology, 184–85

Francis of Assisi, dialogue with sultan, 97–98
fraternal dialogue, 102, 151, 159
Global Civilization Dialogue, 165
International Day for Dialogue, 166
interreligious dialogue, 12, 22, 52, 64, 155, 158, 190
patience, dialogue requiring, 156
Pope Francis on, 65, 101, 137
in Sino-Vatican relations, 151–52, 152–55, 160–61, 173
in Trinitarian relationship, 1–2, 162, 183
unity in diversity, as helping to maintain, 103–4
urgent challenges, facing through dialogue, 63
Ding Yuanzhi, 28
Dong Zhongshu, 38

ecclesial base communities (CEB), 143
ecological civilization, 34, 76, 182
as a Chinese goal, 78, 118, 128
initiatives on ecological civilization, 71–75
integral ecology, in dialogue with, 184–85
Xi Jinping, in the speech of, 69–71
ecological conversion, 60, 64, 65, 66, 68
ecological crisis, 62, 65, 184

Economy of Communion (EoC), 141–43, 145–46
Economy of Francesco (EoF), 140–47
EcoOne (cultural initiative), 66–67
Eh, Edmond, 145
Einstein, Albert, 31
El-Tayeb, Ahmed, 98, 100, 102, 186
Empty Your Plate campaign, 51
encounter, 15, 23, 90, 106, 108, 180, 181
  between Christianity and Latin culture, 1, 158
  Church's encounter with China, 179
  culture of encounter, 136–37, 151, 159–63, 164, 178, 196
  political sphere as a place of encounter, 140–41
  in the Trinitarian relationship, 58–59
  Xi on the encounter of civilizations, 164–65
Evangelii Gaudium apostolic exhortation, 159

Fan Meijun, 71
feigong (Condemnation of Offensive War), 85, 105
Feng Youlan, 10, 54, 84, 106
Fides et Ratio encyclical, xxiv
Focolare Movement, 65–66, 115, 142, 172
Foglizzo, Paolo, 63
food waste, 51–52

Foucauld, Charles de, Saint, 138, 189
Francis, Pope, 12, 56, 67, 107, 110, 117, 137, 179
  Abu Dhabi address and declaration, 98–100, 102, 109
  on the Chinese faithful, 176–77
  common good, on working for, 114
  on the COVID-19 pandemic, 175, 188
  culture of encounter, emphasizing, 196
  dialogue with China, desire for, 164, 173
  on earth as a shared inheritance, 71
  ecological conversion, stressing the need for, 68
  Economy of Communion meeting, addressing, 145–46
  on food waste as akin to stealing from the poor, 51
  on fraternity, 97–101, 105, 115, 159
  on harmony of diversity, 99, 103, 104
  Holy See–China relations under papacy of, 190, 191–92
  on integral ecology, 64, 65
  Jinde Charities, donating to, 135
  joint declaration for fraternity and peace, signing, 185–86

Index   219

love, on humanity as made for, 111
new economic system, calling for, 118, 127, 145
racism and radical individualism, denouncing, 112
rights, on young people fighting for, 106
simple lifestyle advocated by, 138
synodal church, emphasis on, 151, 160
World Day of the Poor message, 136–37
young people, inspiring, 194–95
See also Fratelli Tutti and *Laudato Si'* encyclicals
Francis of Assisi, Saint, 55, 64, 78, 96, 97–98, 138, 172, 189
Fratelli Tutti encyclical, 22, 80, 138, 141, 144, 147
exemplary figures of, 188–89
on fraternity and social friendship, 109–12
Good Samaritan parable, building on, 140, 146
fraternity, 64, 90, 105, 107, 127, 159, 181, 182
Catholic social teaching, as part of, 149
Document on Human Fraternity for World Peace and Living Together, 80, 100, 101
extending fraternity to others, 102–3, 179
Francis, Abu Dhabi address on, 98–100, 102, 109
in *Fratelli Tutti*, 109–16, 140
fraternity in the spirit, 147, 193
from fraternity to universal love in Chinese language, 80–82
freedom without fraternity as contradictory, 112–14
Letter to Galatians, Paul discussing in, 94–95
"liberty, equality, and fraternity" triptych motto, 79, 80, 96–97, 115, 186
in the Old Testament, 92–93
peace, fraternity for, 108–9, 185–87
testimony and pact of fraternity, 97–98
universal fraternity, 112, 138

Gandhi, Mahatma, 30, 138
Gao Pengcheng, 80–81
gaokao (college entrance exam), 131, 168
Global Catholic Climate Movement, 65
Golden Rule of Reciprocity, 83, 153, 189–91
Good Samaritan parable, 140, 146
Gross Ecosystem Product (GEP), 118, 125

Han Yu, 89
he (harmony), 11, 12, 24
Hegel, Georg Wilhelm Friedrich, 8–9, 183
Hillel, Rabbi, 111
Hofman, Bert, 120–21

Hofrichter, Peter Leander, 165
Holownia, Szymon, 137
Hua Hua, 131
Huineng, Patriarch, 40
Huntington, Samuel, 136–37

inculturation, 25, 178, 181, 183
   of Christianity in China, 29, 159
   interculturality as a preferable term, 179–80
   interculturality *vs.* unidirectional inculturation, 163–66
   Second Axial Age efforts toward inculturation, 21–23
   Sinicization *vs.* inculturation, 155–58
Inglehart, Ronald, 132
integral ecology, 76, 78, 182
   ecological civilization in dialogue with, 184–85
   initiatives on integral ecology, 64–68
   in *Laudato Si'*, 61–64, 159
   lifestyle conversion for, 198
I-Thou relationships, 23, 56–57
Ivanhoe, Philip, 26

Jaspers, Karl, 21, 53
Jesus Christ, 16, 26, 29, 91, 92, 162, 177, 195
   anthropocentrism of Christ, 59–61, 185
   followers of Jesus as brethren in Christ, 93–94
   forsaken Jesus, 1, 20, 58, 65, 95, 115
   fraternity in Christ, 79, 96, 108
   Golden Rule of Jesus, 89, 153, 189
   kenosis of, 20, 24, 183
   Lubich, Jesus in the spirituality of, 1, 57–58, 65, 78
   as the New Adam, 44–45, 59, 185, 198
   oneness of God, as praying for, 103
   phenomenological comprehension of, 23
   Trinitarian relationship and, 17–19
   as the Word, 14, 15, 17
jian'ai (all-embracing love), 90, 185
   bo'ai, as substituted for, 88
   as a concept of love, 83, 186
   in Mohist tradition, 80, 84–87, 106, 108
Jin Luxian, 169
Jinde Charities, 134–35, 176
John Paul II, Saint, 22, 163, 164, 173, 180–81, 193, 196
Jubilee Year (2000), 2, 159
justice, 62, 95, 100, 140
   peace, justice as the second wing of, 99
   social justice, 127, 145
   true justice as universal, 107–8, 112

Kang Youwei, 81, 82, 89
kenosis (self-emptying), 20, 24, 183
Keyu Jin, 133–34
Kezamutima, Steven, 67
kingdom of God, 95

Index

Lai Panchiu, 39
Laozi, 4, 6, 9, 11, 21, 36
   on the dialectic of harmony, 7, 104, 182, 183
   on the Great *De*, 27, 28
   wu-wei, on the concept of, 8, 16
Laudato Si' encyclical, 22, 66, 69, 73, 140, 172, 176, 185
   Birthday Tree Planting in response to, 67
   Canticle of St. Francis, title taken from, 55
   convergent points with spirit of, 70
   on the divine principle of the Trinity, 12
   ecological conversion, encouraging, 60, 64
   Holy See Pavilion as highlighting theme of, 32, 33
   integral ecology, calling for, 61–64, 159
   on rupture of the original human mandate, 43
   theme as highlighted at Beijing Expo, 32–33, 174, 184
Leaman, Oliver, 39
left-behind children, 125, 167
Lent, Jeremy, 75, 76
li (propriety), 27, 83
Liang Zhi, 132
Liao Xiaoyi, 72–73, 128
liberation theology, 143
Liu Kezhuang, 41
Liu Xiang, 88
Logos, 13, 22, 26, 28–29, 183
LoHo Homelands, 72–73

Lubich, Chiara, 19, 65, 183
   abandonment of Jesus, basing spirituality on, 1, 18, 78
   on the charism of unity, 57–58, 178
   Economy of Communion, establishing, 141, 142–44, 145
   on politics as the love of all loves, 115–16

Ma Huateng, 132
Ma Yun, 132
Marxism, 1, 90, 131, 158, 183
Mencius, 38, 83, 84, 86, 90, 108, 181
mercy, 16, 105, 143, 159
Moeller, Hans-Georg, 36
Mohism, 54, 80, 84–88, 90, 108
Mozi, 21, 84–86, 87, 105, 108, 181, 186

one-hundred-day formation program, 167–68
open-door policy, 119, 121, 157
original sin, 44
Our Lady of Sheshan, 177
Our Lady of the Knots, 196
Ozouf, Mona, 96

Parolin, Pietro, 192
phenomenological perspective, 4–5, 23
pingdeng (equality), 40, 41, 81
Pontifical Council for Interreligious Dialogue (PCID), 154, 155, 190
Poupard, Paul, 58

poverty, 144, 160, 182
  China, poverty alleviation in, 117, 118, 119–25, 148–49, 177, 193, 197
  common good, eradication of poverty as part of, 114, 116
  incorrect interpretation of religious texts on poverty, 100–101
  new economic model and Chinese poverty alleviation, 126–30, 187–89
  preferential option for the poor, 143–44
  spiritual poverty, 118, 130–31, 135–37
  Targeted Poverty Alleviation Strategy, 124, 128, 187
  World Day of the Poor, 136, 145–46

qi (vital force), 11–12, 24–25, 26

Ratzinger, Joseph, 163–64, 180. *See also* Benedict XVI, Pope
Ravasi, Gianfranco, 69
ren (benevolence), 39, 88, 111
  bo'ai as an expression of, 89
  in Confucian tradition, 83, 181, 187
  jian'ai, as part of, 87
Ren Jiyu, 8
ren'ai (human-heartedness), 82–84, 90, 108, 110, 185–86
revelation, xxv, xxvi, xxxiii
  the principle of revelation, xxii–xxiii
  the reality of revelation, xxiii–xxiv

self-revelation of God, 15
Trinitarian dynamism of revelation, 178, 195
Ricci, Matteo, 1, 2, 158, 164, 182
Ricci Volunteer Program, 135
righteousness, 83, 89, 90, 107, 108, 181
Rondinara, Sergio, 48–49, 59, 60
Rossano, Piero, 180

Schnackenburg, Rudolf, 14
Second Axial Period, 21–23
Second Vatican Council, 22, 25, 166, 173, 191
Shanghai Academy of Social Sciences (SASS), 131–32
Shanghai Universal Expo (2010), 120
sheng (to manifest), 7, 11
Smith, Richard, 75
subsidiarity, 115, 145, 149, 174
Sun Yat-sen, 81, 82, 88, 89, 108, 186
synodality, 159, 160

Tao Yuanming, 138–40, 189, 194
Tertullian, 96
Thérèse of Lisieux, Saint, 16
tianxia (under the sky), 103, 111
Tighe, Paul, 69
Trinity, 1, 12, 23, 57, 116
  charism of unity, Trinitarian vision in, xxvii–xxviii
  China-Christianity dialogue, Trinitarian logic in, xxv–xxvi, 178
  Chinese thought, contribution to Trinitarian relationships, 26–29

Index

dialectic of harmony, interpreting Trinity via, 24–25, 29, 159, 183
Jesus Christ in the Trinitarian relationship, 17–19
perichoresis in Trinitarian language, 25–26
Trinitarian relationship, 19–20, 58–59, 162
Trump, Donald, 77, 150

UN Sustainable Development Goals (SDGs), 33, 70, 185
Universal Declaration of Human Rights, 102, 152, 189

Wang Anshi, 10
Wang Bi, 10
Wang Zhihe, 71, 72, 73
Weber, Max, 144
Wenzel, Peter, 33, 198
Westermann, Claus, 47
White, Lynn, 46–47
Winkler, Dietmar, 165
World Council for Interreligious Dialogue (PCID), 154, 155
World Council of Churches (WCC), 154, 190
World Day of Peace, 159
World Day of the Poor, 136, 145–46
World Evangelical Alliance (WEA), 154, 190
World Youth Day (2023), 195
wu (nothingness/non-being), 7, 9–11, 24, 28, 29, 30
Wu, John Ching-hsiung, 22
wu-wei (non-action), 8, 16, 27, 182

Xi Jinping, 33, 103, 120, 151, 157, 185, 186, 191
common destiny for mankind, promoting, 111–12
emission reduction goals, 76, 77
on the encounter of civilizations, 164–65
on food wastage, 51, 52
Go West development plan, launching, 127
nature, on respecting, 69–70
two centenaries goals, 129–30
UK state visit, 30, 91
xiongdi (brothers), 80, 82
Xu Guangqi, 2, 30

yi (righteousness), 83, 87
yin-yang, 3, 183
in *Daodejing*, 9, 11
harmony arising from, 7, 12
in *qi* of harmonious blending, 24–25, 26
in Trinitarian language, 25–26
you (being), 7, 9–11, 24, 28, 29, 30
youshan (friendship), 91, 186

Zamagni, Stefano, 146
Zhang Zai, 3, 38, 77–78, 189, 194
Zhao Zhengping, 81
Zhen Bin, 72
ziran (naturalness), 16, 35, 36–37, 53
ziyou-pingdeng-bo'ai motto, 81–82